Toward a More Perfect Rebellion

The publisher and the University of California Press Foundation gratefully acknowledge the generous support of the Kenneth Turan and Patricia Williams Endowment Fund in American Film.

Toward a More Perfect Rebellion

MULTIRACIAL MEDIA ACTIVISM
MADE IN L.A.

Josslyn Jeanine Luckett

UNIVERSITY OF CALIFORNIA PRESS

University of California Press
Oakland, California

Library of Congress Cataloging-in-Publication Data

Names: Luckett, Josslyn Jeanine, author.
Title: Toward a more perfect rebellion : multiracial media activism made
    in L.A. / Josslyn Jeanine Luckett.
Description: Oakland : University of California Press, 2025. | Includes
    bibliographical references and index.
Identifiers: LCCN 2024041734 | ISBN 9780520402133 (hardback) |
    ISBN 9780520402140 (paperback) | ISBN 9780520402157 (ebook)
Subjects: LCSH: Minorities in the motion picture industry—California—
    Los Angeles—History. | Independent filmmakers—California—Los
    Angeles—History. | Political activists—California—Los Angeles—
    History. | LCGFT: Film criticism.
Classification: LCC PN1995.9.M56 L83 2025 | DDC 791.43/6552—dc23
    /eng/20240913
LC record available at https://lccn.loc.gov/2024041734

GPSR Authorized Representative: Easy Access System Europe,
Mustamäe tee 50, 10621 Tallinn, Estonia, gpsr.requests@easproject.com

34 33 32 31 30 29 28 27 26 25
10 9 8 7 6 5 4 3 2 1

Contents

Acknowledgments

Roberto Miranda playing a solo bass rendition of Duke Ellington's "Come Sunday" and Dwight Trible singing "My Shining Hour" a cappella: these are two musical moments from the late spring and summer of 2009 in Los Angeles that I will never forget. Trible and Miranda's ensembles were the opening and closing concerts of a series I curated, "Come Sunday: Jazz on the Sacred Side" in the year leading up to my departure to the east coast for "round two" (and then "three") of graduate school. Both men were frequent collaborators with pianist/community organizer/"musical griot" Horace Tapscott. Little did I know they were sending me off on a journey that would circle right back to Tapscott, who provided music for multiple films discussed in this book. The day of Miranda's show, featuring James Newton on flute, Kei Akagi on piano, and Sonship Theus on percussion, Buddy Collette was present in the audience, causing the musicians on stage to beam with gratitude. Later that summer, a third featured artist from the Sacred Side series, vocalist extraordinaire Nailah Porter, threw a backyard farewell bash for me before I headed east. The World Stage poet loved ones were there, and all at once Dwight rose from his seat and started to sing "Shining Hour" to me. It's a song that speaks of light and home and angels watching over . . . with that and Miranda's arco solo

"Come Sunday" still fresh ("please look down and see my people through")—I was set. Blessings and traveling mercies received. This is the Los Angeles I left. This book is my decade+ attempt to return the thanks and praise.

There are many people to thank from Boston, Philly, New York, and beyond. During my time in the Boston area while an MDiv student at Harvard, the writing, teaching, preaching, and musicking of the following people were especially meaningful for me: Rev. Charles Adams, Rev. Dr. Kirk Byron Jones, Leonard Brown, Emmett Price, Josef Sorett, Kay Kaufman Shelemay, Henry Louis Gates, Jr., José Cuellar, Davíd Carrasco, Carolyn Wilkins, Willie Sordillo, Rev. Dan Smith, and all the musicians of the Makanda Project.

My years in Philadelphia while working on my PhD in Africana Studies at Penn were especially rich. My committee was comprised of scholars who are three of the most beautiful, generous, wise souls imaginable and who gave so many gifts beyond their attention to the manuscript: Karen Redrobe, Guthrie Ramsey, and John Jackson (advisor), you have my deepest bows of gratitude. Thank you also to Deborah Thomas who, with John Jackson, included me on the South African tour of their documentary, *Bad Friday: Rastafari after Coral Gardens,* along with the film's composer and coproducer, Junior "Gabu" Wedderburn and his ensemble of Nyabinghi percussionists. That trip planted so many seeds and modeled the kind of academic generosity for which I will always be grateful. Deep love to my fellow dissertating comrades in Africana, especially Khwezi Mkhize, Osei Alleyne, and Celina da Sa. Lyndsey Beutin, you especially deserve a million thanks for every gift of support, guidance, joy, and listening along this bumpy blessed road. Scribe Video Center, Blackstar Film Fest, Philly Jazz Project, Painted Bride, Mother Bethel AME, the transformative dance projects of Germaine Ingram and Leah Stein. . . . I stayed so fed. Thanks especially to Louis Massiah and his then colleague Hye-Jung Park at Scribe for supporting my efforts to "import" my L.A. research. Thanks too go to Fariha Khan in Asian American Studies. We were able to host Zeinabu irene Davis, Duane Kubo, Alile Sharon Larkin, Robert Nakamura and Karen Ishizuka, Barbara McCullough and Billy Woodberry in Philly during those years, amazing! Receiving a 2017 Ford Foundation Dissertation Fellowship also allowed me to travel multiple times to Los

Angeles to interview more of the filmmakers. I thank Karen Redrobe for her introduction to B. Ruby Rich, who invited me to interview Woodberry for *Film Quarterly*. That piece began a remarkably generative relationship with *Film Quarterly* and B. Ruby, who means the world to me and so many of us. Finally, while a student at Penn, I had the great fortune of taking a class with visiting professor Terri Francis. Without her presence on campus in my coursework years, I very likely would not have switched my focus from South African jazz to the filmmakers of UCLA. Grateful for you, Terri!

The filmmakers I interviewed for this project were so generous and so patient and so illuminating. I hope the energy of the exchanges will be clear in the pages ahead. It has been a profound gift to spend time with you all and receive your support for this project. The archivists at the UCLA Film and Television Archive, Mark Quigley and Maya Montañez Smukler, ROCK, as does the archive's director, May Hong HaDuong. So happy for all the work you are doing to program and preserve the student films of the great directors I write about here. I thank Chon Noriega and Xavier Flores for making films from the Chicano Studies Research Center at UCLA available to me (repeatedly). I thank Abraham Ferrer at Visual Communications (VC) for literally clearing his desk and setting me up on his computer to watch VC archives. Thanks to everyone at Visual Communications for all your generosity. I thank Rockefeller archivist Mary Ann Quinn for all of her help locating materials back when I was working on the dissertation. Deep bows to every library worker everywhere, especially those at Penn, UCLA, and NYU, for the endless interlibrary loan requests.

So honored and grateful to have met the late Elyseo Taylor's daughter Karen Taylor in the last moments of this research, and I thank her so much for all the archival materials she shared. For her special persistence helping me find contacts and for so much more, I thank the late Carroll Parrott Blue, whose death was a shock for many of us. The list of filmmakers and film educators who passed since I started this project in 2015 is painfully long; I hold my heart thinking of Danny Kwan, Betty Chen, Ntongela Masilela, Luis Ospina, Robert Grant, Mario da Silva, Lourdes Portillo, and featured in the films themselves that I discuss ahead there are many more yet I must acknowledge—Barbara O, Kaycee Moore, Elizabeth "Betita" Martinez, and Gena Rowlands. The deaths of Colin

Young and Clyde Taylor hit me hard. I am so grateful to have known them both, to have had the opportunity to spend long hours with Colin in England, and for many rich gatherings over decades of friendship with Clyde's daughter, Rahdi, to behold the full Taylor family glow in action.

I'm grateful to the places that welcomed me to share this research in early stages. Special thanks to Ajay Heble and the Guelph Jazz Festival Symposium and all the great improvisation scholars and musicians up there; thank you also to all my colleagues at ASA and SCMS for feedback along the way.

I am fortunate to teach at NYU's Martin Scorsese Department of Cinema Studies with colleagues I both respect thoroughly and honestly enjoy. There is this bank of offices where I get to see and laugh with Robert Stam, Michael Gillespie, Dan Streible, and Manthia Diawara, and if I'm lucky some days I run into Performance Studies colleagues Fred Moten and Alexandra Vazquez a little further down the hall. I want to thank all of the supportive Cinema Studies staff, the helpful student workers, the fantastic teaching assistants I've been able to team with, my two department chairs since I've been here (Anna McCarthy and Dana Polan), as well as fellow faculty members Toby Lee, Juana Suarez, Laura Harris, Jacob Floyd, Marina Hassapopoulou, Feng-Mei Heberer, Allen Weiss, Antonia Lant, Chris Straayer, and Zhen Zhang. I want to give an extra shout of gratitude to Dana Polan for all his support for this manuscript, including arranging for me to be the inaugural recipient of a new Tisch Center for Research and Study (CRS) Manuscript Workshop initiative. Thank you to André Lepecki and Hali Alspach at the CRS for your support of the workshop (and for providing a publication grant for the index) and to Gayle Wald and Chon Noriega for traveling to New York to participate. Special thanks to Gayle for all your notes and care with this project and the next one! Thanks also to Dan Streible, my co-representative from NYU for the National Film Registry Board of the Library of Congress, for all his guidance there and for all the joy of the Orphan Film Symposiums, especially the All Television Edition at UCLA in 2023! In the wider Tisch community, I'm grateful to have a wonderful dean, Allyson Green, and associate deans, Karen Shimakawa and Fred Carl; the unstoppable and endlessly inspiring Deborah Willis as the director of the Center for Black Visual Culture; and I give deep thanks to Matthew Morrison (Clive Davis) and again to Toby Lee and Alexandra Vazquez for their listening and guidance in all things publishing and promotion related. I thank my retired colleague Sam Pollard for his joy and extraordinary films. I'm grateful to Faye Ginsburg and Pegi Vail at NYU's Center for Media Culture and History for multiple opportunities to be in post-screening conversations with Pollard. There is one final NYU colleague I must thank, who I first met over thirty years ago when I was his graduate assistant in the Department of Dramatic Writing: Professor Donald Bogle, the one and only! Thank you for three decades of the best conversations that never fail to mention our mutual friend, Mrs. Geraldine Branton, and her dearest friend, Dorothy Dandridge, and most recently thank you for all your guidance with my research and publishing journey.

Enormous thanks to Raina Polivka at UC Press: we made it after so many years! Thank you for your enthusiasm for this project and my passion for it and for all your patience and support. Thank you to Sam Warren and Jessica Moll at the press and to the fabulous copyeditor, Catherine Osborne, for working miracles in the final weeks. Thanks also to Cathy Hannabach and the wonderful indexers at Ideas on Fire. I so appreciate the anonymous reader's expansive feedback as well as the fantastic and encouraging notes from Glen Mimura. I also want to give special thanks to my creative writing community in San Antonio, Texas, the Macondo Writers Workshop, and especially to its founder and visionary Sandra Cisneros. Love to her and to our O.G. Macondistas Pata Alderete, Anel Flores, Amelia Montes, Arturo Madrid, Erasmo Guerra, Bill Sanchez, and special love to Leslie Larson and to Carla Trujillo who first connected me with Sandra. I also want to thank Dr. Michelle Boyd and her Inkwell Academic Writing community for her magnificent coaching these last few years. And for their exquisite care for my mind, body, and soul I thank my many doctors, nurses, therapists, and wellness workers, most especially Dr. Robert Tuttle, Dr. Allan Goldberg, and the phenomenal Chavel Guarino.

I thank my beloved friends and comrade culture workers, who inspire me to keep keeping on. I'm thinking of you, Sheila Schroeder, Joni Jones and Jay Floyd, Claire Olivia Moed and Ted Krever, Deborah Mukamal, Lyndsey Beutin, Rona Taylor and all the Taylor-Jack family, Nina Crews, Sarah Pirozek, Sifiso Ntuli, Valerie Smith, Shirley Jo Finney, Imani

Tolliver, Esther Chae, Alva Rogers, Gabrielle Petrosian, V. Kali, Curtis Roberston, S. Pearl Sharp, Ruth Forman, Damon Reeves, Erica Woods, Erica Wilson and Zack Wilson, Roy Wilson, Nina Harawa, Angela Ards, Arleigh Prelow, Vivek Bald, Kym Ragusa, Umang Kumar, Aishah Shahidah Simmons, Hye-Jung Park, Michele Prettyman, Ellen Scott, Racquel Gates, Samantha Sheppard, Laura Pulido, and Mike Murashige. Special L.A. thanks to Janet Hicks for bringing me Sophie. To Paul Beatty for gifting me with the *Central Avenue Sounds* book long before either of us could have known it would be so meaningful to this research. To Roger Guenveur Smith for all of your inspiring work in and about this L.A. and that LA. To Sarita See and David Lloyd for hosting me so sweetly on research trips back home. To Shaz Bennett, ah, for so many years of good stories, love, laughter and for the gift I could never have imagined of a chance to dip my toe back into tv writing for the final season of *Queen Sugar*. Deep bows to Ms. DuVernay for making that last part possible . . . not to mention your LONG love for and championing of the filmmakers of the L.A. Rebellion and for all you do for independent filmmaking culture in Los Angeles. Having a home, with a porch and backyard, in Los Angeles during Covid was the most lifesaving gift, and I was so aware during that time if it hadn't been for my earlier tv-writing years and the support of Stan Lathan and Winifred Hervey, I never would have been able to take care of my family in the way that I could during lockdown. So my gratitude to both of you is as deep as it gets. And to my recently departed brother and "mid-level" elder, Peter J. Harris—the Black Man of Happiness—rest in eternal inspiration.

To family by blood and family by marriage—I give thanks to you all for your care, and love, delicious meals, good times, and deep prayers through the darkest times. Love to all the Spiller family (and the Thurlows and the Petersens) in Georgia, Alabama, Massachusetts, and all the way to Raymond, Maine. To my "other mother" Barbara Wallace and all the Wallace family now in Atlanta, appreciate you more than you know and thank you for your decades of friendship with my mom. To my Jackson, Mississippi, family, love you all; special shouts to cousin Vincent, cousin Ramona, and my uncle James Powell, for keeping your wayward, no-social-media cousin in the family loop. To my stepmother, Dr. Remedios "Remy" Almirante, my dear sister Lillian and her son, the amazing

Giacomo, to all the Pinzons, to Greg and Jake, Cousin Terry and his family, and all the extended/blended ones from California to Italy to the Philippines, love you! Remy and Lill, thank you for how much you cared for my dad when he was still here.

I gained an incredible new family in the midst of this research. To my brilliant and beloved mother-in-law, Loretta Lewis, to Christa Lewis and Aparicio Giddens, to Amirh and the mighty baby Isis, to Aunt Judy and all the Philly family—thank you for your love and Fly Eagles Fly! To the Brooklyn family, Kahlil, Casey, Violet and Avery, so good to have you close and get to watch the girls grow, and grow. Happy that Kali is in our world now too!

The Lucketts! There's only three of us left now but what a trio we make! Brother Jason, Mama Barbara, aren't we lucky? Ma, thank you for loving us both so deeply and supporting our creative passions and pursuits. And thank you for that gentle sense of wonder that the best social workers and pastors have, really seeing and meeting people where they are; you gave that to us too. Jason, thank you for your music and how it gathers us and for loving Los Angeles and its magical elders as much as I do. For bringing Buddy Collette and Kenny Burrell into our stratosphere alone ... the riches! Thank you for listening to my thinking about this book from the beginning and loving it not just because you are a Bruin (!) but because you could see it was "so me" all the different parts. Love you both, bless you both.

I mentioned my gratitude to libraries and library workers, yet one man from Van Pelt Library at UPenn deserves special mention. One day when I returned a bunch of CDs from interlibrary loan, he leaned over the circulation desk and said, "You have some very serious music taste." This led to an invitation to see two serious musicians, Odean Pope and Andrew Cyrille, live in concert. Mark Christopher Lewis, you and I have been seriously savoring music together since that moment almost fifteen years ago and I have loved every moment, from samba bars in Rio, to slack-key guitars in Honolulu, to that Hiroshima gig outside D.C. where you protected me from a drunk patron by brilliantly schooling him on Duane Kubo's film about the band, *Cruisin' J-Town* ... swoon, just SWOON. Can you imagine having a partner who can disarm a drunk jazz fan by citing your research??? I have no idea how to thank you for the reserves of patience required, through dissertation, job search, wedding plans, major moves, the death of our beloved cat Sophie, the EXTRA full house during Covid. . . . How did you do it? I'm grateful beyond words and love you beyond measure.

In the last stages of this research I was looking for my old copy of Toni Cade Bambara's *The Salt Eaters,* which of course has the greatest first line of any novel, ever: "Are you sure, sweetheart, that you want to be well?" Instead of finding it, I found a book I'd long let go of finding, figured I had lost, a book that contained the only academic essay my psychologist father, Dr. Roland Hayes Luckett (1938–1999), ever published. Toni Cade must have known in that precise moment my wellness required pops's work even more than hers. The book—a collection of essays called *Multiethnic Coalition Building in Los Angeles,* edited by Eui-Young Yu and Edward T. Chang and published by the Institute for Asian American and Pacific American Studies at Cal State Los Angeles—was put together from a symposium on inter-racial coalition building after the 1992 uprising. My dad's piece is called "Multicultural Education and Racism: A Preventive Perspective." My goodness. That's the apple falling *on* the tree.

Before my dad's eldest cousin Alberta Alexander died in 2018, she asked me to bring her a copy of my dissertation for her mantle in Jackson, Mississippi. She had a bound copy of my father's and a bound copy of her oldest daughter Barbara's dissertations, and she wanted mine to join theirs. When I presented it to her, she said, "My grandfather, your great grandfather, Tom Luckett, sold a big part of his land so that his children could have an education. That sacrifice has now produced three Black PhDs. That's why this is important." This book is dedicated to Dr. Roland Hayes Luckett, with gratitude to all of our elders who sacrificed because they believed education was the best preventive investment against racial injustice. As they look down to see us through, let us make this their shining hour.

Introduction

... the province of Hollywood is not action, but illusion.

Mignon invokes Ralph Ellison in *Illusions* (Dash, 1982)

Who cares about a group of Indians talking mumbo jumbo?
Hell, it's a viable story, but there's no audience for that kind
of story.

C. J. Forester in *Illusions* (Dash, 1982)

If all us mad folks unite—like the Indians, Chicanos,
Blacks, Asians—we'd shape up them white folks and they'd
have to act differently.

Angie in *Bush Mama* (Gerima, 1975)

The research for this book—about a group of American Indian, Asian American, Black, and Chicana/o students who began their training in film as part of an affirmative action media initiative at UCLA, the Ethno-Communications Program (1969–1973)—began in an era of hashtags (#OscarsSoWhite, #DocsSoWhite, #TimesUp, #MeToo, #BlackLivesMatter) and "concludes" (if any research ever does) at the end of Roe, the end of affirmative action ... and, yet, an Oscar first for a Native American actor, Lily Gladstone. For many who appreciated the film for which Gladstone's Best Actress nomination made history—*Killers of the Flower Moon* (2023, dir. Martin Scorsese)—a common audience reaction was shock that they'd never heard of this particularly gruesome iteration of white supremacist terror waged on the Osage in the early decades of the twentieth century.[1]

1

Maria Tallchief as Eurydice in Balanchine's *Orpheus* (1948). Photo: George Platt Lynes. Used with permission of the George Platt Lynes Estate.

Due to the work of prolific Makah documentarian Sandra Sunrising Osawa, I had been exposed to this Osage history in her biographical portrait of America's first major prima ballerina, *Maria Tallchief*, which aired on PBS in 2007. Tallchief was born in Fairfax, Oklahoma, in 1925, during the reign of terror. For dance enthusiasts who were eager to hear about Tallchief's days with Balanchine (her first husband), and how her performances in the 1940s of "Orpheus" and "Firebird" launched and ensured the success of the New York City Ballet, Osawa had something more in store. She took her time orally (she poignantly recites the film's narration herself) and visually to ground viewers in the Osage community that formed the Tallchiefs, by presenting archival materials and testimony from family members and Maria herself relating tales of poison, mysterious death, bombings, and insurance scams.

I remember so well the day I watched the *Maria Tallchief* film, early in my PhD program, and shared with an Africana studies professor the way my jaw dropped to know that there was ever even an Osage prima ballerina named Tallchief, that she never changed her name, that she rose out of this moment of murderous siege on her community and danced *the* Firebird that put the New York City Ballet on the map. Picking up his own dropped jaw, he mused: "It makes you wonder what else they're not telling us." And that could easily be a subtitle for this comprehensive BIPOC filmography born out of that short-lived affirmative action program so many decades ago: "Ethno: all the things no one else is telling us about us, caught on film at last!"

What was this affirmative action program gearing up in '69 at UCLA's film school, and wasn't that the year L.A. Panther Party members Bunchy Carter and John Huggins were assassinated on that campus? I certainly knew about the multiracial organizing of the Third World Liberation Front activists at San Francisco State and UC Berkeley that created the earliest Black studies and ethnic studies programs on the West Coast. By the late '80s I'd become a direct inheritor of that campus revolution as an ethnic studies major at Cal. But who were these future insurgent filmmakers rolling up to Westwood?

The place to begin my research was with the Black filmmakers from UCLA, who had their roots in the Ethno-Communications program. Directors such as Charles Burnett, Julie Dash, Larry Clark, Haile Gerima, and Billy Woodberry (who arrived on campus from the late '60s through the mid-'70s) were in the midst of a renaissance of scholarly attention and preservation fervor, most significantly due to the work of Allyson Nadia Field, Jan-Christopher Horak, and Jacqueline Najuma Stewart's multitiered project, *L.A. Rebellion: Creating a New Black Cinema.* Launched in 2009, the project included a major symposium and screening series hosted by the UCLA Film and Television Archive in 2011 and an award-winning edited volume published by UC Press in 2015, both shortly followed by the release of a DVD anthology of the student works from well-known and lesser-known "Rebellion" filmmakers. The UCLA Film and Television Archive's web page devoted to the project explained the "Story of the L.A. Rebellion" as follows:

> In the late 1960s, in the aftermath of the Watts Uprising and against the backdrop of the continuing Civil Rights Movement and the escalating Vietnam War, a group of African and African American students entered the UCLA School of Theater, Film and Television, as part of an Ethno-Communications initiative designed to be responsive to communities of color (also including Asian, Chicano and Native American communities). Now referred to as the "L.A. Rebellion," these mostly unheralded artists created a unique cinematic landscape, as—over the course of two decades—students arrived, mentored one another and passed the torch to the next group.[2]

This project produced the opportunity to experience a treasure trove of rare and restored films and generated a ripple effect of new writing and programming across the country and around the world celebrating these trailblazing filmmakers.

As an Angeleno, something about the web page description's parenthesis had me restless. It set my comparative ethnic studies sensibility/formation on alert, eager to get the other "communities of color" out of those brackets and into the center of the story. I'd been witness and participant in too many multiracial arts communities in Los Angeles over the decades not to feel protective and prideful of the astounding breadth of this city and its artists. Let us pause for a brief Toni Cade Bambara–style roll call to offer a nostalgic tease of that breadth: from the Watts Towers Day of the Drum Festival, to post-screening jam sessions between Dai Sil Kim-Gibson and Charles Burnett at the Japanese American National Museum, to *Refugee Nation* improv workshops with TeAda Productions on the Westside, to parasol-twirling second lines with the Creole Mafia (Roger Guenveur Smith and Mark Broyard) from Dulan's to downtown, on up to Tia Chucha's Centro Cultural for poetry if anyone had enough gas in the tank to make it all the way to Sylmar, then don't miss Peter J. Harris's Inspiration House Choir's "Black/Brown Dialogues for Whole Living" in Highland Park on the way home.[3]

Logistically and politically, those crossings have never come easy, from freeway traffic to nationalist static to overcoming the fear/contempt/hurt behind statements like "they don't want us there." Still, this was a breadth I suspected in the earliest moments of this research must also be reflected in the wider multiracial filmography of this group of students recruited to that campus during that turbulent decade. To my delight and nourishment, the hunch was correct. Bolstered by the comparative/relational work of Laura Pulido and Josh Kun, Gaye Theresa Johnson, Scott Kurashige, Anthony Macías, Luis Alvarez, Daniel Widener, Steven Isoardi, Denise Sandoval, Nery Gabriel Lemus (and more)[4]—whose documentation of the city's multiracial crossings from picket lines to barbershops, big band to punk rock, zoot suiters to lowriders, informs this work—*Toward a More Perfect Rebellion* reaches freeway miles wide to uncover the behind-the-scenes and on-screen tales of a group of activist filmmakers of color who changed the face of independent media made in L.A.

EMPOWERING THE EYE TO SEE MULTIPLE SIGNS

The relational aspirations of the Ethno-Communications program were designed from the start, according to Elyseo Taylor, the first African American faculty hire in the film school at UCLA. A January 4, 1970, *Los Angeles Times*, headline ran: "UCLA Students Will Film Aspects of Ghetto Life as Means to Dialog," and in the article, Taylor described an interdisciplinary program, beginning that spring quarter, organized "to determine to what extent film can be a tool of sociological research (and) to find out what kinds of things minorities would like to see on film and the most effective way to present them." The article states that the students under Taylor's direction—"blacks, American Indians, Mexican and Asian Americans"—would train in filmmaking techniques and take courses in journalism and mass communications. Taylor would teach a new course called "Film and Social Change," designed "to see the effect of films on society" and for the students to *"acquaint themselves with problems and resources of minority groups other than their own."[5]* This pilot affirmative action program became known as the Ethno-Communications Program, and though it only formally lasted several years, the films, filmmakers, and film studies curriculum it produced have had a profound and lasting impact.

Responding to a 1968 UC system-wide mandate for department heads from each campus to address the "urban crises" plaguing communities of color up and down the state, UCLA film school chair Colin Young had hired Taylor to design a pilot program in community filmmaking. Taylor developed the program with a group of student activists (including Moctesuma Esparza) who fought for greater enrollment of students of color, increased hiring of faculty of color, and the immediate establishment of new curriculum relevant to their intellectual, creative, and political concerns. (At least two of these courses first taught by Taylor, "Film and Social Change" and "Films of Africa, Asia, and Latin America," are still part of UCLA's course offerings). Initially referred to as the Media Urban Crisis Committee in the planning stages (MUCC), then the Media Urban Crisis program (MUC) in its trial year (the first recruits declared themselves the "Mother Muccers!"), the program was eventually renamed the Ethno-Communications Program. The trailblazing cohort of Black students who came through the film school during and just after the Ethno days were retroactively dubbed the "L.A. Rebellion" (by Clyde Taylor), the "L.A. School of Black Filmmakers" (by Ntongela Masilela), and the "Black Insurgents" (by Toni Cade Bambara).[6] For Clyde Taylor, the visionary experimental, documentary, and narrative feature films produced by Julie Dash, Charles Burnett, Billy Woodberry, and Haile Gerima "exposed the irresponsibility of Hollywood portrayals of black people" and "rudely smashed" every code of classical cinema as the directors developed their own bold, new film language.[7] Of the three early names for the group, Field, Horak, and Stewart adopted Clyde Taylor's moniker, affirming that "the L.A. Rebellion created a watershed body of work that strives to perform the revolutionary act of humanizing Black people on screen."[8]

Among the early generation of Black scholars to write about UCLA's "insurgent" filmmakers, Bambara was the only one to mention the Ethno-Communications program by name, in her essay "Reading the Signs, Empowering the Eyes: *Daughters of the Dust* and the Black Independent Cinema Movement." She also mentions several of the filmmakers associated with that "multicultural film phenomena," including Sylvia Morales, Moctesuma Esparza, and Renee Tajima.[9] Beyond this early mention of the program she traces examples of cross-racial alliances in the films, including the thread of Black and Native American solidarity that begins in Julie Dash's *Illusions* (1982) and returns in *Daughters of the Dust* (1991). In her analysis of the latter film, Bambara writes that *Daughters* "demands some work on the part of the spectator whose ears and eyes have been conditioned by habits of viewing industry fare." She insists that the film "asks that the spectator honor multiple perspectives rather than depend on the 'official' story offered by a hero" and that the reward for this effort is "an empowered eye."[10] Taking my cue from Bambara, *Toward a More Perfect Rebellion* insists on honoring the multiple perspectives and offerings of the multiracial group of filmmakers from Ethno.

A great deal of the political power, organizing potential, and pedagogical scope of these films can be missed by studying only one racial group from Ethno at a time. When only one group's work is analyzed, we lose the opportunity to read, and become empowered by, critical resonances and signs of solidarity across the wider filmography. L.A. Rebellion discourse is not alone in its single-group focus. Important Chicano and Asian American media histories that have been foundational for this research similarly acknowledge the Ethno-Communications program as ground zero for the formative years of each of their cinemas, then proceed to write exclusively about Chicana/o or Asian American work.[11] All of these studies—as the editors of the L.A. Rebellion collection explicitly state as one of their project's goals—"lay the groundwork for more research on the other students of color. . . ."[12] In the best sense of musical and academic accompaniment, it is my goal here to put this work in rigorous call and response with these earlier studies, trading archives and arguments in order to form more perfect tool kits to analyze, teach, circulate and celebrate the wider multiracial filmography. The MFA thesis films of both Haile Gerima and Julie Dash offer a useful and grounding point of departure for this discussion, and in the spirit of Bambara, I propose that both films empower our eyes to read and honor multiracial signs.

Haile Gerima is on record expressing frustration with the "L.A. Rebellion" moniker because, he says, "it's unfair to Chicanos, it's unfair to Asians. . . . I don't mind people using it, but for me it excludes."[13] His thesis film, *Bush Mama* (1975), centers protagonist/mother/evolving radical Dorothy (Barbara O) and her struggles against the welfare state, the carceral state, and the police state of Watts after the 1965 rebellion. Along with Charles Burnett's *Killer of Sheep* (1977), *Bush Mama* has perhaps garnered more in-depth scholarship than any film made by the first wave of L.A. Rebellion filmmakers, receiving early critical attention from Clyde Taylor, Ntongela Masilela, and Mark Reid, and later close readings by scholars ranging from Mike Murashige and Paula Massood to Cynthia Young and Frank Wilderson.[14] While the gender and class analysis and detailed readings of the film's formal elements in each of these critiques is razor sharp, two scenes that jump out for me and are not discussed directly in any of those works focus on themes of Third World solidarity.[15] In the first of these two scenes, Dorothy's neighbor Angie, a teenage activist/babysitter, drops by to offer a coalition-building geography lesson to Dorothy's daughter Luann. With Dorothy nearby washing dishes, Angie begins her decolonizing efforts by pointing to various countries in a large atlas and telling Luann (and Dorothy) that there are people all over the world who are angry at white people for what they've done, and not just Black people: "The Asian people, the Indian people, people all over Central America angry at them for what they did. But I bet if all us mad folks unite—like the Indians, Chicanos, Blacks, Asians—we'd shape up them white folks and they'd have to act differently." About ten minutes later we enter a scene where Dorothy, after being hounded by her social worker to terminate her pregnancy, reluctantly enters an abortion clinic. Beyond one white nurse at the reception desk, we see a waiting room crowded with anxious and traumatized women of color. The rest of the film has had virtually an all-Black cast to this point, so why does Gerima cast this scene with Asian, Latina, and Black women? We are placed in Dorothy's subjective point of view when she seems to notice the multiracial casting of the waiting room in real time with us, and though we don't know for certain, an echo of Angie's call of unity between the Black, Asian, Indian, and Chicana "mad folks" may be the empowering thought that prompts Dorothy to abruptly change her mind and exit the clinic.

Julie Dash's protagonist in *Illusions* (1982), Mignon (Lonette McKee), is a light-skinned Black woman who passes for white in her job as an assistant to a high-powered white studio executive in Hollywood circa 1942. It is her voice we hear at the top of the film, speaking Ralph Ellison's words about Hollywood as the province of illusion, not action. This line

Julie Dash with Rosanne Katon on set of *Illusions*. From the collection of Julie Dash.

comes from an essay in which Ellison critiques the "problem pictures" of the 1940s, including films like *Pinky* and *Lost Boundaries* that also center racial passing.[16] Yet Dash subverts the tragic-mulatto trope of the earlier films by affirming Mignon's determination to choose action *and* illusion (passing for white) in order to challenge and change Hollywood herself, by any means necessary. She wants to help the talented Black singer Ester Jeeter (Rosanne Katon) who is hired to fix a sync-sound disaster, and she also doggedly pitches to her boss C. J. Forrester (Jack Rader) a major motion picture about the Navajo code talkers. "They're Marines trained as communications experts. . . ." Mignon recounts information we've seen on screen via telegram that reads: "American Indians Fighting to Save Democracy." Toni Cade Bambara connects these two acts as a pattern in Dash's work of women sharing space rather than dominating space: "Mignon . . . presses for the inclusion of Native Americans in the movie industry, and she stands in solidarity with Ester."[17]

The Navajo pitch is always a bit of a surprise, and not just because it would take Hollywood multiple decades before it told the story of the coders in a major motion picture (*Windtalkers*, 2002, dir. John Woo), but because the 1942 date stamp prepares those who are attuned to black film history that a character like Mignon might pitch a propaganda/uplift film like *The Negro Soldier* (dir. Stuart Heisler, producer Frank Capra), made in 1944, with a screenplay by African American writer Carlton Moss (who also stars in the film). Instead Mignon seeks something even wider, films that feature the talent of an Ester Jeeter, as well as films that honor communities of color beyond her own. Clyde Taylor sees this as an example of the way that L.A. Rebellion films were "breaking something and offering something different. I mean the classic is *Illusions*. Julie—she puts it out there: 'Look at what you're doing Hollywood . . . and what you *could* be doing!'"[18] And the irony of course is that Dash made this film forty years *after* World War II, when fully realized, three-dimensional portraits of both Blacks and Indians were still rare in Hollywood. Many, including Haile Gerima, would argue that they still are now, forty years after *Illusions*, as he told the *Los Angeles Times* in 2021: "I'm fundamentally against Hollywood. . . . [I]t's over 100 and something years of a history of exclusion. It has excluded Native Americans, yet it demonized them. Africans demonized by them. . . ."[19] Regarding this same long history, Clyde Taylor once declared, "It was almost like a law: *Thou shalt not show a Black person as a human being*."[20] What these cross-racial solidarity elements of Gerima and Dash's work here emphasize is that Rebellion filmmakers announced the full humanity of their Black characters, and many insisted that their characters also acknowledge and advocate for the full humanity of other people of color.

CROSSING AND CROSSCUTTING IN THE CITY OF LOS ANGELES

In *Pedagogies of Crossing*, Caribbean feminist scholar M. Jacqui Alexander presents notions of fluency and relationality that speak to this project in useful theoretical and methodological ways for the cross-racial film analysis I stage in the chapters to come. Alexander writes that "we were not born women of color, we become women of color" and "to become women of color, we would need to become fluent in each other's histories ... unlearn an impulse that allows mythologies about each other to replace knowing about one another. . . . We cannot afford to cease yearning for each other's company."[21] These lines are deeply moving, as they conjure the depth and sense of high stakes of the comparative training I received at Berkeley from the likes of Barbara Christian, Loni Ding, Carla Trujillo, Rudy Busto, Carlos Munoz, and Albert Johnson. If we studied the Student Nonviolent Coordinating Committee (SNCC), we better also bone up on the United Farm Workers (UFW). And if we studied SNCC and UFW and cared about the arts? We better read up on the Free Southern Theater *and* Teatro Campesino, side by side. The ethnic studies program at UC Berkeley, born of the Third World student strikes of the late 1960s on both sides of the Bay, trained us to become more fluent in each other's histories, empowered our eyes and minds to stay attuned to resonances in our struggles and radical arts traditions.

In Bambara's writing on the Black filmmakers of UCLA, she uses her own empowered eyes and ears to keep attuned to the "intertextual echoes" across the entire radical black filmmaking tradition. The mesmerizing way she moves across the film texts to make meaning of these echoes conjures both the work of the most sensitive film editor (crosscutting) and the supplest improvising musician (call and response). I will work with both metaphors as useful methodological strategies across this book, beginning with crosscutting here and moving to call and response in the later chapters, to present my own analysis of intertextual echoes across the wider multiracial and multigenre Ethno filmography.

In the most basic sense of film editing, crosscutting is the act of cutting together two different scenes, usually in two different places, with the suggestion that the scenes are happening at the same time, or possibly that they bear a visual or emotional connection that is greater in relation than if we were to only see one side of the story or action alone. The most effective way to build a case for the usefulness of considering the wider media rebellion of the multiracial filmmakers of the Ethno-Communications Program, versus studying their work one racial group at a time, is by incisively crosscutting between their student and early career films. It is also an effective way here to contextualize both the motion picture histories and Los Angeles demographic and migration histories that lead up to the arrival of the Black, Asian, Chicana/o, and Native American students to UCLA in the late 1960s.

This crosscutting impulse came as I was reviewing a trio of documentaries about people of color in Hollywood over the long twentieth century that seemed to be telling almost the exact same story. Within the first decade of the twenty-first century, *The Bronze Screen: 100 Years of the Latino Image in American Cinema* (2001, dir. Susan Racho, Nancy de los Santos-Reza, and Alberto Dominguez), *Hollywood Chinese* (2007, dir. Arthur Dong), and *Reel Injun* (2009, dir. Neil Diamond, Catherine Bainbridge, and Jeremiah Hayes) arrived to take stock of the prior century's largely disgraceful treatment of Latina/o, Chinese American, and Native Americans on film. A rhythm was established: 1. We were there from the silent days; 2. We took terrible roles but played them with humanizing dignity; 3. Things got better in the last thirty years when we controlled the image. These films followed two earlier Black film surveys by William Greaves (*That's Black Entertainment*, 1989) and Pearl Bowser (*Midnight Ramble*, 1994, cowritten by Clyde Taylor and featuring Toni Cade Bambara). These two projects put a spotlight on films made by independent Black directors and writers such as Spencer Williams and Oscar Micheaux (whose work the L.A. Rebellion filmmakers studied in many cases for the first time while at UCLA).[22] Arthur Dong's film does highlight several early Chinese American directors as well, including the remarkable Marion Wong, who created her own production company in the Bay Area in the teens, and in 1916 wrote, directed, and appeared in *The Curse of Quon Gwon*.[23] I value and teach these documentaries; still, the frustrated film editor in me wants to crosscut between the projects to demonstrate the parallel stereotypical tropes, the parallel sagas of whitewashing, as well as the parallel tales of phenomenally talented performers who defied the constraints of their material.

To skillfully crosscut between the films would reveal the need to decolonize ALL the images, not just those of one racial group. One might cut between the tropes of the oversexed women of color, whether prostitutes, madams, vixen saloon keepers, or "squaws," contrasted with the sexless servant or prematurely gray-haired mothers. With the men, one could crosscut between virtually the same gangsters, thieves, rapists, drug dealers, or the lazy, illiterate, buffoons unreasonably loyal and subservient to their white costars—the noble savage/magical negro/Uncle Toms that persist to this day. Then there are the interracial sagas, the doomed mulatta or half-breed costars of the "problem films" of each race. Rigid casting restrictions meant that some "interracial" pairs could never even make it to the screen, which seems to have been the case when Anna May Wong was denied the role of O-Lan from *The Good Earth* (1937), a role the Chinese American actress lost to a German American actress, Luise Rainer, who won that year's Oscar for best actress, as once they decided on the white actor Paul Muni (in yellowface) for the lead, his romantic costar could not be Chinese . . . in a film about Chinese village life!

Years later, Mexican actress Katy Jurado became the first Latina nominated for an Oscar for best supporting actress, yet for playing a Comanche woman who pretends to be Mexican in *Broken Lance* (1954).[24] Her character's son, played by Robert Wagner, also suffers from every Hollywood Indian "half-breed" trope. Rita Moreno, the first Latina to win the supporting actress Oscar, is one of the only Puerto Rican leads in *West Side Story* (1961). Her Puerto Rican "Shark" boyfriend, Bernardo, is played by Turkish actor George Chakiris, whose sister, Maria, is played by Natalie Wood (who may actually speak more Spanish to her Mexican maid in Paul Mazursky's *Bob & Carol & Ted & Alice* than she does in *West Side Story*, but we'll get to Mazursky later). Often missed in the bizarre casting matrix of *West Side Story* is the presence of Nobuko Miyamoto, the Japanese American actress, singer, activist, and founder of Great Leap Theater in Los Angeles, who plays one of the Puerto Rican Shark Girls, Francisca.[25] Like Moreno, Miyamoto, listed as "Joanne Miya" in the credits, manages to sing that she likes to live in America, even with the racial absurdities of America's film industry.

Beyond those documentary surveys, we find even deeper parallels between actors who worked *in Hollywood* in painfully limiting roles, but who *in Los Angeles* created theater companies, performed challenging work, and facilitated opportunities for new generations of theater and film artists. LisaGay Hamilton's remarkable documentary about the life and activist career of Beah Richards, *Beah: A Black Woman Speaks* (2003), explores for instance Richards's important theater collaborations with Frank Silvera. We see that in 1964 their hugely successful Los Angeles production of James Baldwin's *Amen Corner* migrated to Broadway and earned the actress a Tony nomination for her role as Sister Margaret. That production also starred Juanita Moore, who had earned an Oscar nomination for best supporting actress in Douglas Sirk's remake of *Imitation of Life* (1959). In the same decade Moore was massaging Lana Turner's feet and being rejected by her tragic mulatta daughter, Moore was starring in an all-Black production of Jean Paul Sartre's *No Exit* at L.A.'s Ebony Showcase theater.[26] This theater was founded by Nick Stewart, who used his television earnings starring as the dimwitted "Lightnin'" in television's *Amos and Andy* to fund one of the most important Black regional theaters in the country at that time.[27]

Crosscut to a parallel career in Jay Silverheels, the Mohawk actor who spent a decade of his career playing Tonto on television and on film—he too established a theater group in the 1960s, the Indian Actors Workshop in Los Angeles, to "circumvent what most Indians who dreamed of film stardom saw as prejudicial Hollywood hiring practices."[28] Crosscut to Mako, who one year prior to his Oscar nomination for *Sand Pebbles* (1966, dir. Robert Wise) teamed with Beulah Quo and James Hong almost a decade before they appeared in Polanski's *Chinatown* to create East West Players, the nation's first professional Asian American theater company, now over sixty years old. The founding actors from East West Players would in turn support the work of multiple projects by the Asian American film students at UCLA, most notably when Mako agreed to star in Ethno alums Robert Nakamura and Duane Kubo's feature film *Hito Hata: Raise the Banner*, considered the first Asian American narrative feature film. These grassroots theater workshops and companies, built by actors of color resisting limited, insulting, absurd casting practices and humiliating content in Hollywood, consistently provided remarkable talent, professional advice, and support for the New Los Angeles cinema on the horizon.[29]

I refer to the body of work generated by the filmmakers of color who trained at UCLA during and just after the Ethno-Communications Program as the "wider Ethno filmography," and the majority of the work I address within this wider filmography was made (or at least "in production") between 1970 and 1992.[30] And while I respect the designation and distinction of "L.A. Rebellion" for the Black filmmakers of this group, and will often speak of the Black UCLA-trained filmmakers as the Rebellion directors, I include their work within this wider Ethno filmography. I see this filmography as the roots of a New Los Angeles cinema that honors and was always attuned to the concerns of and in a cocreative relationship with the culture workers and the everyday people of the Black, Asian, Native, and Chicana/o communities in the city. I understand that "New Los Angeles" does not contain a racial signifier, just as the L.A. Rebellion is not called the Black L.A. Rebellion, but was a name chosen to describe the work of Black independent media makers trained at UCLA. I choose New Los Angeles to gather and center the collective filmography produced by media makers of color who trained at UCLA in the 1970s and whose work prioritizes the stories, struggles, the mundane and majestic of their Black, Asian, Chicana/o, and American Indian communities. If L.A. Rebellion is Black, New Los Angeles is Black, Indigenous, Chicana/o, and Asian American.

I am also, of course, preparing to rumble or rumba with the New Hollywood filmmakers and discourse in film studies. American film history gives an inordinate amount of attention to the decade of the 1970s, referred to as Hollywood's New Wave, its Renaissance, or its "last golden age," a period where mostly white men were responding to the upheaval of the 1960s with a slate of daring, character-driven stories that unlike Classical Hollywood favored "unmotivated heroes" and savored ambiguous narratives "shifting and modifying traditional genres and themes, while never quite shedding their support."[31] Yet of late, even scholars of this last "golden" period are questioning the "assumption that the American New Wave was a good thing," admitting to and grappling with the period's severe underrepresentation "both on-screen and behind the camera" of African Americans, "together with the extreme marginalization of women (on-screen, in the production process, and also in the audience)."[32] Note of course that this scholarship does not even bother to mention the lack of Asian American, Native American, or Latina/o representation, which is one of the reasons an engagement with the New Los Angeles cinema I propose here is critical in its insistence that academia and Hollywood itself remember that race in the United States, and in the City of Angels in particular, is never only a question of black and white.

WE ARE ALL STRANGE IN THIS PLACE OF RECENT INVENTION: INSISTING ON THE MULTIRACIAL

> There are strangers above me, below me and all around me and we are all
> strange in this place of recent invention.
> This city named for angels appears naked and stripped of anything
>   resembling
> the shaking of turtle shells, the songs of human voices on a summer night
> outside Okmulgee.
> Yet, it's perpetually summer here, and beautiful. The shimmer of gods is easier
> to perceive at sunrise or dusk,
> when those who remember us here in the illusion of the marketplace
> turn toward the changing of the sun and say our names.
> We matter to somebody . . .
>
> *Joy Harjo*

The racial demographics of Southern California reflect a diversity that has historically not been reflected in Hollywood. These opening lines of Joy Harjo's poem "The Path to the Milky Way Leads Through Los Angeles" capture the simultaneous sense of displacement, yearning, and wonder of any recently arrived migrant.[33] The turtle shells and mention of the Muscogee Nation capital in Oklahoma suggests the "we" who matter here are American Indians, likely part of the federal urban relocation program, which by 1970 contributed to Los Angeles being second only to the Navajo reservation as the largest Native concentration in the country.[34] An understanding of the known and lesser-known flows and forced migrations of communities of color in Los Angeles over the twentieth century, leading up to the time of the formation of the Ethno-Communications program at UCLA, provides important grounding for analyzing the creative and political forces at work in their student films and early professional work. The breadth of stories and the communities captured in the Ethno filmography, I argue, could only have come out of a program based in Los Angeles, and yet the city's vast multiracial and multiethnic landscape so richly captured in this filmography is still so infrequently captured in mainstream media.

Returning now to the arrival narrative of Harjo's poem, where nothing in this city of "recent invention" looks familiar, nothing resembles the summer night songs from home, *yet*. Harjo hints with her "yet" that there may be an opportunity for new music in this "beautiful" and new land of perpetual summer. If the turtle shell shakes above were replaced by tambourine, and the location tossed off some sanctified location around New Orleans's 6th ward or Houston's 5th, this poem might just as easily describe the thousands of African Americans who, fleeing pastoral scenes of the blood-soaked, "separate-but-equal" South, made their way west to Los Angeles during the Great Migration. Historian Gerald Horne writes that in 1910 Los Angeles had fewer than 8,000 Blacks, but by 1940 the number rose to over 55,000, and in just four more years approached 120,000.[35] While the city of L.A. in the prewar period was home to both the largest Mexican American and Japanese American populations in the United States, both communities during the 1930s and 1940s had reason to doubt if they *mattered* to anyone, considering that they were alternately deported, imported, or incarcerated. So, again, the mass migrations of African Americans to cities like Los Angeles meant that they were encountering "strangers all around" who were Asian American, Mexican American, and Native American. Racially restrictive covenants "supported by real estate companies, developers and banks," writes Gaye Theresa Johnson, meant that Blacks and Mexicans had very few options of where they could purchase homes in and around the city.[36] George Sanchez points out that these restrictive covenants, set up as early as 1902, used "the all-inclusive term of 'non-Caucasians' to define those who could not purchase property," and ultimately targeted "Chinese, Japanese, Mexicans, African Americans, and sometimes Armenians, Jews, Italians, and others seen at the time as racially undesirable." In his comparative work on interracial communities in Los Angeles, Cape Town, and Hawai'i, Sanchez points out the irony that what made these neighborhoods thrive culturally and politically was often the fact that their residents were unable to live anywhere else in the city.[37]

Neighborhood demographics continued to shift both due to local residential restrictions and national and international policies. In *From Coveralls to Zoot Suits: The Lives of Mexican American Women on the World War II Home Front*, Elizabeth Escobedo describes Depression-era nativist fears of "outsider" Mexicans stealing the scarce jobs of "real Americans," and from 1930–1939 nearly one-third of L.A.'s Mexican community, "regardless of citizenship," was deported.[38] Ironically, by August of 1942 the Emergency Farm Labor Program, also called the

Bracero program, would bring thousands of Mexican laborers back to the States. The binational agreement between Mexico and the United States was made to meet "temporary" agricultural shortages, caused in part by the relocation of Japanese American tenant farmers to concentration camps located as far away as Wyoming and Arkansas.[39] Reverend Hamilton T. Boswell, as noted in Scott Kurashige's *The Shifting Grounds of Race: Black and Japanese Americans in the Making of Multiethnic Los Angeles,* wrote passionate columns in L.A.'s most important African American paper, *The California Eagle,* condemning "the undemocratic evacuation of Japanese-Americans," which Boswell called "the greatest disgrace of Democracy since slavery." Boswell further warned that if Blacks allowed this kind of "race mongering" to go unquestioned, they could "expect similar action against us."[40] Reverend Boswell was himself an African American migrant, originally from Texas, who once in California came to understand his connection with his forcibly removed Japanese American neighbors.

Reversing Reverend Boswell's migration, Japanese American poet Lawson Fusao Inada was born in California, but spent part of his childhood incarcerated at a camp in Jerome, Arkansas, a town near the Mississippi border. Inada, whose jazz-inspired poetry became the focus of an early film crewed by Ethno students, writes about his early jazz education in his poetry collection, *Legends from Camp.*[41] Deprived of his father's turntable while interred, young Lawson learned the sounds and stories of his father's beloved musicians (Fats Waller, "Fatha" Hines, Art Tatum), from tales and whistles his father shared on the walk back and forth from the camp showers: "Coming back, warm and clean, glowing, all the stars were out. We paused; he was teaching me how to whistle. So, I whistled, and then we whistled, 'Melancholy Baby,' his song, loud and clear. . . ." Inada later describes this "Negro" music, "in our distorted reality of aliens and alienation," as a kind of *"citizenship."*[42] So, where Harjo remembers shaking turtle shells as the sound of home, Inada's father's renditions of Fats Waller were a sound of belonging, a sound that even in a concentration camp meant that they mattered to somebody.

In the introduction to *Legends from Camp,* Inada reminds us that the chief camps administrator "went on to become chief of the Bureau of Indian Affairs, where he 're-deployed' his policy of 'relocation.' Which included, yes, 'termination.'"[43] He speaks here of B.I.A. commissioner Dillon Myer, appointed in 1950, "based in part on his experience as the director of the agency that managed the relocation and internment of Japanese Americans during World War II."[44] Nicolas Rosenthal, in his *Reimaging Indian Country: Native American Migration and Identity in Twentieth-Century Los Angeles,* confirms that "Myer saw relocation as a corollary to 'termination policy,' the federal government's efforts to end its government-to-government relationship with Indian tribes, to remove Indian land from trust status, and to cease providing services to Indian people." Myer also believed in "depopulating reservations to the point that they would be 'self-sufficient' and no longer in need of federal services."[45] These policies were designed to "break down tribal ties and assimilate Indian people."[46]

These policies also influenced at least one film school grad in the late 1950s—from the *other* school in Los Angeles, USC—to direct a hybrid documentary feature. Kent Mackenzie's *The Exiles* is about one night in the lives of a group of "urban" Indians who are filmed living, partying, dancing, and encountering police violence in Bunker Hill. Yet the film also offers quiet glimpses of its central characters, especially Homer and Yvonne, attempting to create space for themselves in overcrowded apartments, daydreaming about family back on the reservation, and insisting on carrying out sacred drumming traditions in the wee small hours at the top of hill "X." Shot in black and white a good decade earlier than the first "Ethno" films, *The Exiles* is sometimes grouped with the Ethno filmmakers in discussions of "minority cinemas," for example by David James in *The Most Typical Avant-Garde: History and Geography of Minor Cinemas in Los Angeles.* And in the closing scenes of Thom Andersen's *Los Angeles Plays Itself,* Mackenzie's film is framed as the beginning of a "neorealist movement" in Los Angeles that finds its ultimate examples in the first features (all student films) by Charles Burnett (*Killer of Sheep*), Billy Woodberry (*Bless Their Little Hearts*), and Haile Gerima (*Bush Mama*).

> There is another city . . . and another cinema. . . . It begins with *The Exiles* by Kent Mackenzie. You could call it neo-realist. Since it comes from outside the Hollywood studios, you could call it independent, but it's not exactly *Pulp Fiction.* . . . Fifteen years later, there was finally a neo-realist movement in Los Angeles, led by young black filmmakers. . . .

In the year following *The Exiles*'s release, Colin Young, in his capacity as the L.A. editor of *Film Quarterly,* convened a roundtable of critics, producers and directors, including Mackenzie, who was still shopping for a distributor for *The Exiles.* The roundtable prompt was "Personal Creation in Hollywood: Can it be Done?" Mackenzie answered emphatically: "I am not of Hollywood." He claimed that he wanted to make films that made statements, but that no one else in his circle seemed to want the same: "They all want to get into a position, they all want to be directors, they all want to have Cadillacs or security or something like that."[47] Ultimately, we hear Mackenzie suggest that a story with a "statement" about contemporary urban life for American Indians can be made, but not in Hollywood. And if that sounds familiar, twenty years after *The Exiles,* Julie Dash would write and direct a film about Hollywood, *Illusions,* in which her protagonist Mignon Dupree pitched a "viable story" about Navajo codetalkers in the US Marines, and her boss shot it down: "Who cares about a group of Indians talking mumbo jumbo. . . . There's no audience for that kind of story." Who cares? The filmmakers of the Ethno-Communications Program care, as well as the communities that they served and serve still. These narratives matter to somebody, if not in Hollywood, then in Los Angeles. This book tells that story.

This book arrives in the wake of so many literal and metaphoric wakes and wars. If anything, Hollywood seems to be on an upswing in terms of issues of representation both in front of and especially behind the camera, while academia bans, silences, excludes, and increasingly lays out a path that accommodates only the insanely wealthy. In this moment, the formation and (too) short tenure of UCLA's Ethno-Communications Program unfolds as both an inspirational and cautionary tale. I begin the first chapter by providing an overview of the scene at UCLA, both within and beyond its storied film department, in the tumultuous late 1960s, charting not only the innovations in curriculum introduced by then-Theater Arts chair Colin Young, but also the fight for ethnic studies across the wider campus. Chapter 2 begins with the specific battle led by the film department's first black professor, Elyseo Taylor, to establish the affirmative action initiative, originally named the Media Urban Crisis program (MUC). From there we meet the program's first-year class, the original Mother Muccers, and hear directly from them about their multiracial media activist adventures filming their communities from Westwood to Compton, from Chicano Moratorium marches to Asian American rehab facilities to L.A. Panthers headquarters. Through original interviews with dozens of the MUC and Ethno alums, we come to understand that though the program may have formally only lasted three to four years, the filmmakers' political and creative formation in the program would impact their political/creative/professional work for the rest of their lives. The third chapter takes on the Ethno filmography directly, as I comparatively analyze their work, crosscutting between groups of films with shared political themes, demonstrating that the cross-racial relational study of the wider Ethno filmography enhances the study of any of the individual racial groups' body of work. In chapter 4, "Uses of Ethno: The Ethno Filmography as Power," I borrow or improvise on Audre Lorde's iconic title to put the pedagogical power of this filmography to work in two fields, jazz studies and cinema studies, particularly studies of US cinema of the 1970s. Here, I once again crosscut between the fixed "Jazz Tradition" offered up in a series such as Ken Burns's *Jazz*, and the vibrant West Coast scene—especially the legacy of Central Avenue with figures such as Clora Bryant and Horace Tapscott—portrayed so abundantly in the Ethno filmography, which remembers and includes the Asian American and Native American contributors to "America's original art form." I then take on several iconic films and filmmakers of the "New Hollywood," primarily works that are themselves centered in Los Angeles, in conversation with works from the New Los Angeles filmography that tell the stories of the city the industry won't touch. Conversations about class, gender, sexuality, and especially race in the New Hollywood films from Hal Ashby (*The Landlord*) to Mazursky (*Bob & Carol & Ted & Alice*) to Polanski (*Chinatown*), once thought cutting edge, are challenged when juxtaposed with works by the New Los Angeles filmmakers that address subaltern portraits of evictions and forced removals, intersectional portraits of sexism for working class women of color, and humanizing portraits of Japanese gardeners and Chinese American laundrymen, among others. Unlike the infamous closing line of Polanski's film ("Forget it, Jake, it's Chinatown"), the New Los Angeles films insist that we NOT forget about the complex histories of California's Chinatowns and "J-Towns."

Regarding this book's title nod to the Preamble of the Constitution: if any group of directors ever created a filmography that both aspires toward and meaningfully delivers on the inclusive gesture of a "more perfect union," it is the Ethno filmmakers. While far from a traditional portrait of patriotism, their filmography presents an America, and a Los Angeles, I finally recognize. The Ethno filmography features an America that remembers that there are Japanese koto players who grew up in predominantly African American communities, there are Chicana SNCC workers who were part of Freedom Summer, and once upon a time there was even a Kaw/Creek jazz saxophonist who made the Billboard Hot 100.[48] This filmography does include fictional characters Yellow Mary and Trula, whose laughing and lace-cloaked pas-de-deux in *Daughters of the Dust* is lovely, luscious, and . . . exceptional. There is notably little queer representation in the wider Ethno filmography.[49] It is not until we get to Sylvia Morales's *A Crushing Love: Chicanas, Motherhood and Activism*, which I discuss in chapter 3, that we find Cherríe Moraga speaking out directly to the camera about queer desire.[50] Author Peter Sagal has said of the "more perfect" gesture in the Preamble that "progress towards perfection will be unending and uneven,"[51] and nowhere is the unevenness of this Ethno filmography felt more than in the scarcity of narratives about LGBTQ communities of color in L.A. in the '70s and '80s. Even with this growing edge, the insurgent Asian American, Black, Chicana/o, and Native American filmmakers associated with the Ethno-Communications program created one of the most expansive and recognizable portraits of multiracial America that any university-trained cohort of filmmakers has ever produced, and I muse in the book's conclusion as to what it would take to create and sustain a program as generative as the program that happened once upon a rebellious time in Westwood.

1 The "Urban Crisis" in Westwood?

FILM AND SOCIAL CHANGE AT UCLA AFTER WATTS

This is "The University of California" . . . the University of
this State. It must be adapted to this people . . . to the
requirements of their new society and their undeveloped
resources. It is not the foundation . . . of private individuals.
It is "of the people and for the people." . . . It opens the door
of superior education to all.

UC President Daniel Coit Gilman, inaugural address, 1872

What I wish to propose is a new coalition, a new partnership combining the dedication, the moral concerns, and the
spirit of brotherhood of today's younger generation and the
full intellectual resources of our universities in what could
be an unparalleled attack on the social ills of our times . . .
those economic and social and racial and environmental
problems that are encompassed in the term "urban crisis."
As we face the new century ahead, let us pledge our united
efforts to build a University that is as large in spirit as the
times demand.

UC President Charles S. Hitch, inaugural address, May 1968

Francis Ford Coppola had just completed his MFA. There
were two Chicanos in the graduate and undergraduate programs combined with a handful of other minority students.
If the media industry was a bastion of the status quo, then
film schools trained its palace guard. In 1968, film studies
at UCLA was as it had always been.

Renee Tajima, "Lights, Camera . . . Affirmative Action"

The University of California was established in 1868. Five years earlier, Abraham Lincoln delivered his landmark Gettysburg address following the deadliest battle of the Civil War; twenty years earlier, Alta California was still a part of Mexico; and by 1882, California representatives would push the Chinese Exclusion Act through Congress, establishing the first federal law banning a specific ethnic or national group from entering the United States. Out of context, the remarks above by two University of California presidents, delivered a century apart, might appear as if Gilman entered his tenure in a period of calm versus the turmoil under which Hitch assumed his post. What is certain is that the university, both at its inception and its centennial, was in the throes of extraordinary local, national, and international crisis and transition to which it was gearing itself to respond. In 1872, we hear President Gilman adopt the familiar unifying and inclusive language of Lincoln's "of the people and for the people." Yet did the "all" who deserved an open door to superior education include the state's original stewards, the multitudes of Native peoples navigating settler violence, dispossession, incarceration, disease and death? Gilman suggests this public university must adapt to the requirements of a new society, yet in the ensuing decades how well would it adapt to the great and small migrations, forced removals and federal relocation programs that brought Black, Brown, and Asian huddled masses to the Golden State? One hundred years (and eight additional campuses) later, it could be argued that at least part of the social ill and urban crises lamented by President Hitch had to do with the public university's failure to be truly of and for *all* the people of the state. If it had, surely there would have been more than two Chicanos in the Los Angeles campus's film school by 1968.

The escalation of troops in Vietnam and the assassination of Dr. Martin Luther King in Memphis; rebellions in Watts, Newark, and Detroit; Black and Brown bodies dying in disproportionate numbers on battlefields abroad and at the hands of police at home—these global and national pressures were only part of what Hitch was staring down as he prepared his inaugural address in 1968. Within and beyond the UC system, the late 1960s in California witnessed dramatic pendulum swings between protest, progress, and backlash, from the East L.A. Chicano Walkouts, to the Third World Liberation Front–led battles for Black studies and ethnic studies at San Francisco State and UC Berkeley, to the campus shooting deaths of L.A. Chapter Black Panther Party (BPP) leaders John Huggins and Bunchy Carter, who only months earlier had been recruited by UCLA's High Potential Program (HPP). Important Black faculty hires such as Arthur Smith (eventually known as Molefi Asante), Clyde Taylor, and Angela Davis were recruited to UCLA in this period too, although before she gave her first lecture, the Board of Regents attempted to fire Davis for her association with the Communist Party. Even up in North campus, a daring Scottish immigrant chair, Colin Young, was staging his own quiet revolt within the film department. Already a part of the joint student/faculty task force set up in 1968 to support the Black Student Union (BSU) and the United Mexican American Students (UMAS) proposal for the creation of the HPP, Colin Young took seriously President Hitch's call for each department head of every program across each of the nine UC campuses to take concrete steps to address the "urban crises" plaguing the nation.[1] In the case of UCLA's film department these steps would lead to the implementation of a pilot affirmative action media training program for American Indian, Asian American, Black, and Chicana/o students. The activist students who entered this program, learning their craft against the backdrop of so much trouble in the world and in their communities, would soon change the face of independent film and media.

Opening up the field of media was of course a national concern in this period. When President Lyndon Johnson commissioned the Kerner Report (formally titled the "National Advisory Commission on Civil Disorders Report"), a critical aspect of his query into the civil unrest of 1967 was the role of media. The oft-quoted line from the commission (released in March 1968) warned: "Our nation is moving toward two societies, one black, one white—separate and unequal," and part of the commission's analysis included an indictment of the media for exacerbating that gulf instead of using its resources to build bridges. "[We] believe," they wrote, "that the media have thus far failed to report adequately on the causes and consequences of civil disorders and the underlying problems of race relations." The task force interviewed Black residents of "ghettos" who claimed to distrust the "white press" and feel contempt toward media that "acts and talks about Negroes as if Negroes do not read the newspapers or watch television, give birth, marry, die, and go to PTA meetings. . . . When the white press does refer to Negroes and Negro problems it frequently does so as if Negroes were not a part of the audience . . . such attitudes . . . feed Negro alienation." The report repeatedly recommends the recruitment of Negro journalists; it also suggests "Negro reporters and performers should appear more frequently—and at prime time (and) in dramatic and comedy series." Overall the media must "exercise a higher degree of care and greater level of sophistication than they have shown."[2]

Back in Los Angeles, reflecting in 1967 on the need for care and greater communication between the "two" worlds, screenwriter and founder of the Watts Writers Workshop Budd Schulberg wrote, in language that reads like a direct precursor of the Kerner document: "One of the tragedies is that there has been no real channel of communication between Watts and the prosperous communities, between Watts and what you might call 'The outside world.' Watts has been made to feel cut-off, neglected, ignored, rejected." In his introduction to *From the Ashes: Voices of Watts*, Schulberg describes a scene of watching television with some teenagers in Watts and squirming at the way the box was "selling swimming pools and golf courses and at the same time warning them to keep off the grass. I remember feeling, after watching them watch that absurd American Dream of a commercial, that the burning of a supermarket (offering substandard meats and vegetables at higher prices than in Beverly Hills) was, if not forgivable, at least understandable." The Watts Writers Workshop, while mostly Black, would also, according to the collection published by Schulberg, include writers who identified as children of Mexican migratory workers and/or of mixed Negro/Mexican/Apache/European ancestry.[3]

Two societies, separate and unequal . . . only two? While the writers of the Kerner Report sound a clarion call against the absence of Black reporters, Black stories, Black presence in primetime beyond images of burning and looting, the sizable numbers of other people of color in regions such as Southern California go largely unacknowledged in the report. In other words, the tidy binary of "two" societies in a place like Los Angeles was insufficient from the start. Renee Tajima reminds us that Los Angeles in this period was home to the nation's largest Asian and Chicano communities, not to mention the large concentrations of urban Indians.[4] The needs of these multiple societies were going unmet by both the media and the state's major universities. Fortunately for a campus like UCLA, there was a convergence of mobilized community and student activists in the greater city (who were themselves energized by the explosion of creative arts and music from communities of color east and south of Westwood) who were met by a window of willingness by several administrators and faculty open to change. One center of this change on campus took place in the film school led by Colin Young, who was not only receptive to but desirous of change. In the pages that follow, I chart the evolving scene in the film department under Young's innovative leadership in the mid-1960s in conjunction with the wider campus battle for increased enrollment of students of color and for the establishment of Black studies and ethnic studies at UCLA. By doing this I lay the groundwork for my larger argument that the Ethno-Communications Program—which film historian David James has called "the main point of origin for early minority filmmaking in Los Angeles and hence in the nation"[5]—could only have happened on this campus, in this city, at this turbulent time.

EVERGREEN AND THE EVOLUTION OF THE FILM DIVISION UNDER COLIN YOUNG (1964–1970)

Evergreen, a short student film made at UCLA in 1965, captures a sensual though short-lived romance between a jazz saxophonist and an art student in Los Angeles.[6] It is shot in black and white and features music by Herbie Mann and Bill Evans, as well as a single, "Henrietta," by the rock and roll band Rick & The Ravens. The piano player and vocalist for the Ravens, Ray Manczarek, was the graduate student director of this film. A year after the film, the Polish American Manczarek would drop the 'c' from his last name, explaining, "I'm third generation."[7] The Mexican American actor who played the saxophonist changed his name *for* the film from Hank Olguin to Henry Crismonde to sound more "New Wave."[8] And Dorothy Fujikawa, the Japanese American art student who played a Japanese American art student in the film, seems to have kept her name until she married the director. Manzarek's pre-hippy, post-beat short (the title is taken from *Evergreen Review*, the beat literary journal pointedly on display in Dorothy's pad), is filled with shots of the couple making love, running toward each other

Screenshot from *Evergreen* (Ray Manzarek, 1964).

across campus, rolling around on Venice Beach while rapping about alienation and improvisation. Yet, once Dorothy's character utters the word
"marriage," Hank's character runs for the hills. The nude love scenes in this
short were considered so racy, UCLA faculty insisted that Manzarek re-edit
the film before the public screening of selected student work in late May of
1965. Considering that the film was pre-*Loving v. Virginia*, one might
wonder if the interracial aspect of the steamy shower scene had anything to
do with the film's controversy (though anti-miscegenation laws had been
overturned in California since 1948 when the state, in *Perez v. Sharp*, ruled
in favor of the marriage of Mexican American Andrea Pérez and African
American Sylvester Davis).[9] Hollywood barely allowed an interracial
embrace between Dorothy Dandridge and John Justin in *Island in the Sun*
(1957), and television fans would have to wait several more years for the
BIG KISS between Captain Kirk and Lieutenant Uhuru.[10]

Are there obvious progressive politics at work in *Evergreen?* Is it problematic that the Asian American woman lead is topless for much of the
film? Regardless of how the viewer might answer these questions,

Manzarek's casting is worth further consideration. The city of Los Angeles boasted one of the largest populations of both Mexican American and Japanese American residents in the nation; yet, Hollywood was not ready to present an interracial love story (doomed or not) between lovers from these two communities whose demographic numbers and proximity meant this kind of affair was highly likely. Furthermore, an Asian American artist who cogitates on Bertolt Brecht and digs Andre Previn and Miles Davis too? We barely see this level of eclecticism for Asian American women's roles now. A Mexican American military vet and musician who worships avant-garde saxophonist Eric Dolphy? To this day that kind of stereotype-busting character in a Hollywood film is rare, even if his character—for those who know Los Angeles jazz history—might call to mind Watts-born saxophonist Anthony Ortega, who in the 1940s studied with Lloyd Reese, the African American music teacher well-known for tutoring Charles Mingus and Eric Dolphy.[11] Whether intentionally or not, one can read *Evergreen* as offering a tease of the New Los Angeles cinema to come, one that would include more of its communities of color featured in non-traditional/non-stereotypical roles. Even Ray Manzarek, a white ethnic Polish American, male, heterosexual director, lamented the futility of his future in the exclusionary film industry of the 1960s: "Here I am, I've got a master's degree in film from UCLA, I want to be a filmmaker—a director—I love making movies . . . and I don't know a single person in the film business! How the fuck am I going to break into this closed circle of Hollywood?"[12] As rock and roll lore has it, in the summer of '65 he instead bumped into fellow UCLA film school classmate Jim Morrison on Venice Beach and decided to give the music industry another go.[13]

I begin with *Evergreen* and Manzarek's story in an effort to build a case against the idea that UCLA, like its crosstown rival film school USC, was spitting out directing icons or entertainment industry moguls by the dozens as early as the mid-'60s. As galvanizing a term as the "L.A. Rebellion" may be, the expression's implicit characterization of UCLA's film school as "Hollywood" or a "mainstream" bastion that had to be overturned is on some levels misleading. Even before Clyde Taylor dubbed the Black filmmakers from UCLA the "L.A. Rebellion," others such as Renee Tajima, in a 1984 article for *The Independent,* poetically characterized the film school as training the palace guard for the status quo industry.[14] As Colin

Young would repeatedly point out, it was not until the late 1960s—when Francis Ford Coppola (UCLA), George Lucas (USC), and Martin Scorsese (NYU) burst out of university film training programs—that "the studios" even remotely considered film school graduates.[15] UCLA in 1968: overwhelmingly white, yes, but overwhelmingly Hollywood? Not exactly.

The exceptional case of Coppola, according to film critic Michael Sragow, suggests the opposite: "In the sixties, moviemakers coming out of film programs at places like USC and UCLA hoped to revitalize American movies as an art form and overturn the Hollywood status quo. Coppola, as writer-director John Milius recently told me was, 'the rebel envoy, the guy who had gotten into the walled city.'"[16] Considering Tajima's vantage in 1984, by which time Coppola had been nominated for a dozen Academy Awards and taken home five, it is easy to imagine how one might recall the film school that produced him as one that delivered only Oscar gold and golden boys. However, Coppola was an outlier then, the exception and not the rule. In a 1968 interview with John Gelmis, one year after offering his studio feature film *You're a Big Boy Now* as his MFA thesis, he chided, "Oh yes, I'm the famous sell-out from UCLA. Dating back to 1961, when I got my job for $300 a week to write *Reflections in a Golden Eye*. There was open resentment." In the same interview, when asked about Jean-Luc Godard, Coppola suggested that there were "kids" at UCLA and USC who were "incredible Godard addicts," and that "the kids at school are the most narrow-minded of any age group."[17] Gelmis surmises that Coppola's "willingness to work within the system alienated him from the student filmmakers whose heroes are rebels like Godard."[18]

Ray Manzarek, Jim Morrison, and UCLA classmate and later Doors photographer Paul Ferrara were among the "kids" who did in fact idolize Godard. Manzarek reflected in his memoir:

> The actual schooling at UCLA, was incredible. Jim and I learned the "art of the cinema" from some truly wise and inspirational men. The prevailing philosophy of the time was "art first, commerce second." ... [I]n the sixties we were taught to emulate the French New Wave. Directors like Godard and Truffaut and Robert Bresson.... The Maysles brothers and Leacock/ Pennebaker from America. Artists, filmmakers, poets all ... who dared to go against the commercial grain and attempted to make a statement about the human condition.[19]

Manzarek recalled a specific occasion when Morrison passionately defended Godard's *Breathless* to someone who couldn't stand how "cutty" it was. He says Jim went wild: "It's supposed to be cutty, man. It's called jump cutting. It may not be correct for the 'cinema of your papa,' but it's correct for today. It's at our speed, our tempo."[20] If anyone, especially a fellow UCLA film student, didn't agree with their assessment of the "correct" cinema of the day, Manzarek recalls they'd laugh and shout, "Why don't you go to USC where you belong, fascist!"[21]

The University of Southern California (USC) launched its film department, the first in the nation, in 1929; it would be almost two decades before UCLA established its Department of Theater Arts in 1947. Theater Arts was designed to include concentrations in theater, motion pictures, radio and eventually television, but according to Colin Young, initially the film division was "very much second fiddle" to the theater division. Young was a graduate student in the department in the early '50s, under the chairmanship of retired Hollywood producer Kenneth Macgowan. In a special for Scottish television, Young confessed that Macgowan, being "of Scottish extraction . . . thought he had a good thing on his hands when a Scottish philosophy graduate came through his door, and just on that basis he let me in."[22] Sympathy and special treatment for the recently arrived immigrant trying to make his way in the media industry . . . perhaps a seed was planted for Young's later advocacy for programs like the High Potential Program and eventually the Ethno-Communications Program.

Young was born in Glasgow in 1927, the son of a confectioner whose business was destroyed during the Depression. After serving in World War II, he studied philosophy at St. Andrews, wrote film reviews for the *Aberdeen Bon Accord,* and eventually received a scholarship to study philosophy at the University of Michigan. A chance visit with friends in Los Angeles who lived close to Westwood contributed to Young's decision to switch gears, stay put, and earn an MA in film at UCLA in 1954. After completing his degree, he taught editing in the department; became the Los Angeles editor of *Film Quarterly;* and eventually became head of the Motion Picture division of the department. In 1964, Young became the first faculty member from the film division to be named overall chair of the Theater Arts department, a position he held until the summer of

Colin Young with Student Film soup can. Courtesy of the family of Colin Young.

1970. During his decade and a half at UCLA, Young was both witness to and catalyst for many changes in the film division, not to mention the stream of innovative faculty he corralled through the department during his tenure (from Josef von Sternberg and Dorothy Arzner to Basil Wright and James Blue).

In a 1964 article called "Teaching Film at UCLA," Young wrote that when anyone asked how filmmaking was taught at UCLA, his simplest answer was: "The students are encouraged to make a lot of films."[23] He was then anticipating the department's shift from the traditional approach of first teaching students the technical aspects of film (camera, editing, sound, etc.) and then allowing students to make their own films, to the Project system, which gave students the opportunity to write and direct short 8mm films, called "Project Ones," in their first quarter.[24] When I spoke with Young on the verge of his ninetieth birthday, he remembered vividly that "junking" the old system made for much more original films: "The work improved enormously." Also, because no formal selection criteria were in place in those days for undergraduates, the Project One films allowed faculty to see who might have real talent or not.[25]

Even before the project system, Young stressed: "Although close to Hollywood we pay little attention to the Hollywood practice of rigid specialization. We are training filmmakers or writers, rather than technical specialists." Yet, he did lament that due to the school's proximity to Hollywood, it still attracted undergrads who were "academically respectable and artistically vacuous—one eye on his academic record, the other on Hollywood."[26] When I asked about the difference between UCLA and USC during his tenure, Young echoed the notion that USC was "much more Hollywood-tied," but then on further reflection he added:

> It wasn't that there were no ties to Hollywood [at UCLA], but ... it was not clear to me how we could justify having two schools of the same kind almost next door to each other. So ... two things happened, one was that for some reason ... we became more aligned with what you might call the independent filmmakers. The other thing that happened was that we became more and more interested in documentary. There was a very definite attempt to get to the bottom of how to tell stories which were documentaries rather than fiction. Not polemical films but films that told stories.

No matter which school, Young joked, "there was a big tendency of people to think they were the center of the universe." Chuckling, he continued, "it happens to poets and filmmakers."

As a teacher and department chair, he began to wonder how he could get these students to open their eyes to "a larger horizon." As a campus administrator, he began to realize that his natural allies in his determination to open eyes were "not necessarily in the film department," but rather "in sociology, anthropology, ethnomusicology."[27] To this end, by 1966, Young decided to partner with UCLA's anthropology chair, Walter

Goldschmidt, and create the nation's first ethnographic film program.[28] "The approach that we took was, it's the camera that's got to see something, but you'll be behind the camera, so there's no way you can separate yourself from what you're filming. It will not be an objective record, but it will be your experience of looking, and listening. So, this became known eventually as observational documentary."[29] Filmmakers later considered "pioneers" of this tradition of "observational documentary," such as Herb Di Gioia, David and Judith MacDougall, and Jorge Preloran, were students of Colin Young at UCLA. They, along with award-winning cinematographer and director Joan Churchill, transitioned from UCLA film school students to colleagues when he hired each of them to teach at UCLA and/or the National Film School in England (which he founded in 1970 and ran until 1992).

Writing about his days as a student of Young's at UCLA in the mid-'60s, one of the first points David MacDougall emphasizes is how significant the advances in equipment were at the time: "We were the first generation of film students to have access to the new synchronous sound cameras. The Eclairs and Nagras we were allowed to use were the same as those being used by the professional filmmakers on the forefront of documentary. It made us feel professional ourselves. . . ."[30] Joan Churchill and her partner, sound recordist Alan Barker, also a UCLA film alum, hammered home to me how the new equipment changed everything for documentary shooting. They recall that UCLA had some of the first Eclairs, and Barker explained, "The invention of the small camera that was noiseless—'cause there were small cameras before but they made a lot of noise so you couldn't shoot sync sound with them. And then the crystal control recorders, where there was no physical connection between the camera and the recorder—that's what really made 'life on the hoof' documentaries possible." Churchill added, "The other thing was the magazines, you could preload the film into these magazines and (they) would just snap on. So, you didn't have to stop and load, which was very liberating also."[31]

This physical freedom supported one of the key aspects of the approach to filmmaking MacDougall was learning in the Ethnographic Film Program: "The new kind of documentary required a form of immediate decision making which could not be achieved within the industrial model of documentary production, where films are scripted and responsibilities are divided among director, camera operator, and other technicians." This new kind of documentary was also not about technical expertise. In the spirit of the Project One films, MacDougall also noticed when he taught ethnographic workshops at Rice University (in a program he later codirected with James Blue), the first films by the anthropology students were "much more original" than the first films of the film students. MacDougall learned from Young, then taught his own students, that this new kind of filmmaking was "a language that could be used by anyone, thus depriving the professionals of their exclusive hold on the medium."[32]

Two final observations of Young by MacDougall bear mention with the elements discussed above, as together they weave an important prelude to the formation of the *other* "ethno" program to come. MacDougall spends considerable time assessing how Colin Young's philosophy training impacted his own filmmaking practice and future teaching style: "It was probably his training in philosophy that made him focus our attention on the problems of knowledge. How can you know things and how can you know them through film? The new cameras permitted a new form of observation, but what use could this observation be as evidence?" These kinds of questions led to a revaluation of the relationship between the filmmaker, the subject, and the audience. MacDougall, and Young's other students, were tasked with refiguring a more equitable "triangulation," one where the "audience and the film subjects had to be drawn more fully into the filming process as confidants and participants. We should be more involved in a common quest for knowledge and the filmmaker less of a magician, pulling rabbits out of hats."[33] Ideas about a "common quest for knowledge" informed Colin Young's theoretical/pedagogical approach to ethnographic film, and these same ideas significantly informed his practical approach as a campus administrator.

Long concerned with advancing the cause for the "intellectual respectability" of film studies, Young's creation of the joint film and anthropology venture was part of a strategy to convince the larger university administration of the academic seriousness of the motion picture division (even vis-à-vis the theater division).[34] In my conversation with Young he recalled, "I was aware . . . we were not communicating our message very articulately to the rest of campus, who saw us as 'these people up at the North campus who cause trouble and were far too expensive,' cost per student, 'all the other things we could do with that money!' I took it upon myself to become useful to the academic senate. I became a member of the education committee and eventually its chair."[35] In a 2009 interview with the *Journal of British Cinema and Television,* Young addressed specifically his administrative strategy of making links with social science departments (which he did for both the Ethnographic Film Program and later in his conception for what became the Ethno-Communications Program):

> The reason I wanted to make the link with the social sciences was to attack the argument that film was something you went to when you were too tired to do anything serious. The Academy always had that attitude towards it. So getting social scientists on board with us was a quite conscious attempt to attack that argument and to get them committed to film in a way that allowed us to say "look, the real comparison to what we are doing in the film school is not the humanities but the social sciences and the sciences and that is why we need to be given an opportunity to practice what we preach."[36]

By cultivating a productive relationship with UCLA's Chancellor Franklin Murphy, Young consistently received support for most of his proposals. "He was very interested in the Ethnographic Film Program," Young recalled of Murphy. "In fact, he really supported me in all my wild endeavors. It just takes that kind of relationship between administrators (and) all sorts of things can happen in a university."[37]

Young's creative pedagogy and proactive engagement with university administration positioned him to be willing and able to take on President Hitch's charge that the University of California step up its commitment to addressing the "urban crisis." At a Board of Regents meeting on May 17, 1968, one week before his inaugural address, Hitch delivered a report called "What We Must Do: The University and the Urban Crisis," which was described by the *Los Angeles Times* the following morning as: "Massive UC Attack on Urban Problems Called for by Hitch." Sounding like a harder-hitting early draft of his pending inaugural, Hitch fired:

> Our nation, our state, and our cities are in the grip of crisis. It is a moral, economic and racial crisis. . . . [P]erhaps we are mistaken to call it a crisis, for crisis implies brief climax and muted aftermath. We have . . . to face the fact that the trouble of our time is rooted deeply in past inequalities and

injuries, and we have . . . to work for the elimination of the . . . frustration of many, the indifference of many more, and the fears that are corroding the institutions of our democracy. This trouble will be with us until every man is allowed his full measure of human dignity.[38]

Hitch then set forth recommendations for how the university must focus each of its three missions—research, public service, and education—to better serve, recruit and financially support educational opportunities for children of "poor and uneducated parents." And while he avoided the phrase "affirmative action," he did say that more often than not, "to be poor and to be the child of parents who have not had the advantage of education is also to be black or to have a Spanish surname." The following week, before then-Governor Reagan and a crowd of five thousand in Pauley Pavilion, home to so many Lew Alcindor–led Bruin basketball victories, Hitch closed his inaugural address, perhaps channeling Coach Wooden, championing a sense of shared responsibility for the work ahead: "Our ability to carry out our social responsibilities will depend on all of us. . . . Let us pledge our united efforts to build a University that is as large in spirit as the times demand."[39] The speech and earlier report by President Hitch played a critical role in Colin Young's move, in conversation and collaboration with the departments of Sociology and Journalism, to formulate a program to recruit and equip students of color with filmmaking tools so they might make community based media to address the so-called "crisis" in their own neighborhoods. Hitch's charge may have also prompted Young to hire UCLA's first Black film professor, Elyseo Taylor.[40]

Elyseo Jose Taylor joined the faculty of the film division in the 1968–69 school year and was tasked with organizing and recruiting students for what was initially referred to as the Media Urban Crisis program (MUC), officially launched in the winter quarter of the 1969–70 academic year. More on Taylor and the creation of and administrative battle for the program (eventually renamed "Ethno-Communications") will follow in the next chapter. The final section of this chapter will now move out from the film school to get a broader sense of the campus-wide battle for Black studies and ethnic studies at UCLA. The uneasy alliances formed between activists, administrators, and funding organizations to forge new programs, expand curriculum, and increase the representation of students and faculty of color create the backdrop for the arrival of the Mother Muccers.

LEST WE FORGET: THE "THICKET OF RELATIONSHIPS" REQUIRED FOR CAMPUS REVOLUTION

The Third World was not a place, Vijay Prashad reminds us; "it was a project." Reflecting on gatherings like the one that transpired in Bandung, Indonesia, in 1955, Prashad continues, "During the seemingly interminable battles against colonialism, the peoples of Africa, Asia, and Latin America dreamed a new world. . . . They assembled their grievances and aspirations into various kinds of organizations, where their leadership then formulated a platform of demands."[41] US Third World Left projects, such as the Third World Liberation Front of Berkeley and San Francisco in the late 1960s, motivated Black, Asian American, Chicana/o, and Native American student activists to imagine and insist upon new worlds, new programs, new relationships with each other and between their communities and the university. The TWLF strikes in the Bay Area have received much more scholarly attention than the multiracial campus organizing that took place in the same period at UCLA.[42] Craig Collisson, in his rigorously researched dissertation "The Fight to Legitimize Blackness: How Black Students Changed the University," builds a particularly strong case for reexamining the organizing of Black and Mexican American students at UCLA. He goes as far as saying that some scholars "mistakenly point to the fall 1968 San Francisco State strike as the spark 'that set the black studies movement in motion'. . . . While the strike garnered tremendous publicity for black student concerns, successful protests at the University of Washington and UCLA both predate the strike."[43]

Galvanized by President Hitch's inaugural charge as well as the July 1968 appointment of the campus's youngest Chancellor, Charles "Chuck" Young (age thirty-six), new and productive collaborations between student activists, faculty, and administration launched a series of programs designed to respond to the educational demands of students of color across the campus and the city at large. Beginning in June of 1968, Vice Chancellor Charles "C. Z." Wilson, an early high-ranking Black administrator at UCLA, worked with Charles Young and student leaders from the BSU (Black Student Union) and UMAS (United Mexican American Students) to create several task forces. Two of the most important outcomes were the creation of the High Potential Program as well as a preliminary plan for a Black Studies Center.[44] Chancellor Young hired members of the Black Student Union's Education Committee, led by political science student Virgil Roberts, to spend the summer writing up a proposal for the center, and at the same time, a group of Mexican American students, led by Ross Munoz, worked to develop the HPP.[45] Collisson contends that with "near miraculous alacrity, the Munoz-led committee proposed and implemented (the) new minority recruitment program ... designed to give gifted minority students an orientation year with a transitional curriculum to prepare them for the academic rigors of UCLA."[46] In the first year, Collisson reports, the HPP recruited fifty Latina/o students and fifty African American students, including Los Angeles Black Panther Party members Elaine Brown, Geronimo Pratt, Bunchy Carter, and John Huggins. The program eventually extended to recruit Asian American and American Indian students as well. Nicolas Rosenthal reports that as a result of both the HPP and the Equal Opportunity Program (EOP) the American Indian population at UCLA increased from seven to seventy in 1969. As an illustration of how politically volatile these times were, by November of '69 many of these new students left UCLA to join activists from San Francisco State and UC Berkeley to take part in the occupation of Alcatraz. Almost half of the original occupiers were from UCLA.[47]

The story of the formation of a Black Studies Center at UCLA (now known as The Ralph Bunche Center for African American Studies) is a complicated one that tragically includes the 1969 shooting deaths of two of the HPP (and BPP) students, Carter and Huggins, at a meeting of the Black Student Union. Roberts was a central though lesser-known figure in the formation of the center, as well as UCLA's larger Institute for American Cultures. He transferred to UCLA as a political science major in 1966, and in the summer of 1967 was selected to participate in the Foreign Affairs Scholar Program, a Ford Foundation–sponsored minority recruitment program at Howard University. It was there, according to Collisson, that the "political moderate" transitioned to a "black power advocate." Roberts became determined to bring Black Studies to UCLA. He organized a popular course in the spring of 1968 called "The Black Man in a Changing American Context," which featured a series of guest lectures by pioneering scholars and activists such as St. Clair Drake, Kenneth Clark, and Amiri

Baraka. With attendance numbers near five hundred students (a large portion of whom were white) Roberts claimed that the course's success "became our argument for a center," demonstrating there was "something of substance worth studying."[48] Roberts also traveled to San Francisco State with fellow UCLA BSU members to witness how Black Studies was evolving there. Historian Martha Biondi writes that Roberts and his comrades "borrowed some of (San Francisco State's) ideas," but they ultimately proposed a four-unit ethnic studies center. Proposing a center rather than a department, which incorporated Asian American, Mexican American, and Native American units, she writes, won praise (and ultimately implementation) from some but harsh criticism from others. Biondi suggests that the small numbers of Black students on UCLA's campus may have partly inspired Roberts's commitment to creating multiracial alliances, but in a time of such "intense nationalism" there were inevitably members of the BSU at UCLA who were outraged by the proposal. Roberts recalled that he and his education committee members were virtually "excommunicated" from the BSU: "There was a meeting in which the BSU members said they felt we were selling out to white folks, and that they were going to kill all of us."[49]

Mike Murase, a UCLA student and cofounder of the Asian American movement magazine *Gidra*, also criticized the Roberts-proposed, Chancellor Young-established plan to create the four organized research units. Calling it "a conciliatory measure dictated by fear," Murase also emphasized that the units held no authority, for example, to hold courses. Murase placed the onus of the plan for the "center" approach (versus the demands for a Third World College at San Francisco State) on Chancellor Young, who Murase believed was "anxious to maintain the image of UCLA as a peaceful campus."[50] Murase reports that in a letter to the Academic Senate, Chancellor Young "reiterated that tension will exist between those who seek change and those who oppose it, and that 'our task is to keep that tension at an absolute minimum.'"[51] In a 1969 *Gidra* article called "UCLA Sells Out," staff writer Irene Miyagawa also takes aim at Chancellor Young and speaks directly about the consequences of "center" status for the Asian American Studies Center:

> The Man, via puppet Mr. Charlie Young, successfully undermined an unprepared student power movement at UCLA. . . . The creation of the Ethnic

Studies Center was paternalistically given to the students of Third World background. The students can effect control of the budget only through a faculty director. Already, the Asian American Studies Center is "promised" an official $100,000. "Center" status means that the program is subject for annual renewal. It can be discontinued. In short, the students accepted a second-class "Center" status . . . not a department, not a separate college. The Center is extremely vulnerable.[52]

And future Ethno-Communications film student Eddie Wong, in an opinion piece for the same issue of *Gidra,* had this message for the Chancellor: "Chuck Young understands that Third World student groups will not tolerate the shuck-and-jive routine Young usually employs to extricate himself from campus conflicts and commitment to minority programs."[53]

Writing about the difference between student demands and their implementation, Craig Collisson and Noliwe Rooks remind us that many Black studies programs were "invariably institutionalized as part of a larger constellation of ethnic studies centers."[54] Collisson holds in tension the claims that university administrators' attempts to create ethnic studies centers were merely strategic with important claims that multiracial solidarity and coalition mattered to these student activists of color. On the administration side, Collisson posits:

> At UCLA, the administration decided early on to include as many ethnic groups as possible in the Institute of American Cultures. This was done partly to avoid future student protest and partly out of a commitment to ethnic studies. But the IAC was also created to avoid charges that black studies centers were yet another example of reverse discrimination. . . . If administrators were to only institutionalize a black studies curriculum, critics could argue they were creating a separatist, racist curriculum. . . . When institutionalized alongside other ethnic studies programs, black studies became one voice among many. They became not a separatist program, but an inclusive one that embraced multiculturalism.[55]

Collisson also suggests that Virgil Roberts took "coalitional politics" seriously. His fellow BSU activist and HPP recruiter Daniel Johnson recalled in an interview with Collisson, "What's wrong with you having your Asian Americans doing the same exact thing? Because that only strengthens our claim and reinforces the notion of what's absent in American history." But again, on the administration side, Collisson lays out the uncomfortably self-congratulatory language of certain UCLA administrators in 1969 about the launch of the Institute of American Cultures (IAC). There was, he says, no mention of the United States "as a race-based caste society." Instead they spoke of the "celebration of the rich tapestry of American cultures." Vice Chancellor Paul Proehl, in an example given by Collisson from a *Daily Bruin* article about the launch of the IAC, announced, "We hope that the project will be representative of America's pluralistic society which is developed neither by separatism nor by assimilation, but by something that partakes of both at the same time recognizing the uniqueness of each individual group but admitting the ultimate goal of a truly integrated society."[56]

Critical ethnic studies scholars continue to grapple with how the "solidarity" framing of the Third World Liberation Front at UC Berkeley and San Francisco State was "co-opted into a liberal politics of multiculturalism."[57] And down in Westwood, brave alliances from student and community activists coincided with hollow "pluralism" platitudes of administrators from the very start. This is not to say that the four ethnic studies centers established there did not go on to serve (and multiply the numbers of) students of color at UCLA, with thriving and generative research centers that are still active today. Even the activist publication *Gidra* was initially housed at and supported by the Asian American Studies Center on campus. Vital academic journals such as the *Journal of Black Studies, Amerasia Journal, Aztlan: A Journal of Chicano Studies,* and the *American Indian Culture and Research Journal* were all founded and/or flourished as a result of these centers.[58] Most importantly for this book, the centers would play an important role in recruiting and providing financial support for many of the first Ethno-Communications film students.

Noliwe Rooks, in her important study on the Ford Foundation, further interrogates what she calls the "thicket" multiracial alliances, not only between people of color but also including white administrators, white university faculty, and white philanthropic organizations. In what may have been fodder for UC President Hitch's spring 1968 inaugural address, Rooks provides details of McGeorge Bundy's early addresses at the start of his new presidency of the Ford Foundation in 1966. Bundy claimed in August that "solving America's racial troubles would define his presidency." At a National Urban League dinner also that year, Bundy announced, "that full equality for all American Negroes is now the most urgent domestic concern," and by 1967, Bundy suggested that "the most deep-seated and destructive of all the causes of the Negro problem is still the prejudice of the white man." Rooks argues that the implementation of Black studies programs "became the primary method through which Bundy and the Ford Foundation would attempt to address the 'Negro Problem,' and they quickly set about the task of convincing administrators in colleges and universities that the new field was a tool for achieving democratic racial reform."[59]

Earlier in her study, Rooks describes her own challenges about the project of reframing this early history of Black studies. Was this a story—to echo Toni Morrison's charged refrain at the close of *Beloved*—that should or should not be passed on? Rooks writes, "I rarely told people that what fascinated me was not necessarily the protest of Black students, but the fact that the first student strike—leading to the first department of Black Studies—was decidedly interracial and democratic." Calling the interracial aspect one of the "unremarked-upon" legacies of the movement for Black studies, she continues, "at San Francisco State, Black, white, Native American, Asian, and Latino students rose up together, joined forces, and made or supported unequivocal demands," and then she repeats: "Overwhelmingly, history has forgotten that any but Black students were ever involved in the student strike that produced Black Studies at San Francisco State."[60] This point is important even if it unintentionally contains a slight erasure of the generations of students of comparative ethnic studies trained at SF State and UC Berkeley for whom this history has not only not been forgotten but is at the center of their academic work.[61] At the heart of Rooks's concern seems to be whether or not the victories of Black studies for Black activists and scholars are somehow diminished by remembering the other people of color as well as their white allies and even their philanthropic benefactors:

> The stories, incidents, and history discussed here as part of the founding of African American Studies mattered profoundly to those involved, and they evoke powerfully remembered emotions from a time before African Americans could assume their acceptance in America's colleges and universities. . . . For them, people who had fought and sometimes suffered bodily

injury and/or material loss for the cause, the formation of hundreds of African American Studies programs on college campuses in the late 1960s and early 1970s meant more than a mere opportunity to engage in study about the history and literature of people of African descent; it represented a hard-won success story from the civil rights/Black Power era. Within that narrative, African American students were the main characters and solely responsible for asking for and receiving racial acknowledgement, acceptance, and most importantly, resources and respect.

Victories and successes matter, Rooks concludes, so she wonders: should historical memory "be tampered with" if the impact of the victories is lessened? Is it a story to pass on? Rooks ultimately answered in the affirmative, given her belief "that there is an important story to be told about the thicket of relationships among white philanthropy, America's changing struggles with racial integration at the university level, and the field of African American Studies," though she concedes that "clarity does not always ameliorate the significance of memory, and that intent cannot control the use of memory in the service of power."[62]

I quote these passages from Rooks's work at length because I take her concerns quite seriously and have at times wondered if my own decision to focus on the multiracial roots and cinematic fruit of the Ethno-Communications Program in any way lessens the "victories" of the L.A. Rebellion school of Black filmmakers. Does the shared multiracial victory dampen the monoracial one? Or could we consider the inclusive and grammatically creative lyrics of Curtis Mayfield, "We're a winner . . . we're all moving on up. . . ."

In Elaine Brown's Panther memoir *A Taste of Power*, she poignantly remembers a New Year's Eve coalitional meeting with the Brown Berets. "Mexicans, or Chicanos, had joined with other Latinos to form the group. Patterning their program after ours, they wore brown berets, à la the Panther black beret, to represent the unity of our common revolutionary commitment. Black Panthers and Brown Berets welcomed in the new year: 1969."[63] Just midway into the first month of the new year, her High Potential Program and Black Panther comrades John Huggins and Bunchy Carter were killed at a meeting in Campbell Hall to determine who should run the new Black Studies Center at UCLA. There were US Organization members who were also participants in the High Potential

Program; it is not clear however if the US Organization members present January 17, 1969, in Campbell Hall—one who shot Huggins and Carter but was never apprehended, another three who were charged with conspiracy and second-degree murder—were even students at UCLA. (US leader Maulana Karenga, who was not there that day, had been a student at UCLA in the earlier 1960s, earning a BA and MA in Political Science). Whether or not this was a clear case of the FBI infiltrating both organizations, as has widely been speculated, I raise these points to further complicate what Rooks called the "thicket of relationships," intra and interracially, during this most turbulent time.[64]

Less than one year earlier, at a Black Power rally in Los Angeles, Bobby Seale, Stokely Carmichael, and Maulana Karenga, among others, shared the stage at the Los Angeles Sports Arena. Future Ethno-Communications Program student and organizer Moctesuma Esparza remembered the rally well because he was one of two non-Black speaker. He told me that years before the tragic shooting at UCLA, after the Watts Riots, the Young Citizens for Community Action, a group of Chicano high school activists who would later be known as the Brown Berets, were "communicating and meeting with Maulana Ron Karenga. We were close to US and later I became very close to the Panthers. In fact, Elyseo Taylor filmed me at the Black Power rally at the Sports Arena (in) 1968. Yeah, he filmed me. . . . He didn't know me then. . . . And I declared war on the United States and racism. The whole auditorium leaped up. . . . It was an astonishing moment."[65] The radio archive of the show confirms that Esparza was invited to introduce Anselmo Tijerina at the rally (Anselmo was the brother of New Mexican activist Reies Tijerina, who was also scheduled to speak but had been delayed). His brief but well-received remarks were as follows:

> Brother Seale said a little while ago that the Black man has been facing a war of oppression from the "Gabacho," that is what we call "whitey!" [huge cheers] for the last 400 years! Well the Gabacho has been in the Southwest for over 100 years and we have been facing a war of extermination for that time. Right now there is a war. A war in the streets, a war in the hills of Northern New Mexico—and right here today is one of the men . . . carrying on that war against the Gabacho, because he is doing us ALL in. And he will do us all in if we don't fight him, so we have got to fight him! And we have got to fight! (cheers) Anselmo Tijerina![66]

Whether this rally was before or after Colin Young recruited Elyseo Taylor, it was apparently the event that inspired Taylor to recruit Esparza to head the student planning group of the Media Urban Crisis Committee. This committee, which laid the foundation for the Ethno-Communications Program, received its first significant grant from the Ford Foundation in 1969, though surely somewhere there was a Mother Muccer who referred to them as the "¡Gabacho Ford Foundation!" Whether the Ford Foundation was seen as "the Man" or as a funding ally, their dollars supplied new Eclairs and Nagras for the incoming class of Black, Chicana/o, Native American, and Asian American insurgent film students—weapons for the fight and the films ahead. The ensuing multiracial solidarities on and behind the camera of the Ethno-Communications film projects might, like Manzarek's *Evergreen,* produce shorts that were shot handheld in black and white, and would definitely feature local music legends and swinging jazz scores. But the similarities end there, as Sylvia Morales insisted: "For us, there was a sense of urgency, so we set aside our desires to make personal films in order to make ones that reflected our communities."[67] The days of whimsical interracial flings on film were over, in order to make way for a more demanding and relevant cinema, in order to form a more perfect rebellion.

Elyseo Taylor and the Ethno Ethos

ONE FOOT ON CAMPUS, ONE FOOT IN THE COMMUNITY

We were all sort of crossing over into whatever the political interests were of the members of the group. So, you were always out and trying to be involved, trying to be relevant at the time . . . trying to use media to expand the political awareness of not only ourselves but the quote unquote, community.

Richard Wells, original Mother Muccer

We did have the camaraderie. I think it was [Taylor's] vision. He actually had a class called "Film and Social Change," so, he had really felt that films were not addressing social problems. I really give credit to Elyseo . . . to this day, [we're] still involved in social change, so our theme is always about social change, social justice, social injustice.

Danny Kwan, original Mother Muccer

Elyseo Jose Taylor (1923–2006) was a soldier (an original "Black Panther" of the 761st Tank Battalion)[1], a filmmaker, a changemaker . . . and a mystery. The course he first taught at UCLA in the early 1970s, "Film and Social Change," is still a popular course on that campus, now in its sixth decade. The students he recruited, taught, or advised there, hailing from East L.A. to East Africa, would create a body of work that changes how we think about filmmaking in the 1970s in Los Angeles and how we understand the multiracial landscape and culture workers of the city itself. Yet after he was denied tenure at UCLA in the mid-1970s, Taylor more or less vanished from the public record. While this chapter does not exhaustively unlock the mystery of his disappearance (though it surely hopes to inspire others to take on that task!), it picks up the theme of film and social change—a focus he shared with his campus recruiter, Colin Young—by outlining Taylor's vision for change at the film school and the battle he faced attempting to implement it. Then, to dispute any claim that the Ethno program's short tenure means that it was a failure, I bring in the voices of the students who directly benefited from and helped to shape the program in its earliest days. These activist filmmakers kept "one foot on campus and one foot in the community."[2] *Communities*, plural, is perhaps more accurate, as the first group of students insist that one of the most gratifying parts of the program was working together, cross-racially, in each other's communities to tell stories that no one else was bothering to tell in the so-called Hollywood Renaissance of the 1970s. They were inadvertently insisting on, then producing, a New Los Angeles Cinema. A Chicago-born son of a civil rights lawyer instigated this Los Angeles story, though its spark may have been set in Geneva, Switzerland, of all places.

In the months leading up to the Watts Uprising of 1965, Taylor was living abroad, working as a photographer and film director for a Swiss ad agency. He had just been hired to shoot a segment for a USIA propaganda film called *Eulogy to 5:02*. Written and produced by future Nixon speechwriter and Reagan adviser Bruce Herschensohn, the Cold War documentary travelogue features voice-of-God narration by Hollywood icon Richard Burton.[3] With convincing charm and veritas, Burton explains that on this particular May afternoon in 1965, world leaders did not sign a treaty. For historians this minute went "unrecorded and unremarked," but "for the two-thirds of the world who live in freedom, 5:02 *was* significant. For it was another minute spent in doing what they *chose* to do—to work if they wanted to work, to dream if they wanted to dream, to live as they wanted to live." The film then proceeds to show exactly one minute of life in a dozen or so nations of the "free world"—a wedding here, a birth there, an afternoon harbor cruise in Geneva. Taylor was tasked with shooting several well-dressed Swiss women catching a sunset cruise, as Burton's narration extols their freedom to choose to savor a spring holiday on the water. Period. *Cut to:* scenes of the next *free* nation.

The correspondence between Taylor and Herschensohn coordinating the shoot for this bizarre project includes telegrams and letters starting in the spring of 1965 and ending in August, at which point Taylor acknowledges that he is leaving Europe to return to the United States and requests a meeting with Herschensohn in Hollywood. There is no evidence that a future California connection ever occurred between these two men. What we do know is that within days of Taylor's request, a young African American man, Marquette Frye, was pulled over by the LAPD just outside of Watts, and the fires of '65 soon followed.

> When the black ghetto of Watts in Los Angeles went up in flame in August of 1965, America was seized with fear and indignation. . . . Fear, for after the initial shock had subsided it realized that it knew very little about these communities. . . . [W]hat chance was there for a white person to know anything about life in the ghetto? As for visiting it, he was discouraged from doing so by the stream of stories in the media of race hatred. . . . It took murderous rioting to awaken the nation to the true extent that mass media had failed them. . . .
>
> When I began teaching filmmaking as a private undertaking in Watts soon after the insurrection, my idea was that art, including film, was a means by which a people could engage in a dialogue with itself. . . . In making their own films, the people would begin their own dialogue, they would be able to become acquainted with themselves as a community. They could look into all of its parts, learn the needs, discover the dreams, search for solutions to common problems.[4]

The return home to the US in the late summer of 1965 is clear, but the precise arrival of Taylor to Westwood is difficult to pinpoint. In several reports about his time at UCLA, he mentions coming back to the States just after the Watts "insurrection." The lines above were delivered by Taylor at a media conference in Bellagio, Italy, over a decade after Watts, but from his emphasis on the flames and murderous rioting, one can't help but imagine that the disconnect between filming the harbor-cruising Swiss elite while reading headlines of the Black insurrection in Watts may have motivated Taylor to redirect his talent toward more meaningful pursuits.[5] After working with various community filmmaking projects around Watts and later the UCLA Extension Media Center,[6] he was eventually recruited by Colin Young.[7]

Elyseo Taylor. From the collection of Karen Taylor.

Young's memory of Taylor's recruitment was less clear by the time of our correspondence: "What I can't recall is how Elyseo arrived on the scene, but he must have been involved in this planning stage." In the same email response to my question about how he first came into contact with Taylor, he did share a detailed account of the first time he introduced Elyseo Taylor to the new UCLA chancellor, Charles Young, who took over in July of 1968. This memory was crystal clear:

> Anecdotally I can cite Elyseo's insistence that he accompany me to the (then new) Chancellor Chuck Young at his annual garden party-cum-reception at

> the end of what must have been his first year with us. I tried to wriggle out of it because it clashed with a wine stomp in Topanga where I lived. I remember Elyseo saying that I had to "take my Nigger along" . . . to meet the Chancellor so I took my university togs with me to the wine stomp. When the time came, I clambered out of the crushed grapes, plunged into the nearby pool and changed rapidly for the drive to campus. One problem only—I had forgotten to bring a pair of shoes. All I had were my grape stained sneakers. Although they had not been in the vat (we were bare footed and bare everything else for the stomp) they were stained neverthe-less. Elyseo was aghast. I just hoped Chuck Young wouldn't notice, but he did—demanding an explanation. This didn't do Elyseo any harm. In fact, the contrary. It gave him status in Chuck's eyes—if he could get me back from Topanga . . . he must be somebody to be taken seriously.[8]

This oddly specific recollection is most unsettling in terms of the snapshot it offers of the code-switching and role-playing Taylor must have per-formed as the "first Black" faculty in film, whether he ended up "gaining status" in the new chancellor's eyes or not. Taylor was a soldier, and the art of carefully navigating the hierarchy, from chancellor to undergrad, in search of useful allies was likely a skill he had cultivated over decades.

There had been very few students of color training in filmmaking prior to Elyseo Taylor's hiring. Several graduate students who were there—including Charles Burnett, Betty Chen, and David Garcia—would become important players in the Ethno program in their role as teaching assist-ants. Earlier African American film students such as Ike Jones and Vantile Whitfield had come and gone before the Ethno students arrived, although Whitfield, as founder of the Black theater workshop PASLA (the Performing Arts Society of Los Angeles) in 1964, continued to contribute to the flourishing of the Black filmmaking at UCLA well into the 1970s by providing much of the phenomenally talented acting pool for early Rebellion films. There were also talented and imaginative students like Nettie Peña and Robert Grant, who made significant contributions to L.A. music lore (Peña) and/or crewed historic music documentaries (Grant); yet their UCLA student films did not necessarily focus on political activ-ism in their communities or on people of color at all.[9] Taylor needed energetic, community-engaged students to launch his "urban crisis" program, and with the help of political organizer/undergrad history major

Moctesuma Esparza, and the support of the brand new ethnic studies centers on campus, he gathered just that.

"UCLA Students Will Film Aspects of Ghetto Life as Means to Dialog" ran the *Times* headline January 4, 1970, to announce that "a group of UCLA graduate and undergraduate students will be taking part in a project aimed at throwing light on life in the ghetto and perhaps broadcasting that light to others." The announcement of the program was just shy of the one-year anniversary of the Campbell Hall shooting deaths of Black Panther Party (BPP) and High Potential Program (HPP) members Bunchy Carter and John Huggins. One year after that campus tragedy there is a new message of hope, especially for the twenty students selected, who are listed as "nearly all members of minority groups ... blacks, American Indians, Mexican and Asian Americans, and a few whites."[10] The program, not yet given the title of Ethno-Communications, was described as being "under the direction of Elyseo J. Taylor, assistant professor of motion pictures," and Taylor's philosophizing about the state of media for "ghetto" residents dominates the article. In fact, he is the only person from UCLA—faculty, staff, or student—quoted in the article.

The impetus for the program, in Taylor's words, had to do with his sense "that most of the problems of the ghetto are either created or magnified because there is no dialog between the minority community and the greater community." Without stronger media produced by people of color from their own communities, "the good things" about these communities are "unknown to everyone." Art is the means by which, Taylor continues, "people communicate, have a dialog, and so far people in the ghettos have been eavesdropping on the dialog the white community has been having with itself." The article provides brief biographical details of Taylor's academic and professional career, describing him as a University of Chicago graduate in sociology and economics, who "also studied at several universities in Europe and taught economics at the University of Basel." He is also described as having owned his own film and advertising company in Switzerland.[11]

Taylor stresses that in the past a number of diversity training programs had been attempted and quickly failed.[12] One project that he saw as an exception to learn from was George Stoney's "Challenge for Change" community media project, created with the National Film Board of Canada in

1967, that trained Indigenous residents of Fogo Island in filmmaking.[13] He also mentions a UC Media Extension precursor to Ethno, under the direction of UCLA film school grad Peter Schnitzler, that had recently begun to train "black and Chicano youths of high school and junior college age . . . in basic filmmaking techniques" with the aim of using film "as a means of self-expression, social perception and acquiring professional skills."[14] In both cases these training programs for people of color were run by white filmmakers. It is worth noting that an article announcing a training program for people of color led, at last, by a faculty person of color, does not make this explicit. Taylor's race, or that he was the first Black faculty member hired by the film school, is not mentioned in the article. With the emphasis on his European training and professional background there would be no obvious way to know.

Colin Young's garden party tale loosely suggests that Taylor made a good impression with Chancellor Chuck Young; however, fellow film school professor Richard Hawkins did not have such a positive assessment of Taylor. In an oral history conducted by the UCLA Film and Television Archive, Hawkins recalled, "Yes, I remember Elyseo. . . . [W]e found him not terribly effective, and the students did not particularly take to him. I don't—I think he was there for a year or so, I don't remember just how long. At that time we were trying to reach out to get more diversity in the department and also among the students. . . ."[15] Though the employment records of Taylor remain private even after his death, it appears minimally from the UCLA catalog archives that Taylor was a member of the Theater Arts faculty from at least 1969 to some point in the 1973–74 school year, more than the "year or so" Hawkins remembered.

A $17,200 Ford Foundation grant was secured in the summer of 1969 for the Media Urban Crisis program (MUC), which in most archival reports Taylor refers to as "his program." This grant was part of a larger $250,000 Ford Grant awarded to the Regents of the University of California "for research and development projects in urban affairs for a one-year period." The early memos awkwardly refer to the UCLA program as the "Communication and Learning Through Film Production Project," and explain: "The specific objective of this project is to relate media training to community development, and to use media (films) as a means for tying the minority community and the University together. Through this project, UCLA seeks to research, establish and develop a new interdisciplinary media curriculum under the administration of the Department of Theatre Arts."[16] A later description stressed that the students themselves were central to the program's implementation: "A staff of students . . . helped to construct the curriculum and to establish criteria by which candidates were to be recruited."[17] Taylor's year-end report captures the program's priorities. Motion pictures and television as means of communication can make "critical contributions" to "community development," Taylor begins, "particularly in the Ethnic Minority Communities." He insists that any such communications "would have to be done by the people in these communities, and not by outsiders"; therefore this pilot program was a means to "devise a program of instruction for young people from the Ghettos and Barrios so that they would be able to make films in, for and about their communities." The recruitment criteria was established as: junior standing or above (a mix of undergrads and graduate students), demonstrated artistic ability, and *"evidence of involvement in community affairs"* (emphasis mine).[18] Taylor's insistence on recruiting students with "community involvement" and the consistent language of film and social change deserves a bit more context.

Taylor and Colin Young both looked to George Stoney and the National Film Board's "Challenge for Change" media collaborations with Indigenous activists as inspiration for what they were launching at UCLA.[19] Between Taylor and Young, the language of media and "social change" was everywhere, from titles of publications, to a publicized guest lecture featuring both professors ("Cinema and Social Change," auspiciously scheduled for May 4, 1970, the day of the Kent State shootings), and it is the phrase Taylor took up for the title of his first course taught on campus.[20] The refrain was so frequent it was one of the first questions I was eager to ask Young about when we met.

Film and social change was, in Young's estimation, hardly an original idea. "It was in the blood of documentary. . . . It goes back in my knowledge to John Grierson, the Scottish/British head of documentary in England, prewar," who later founded Canada's National Film Board (1939). "Their politics were socialist—not a word you hear very often in the US." He interrupted himself to joke: "Except in Vermont . . . good Old Bernie!" Then continued, "British documentary was very much class driven

... giving a lot of time and space to the working class and telling their stories."[21] Young did not recall the planned joint lecture with Taylor on cinema and social change, but he remembered many conversations with him about the topic and was "so pleased to have somebody like Elyseo to collaborate with." What may have evolved into a productive partnership was cut short when Young accepted an invitation to return to the UK and head up their National Film School. Taylor was left to fight for and protect his Media Urban Crisis program unsupported by a powerful departmental chair.

A thorough read through the UCLA special collections records of the memos shared between the faculty and staff connected with the Media/ Urban Crisis Committee (MUCC)[22] from April 1969 through the spring and summer of 1970 suggest that as Colin Young's advocacy and leadership dropped off, Taylor's memos become more frustrated. The ensemble of vice chancellors who at one point appeared enthusiastic toward Young's plans were apparently increasingly skeptical of Taylor's. Memoranda from the four ethnic studies centers included in later stages of the planning become downright heated by the slow pace of the organization and implementation of the program and the questionable support for their students of color associated with it. The directors of the Afro-American Center, Asian American Center, American Indian Project, and the Mexican-American Cultural Center declare that the Media Urban Crisis program has "become a step-child within the Theatre Arts Department—unwanted, neglected and exploited." They remind the chancellors that their initial letters from the prior spring 1969 outlined a sincere commitment to the university's responsibility to address itself to the urgency of the multiple urban crises at hand; yet one year later "the urgency has deepened and the responsibility has been shirked."[23] This impassioned letter from the four ethnic studies centers triggers a series of backpedaling and passing the buck memos from the vice chancellors declaring Elyseo Taylor's actions were "premature" and "went beyond the Committee charge,"[24] and there are more and more doubts about the "leadership of Theater Arts in the Urban Crisis area."[25] Sprinkled into the pile of warring memos are notes from Taylor going to bat for *his* Urban Crisis students to receive the financial aid that they require, and yet he is scolded for not going through the proper channels to secure these funds. One can literally see the administrative undermining at work, with Taylor cc'ing multiple parties and then those parties consulting with one another without cc'ing Taylor.

By the end of May 1970, there is a parting of the ways. A memo titled "Minutes of the Standing Committee on Ethno-Communications" signals the first shift. There is a new name for this program: Ethno-Communications (no information is given about who gave it that title). Film professor John Young is listed as "Chairman," Colin Young is not among the attendees and is nowhere mentioned in the three-page memo, and Taylor is simply listed as "present." There is a clear distinction made between "Mr. Taylor's Urban Crisis program," the two-quarter pilot program now coming to a close, and the new Ethno-Communications Program, whose students would be selected "jointly by the faculty and Ethno-Communications students (on a one-to-one basis) and the Ethnic cultural center(s)." The curriculum would still be interdisciplinary, including courses in "cultural awareness" by the sociology department, as well as courses in "History of African, Asian and South American Film" and "Film and Social Change."[26]

While Elyseo Taylor's role as leader of the Ethno Program may have shifted (there is no mention of Ethno-Communications as "my program," the way he deemed the MUC program his), his impact on the curriculum is undeniable. The UCLA course catalog beginning with the 1970/71 academic year lists Taylor as the professor of "Film and Social Change," and beginning in 1971 he is the faculty of record for "History of African, Asian and South American Film" at least until 1974.[27] And then he seems to disappear. I have not ever been able to secure official documents explaining Elyseo Taylor's denial of tenure nor found any discussion of it in the press.[28] At best we have the closing title card from Ben Caldwell's 1979 student film, *I & I: An African Allegory*, which reads: "Thanks go to Elyseo Taylor who was my advisor until he was fired for racist reasons."[29]

More fallout over his departure will be revisited at the end of this chapter. But it is time to go back now to the beating heart of the matter: the arrival of the Mother Muccers. Other than the existence of a few of their names on a handful of documents held in UCLA's special collections, the student filmmakers' voices are absent in those archival materials. Yet they *are* the story—their personal and political journeys to UCLA and their creative and professional journeys from Ethno onward. The special collections documents characterize MUC and/or Ethno as a briefly promising, ultimately failed departmental nuisance, motivated by the flicker of care the university was supposed to demonstrate in the heat of the multiple crises (local and global, political and economic). The students' stories, told to me in rapturous interviews, deliver an entirely different tale of groundbreaking shifts in the history of media by people of color once they were surrounded by like-minded activist classmates and armed with cameras to document the "good things," the bitter and beautiful struggles in their communities.

INTRODUCING THE ORIGINAL "MOTHER MUCCERS"

While there are discrepancies about the original number of students admitted to the first class of the Media Urban Crisis program (some say thirteen, others twenty), there is general agreement among those I interviewed from that class that the group minimally consisted of Moctesuma Esparza, Luis Garza, Wendell Handy, Sandra Sunrising Johnson, Danny Kwan, David Lazarin, Brian Maeda, Francisco Martinez, Yasu Osawa, Cliff Stewart, and Richard Wells. It may have also included Marie Kodani and Rufus Howard.[30] Of this first group, I was able to speak in person with Esparza, Garza, Kwan, Maeda, Wells, Sandy Johnson (now Sandy Johnson Osawa), and Yasu Osawa. My first stroke of luck came from finding Luis Garza at the moment he was working on a commemorative exhibition of the Chicano Movement publication *La Raza* for a retrospective at the Autry Museum in Los Angeles.[31] This meant I caught Garza—whose role as a photographer for *La Raza* in the late 1960s led him to UCLA—deep at the work of remembering and surrounded by images of the times.

> Each one of us has a different path into Ethno-Communications . . . so I think that those are some of the threads within the storyline: How do you get into it and what do you get out of it? What are you doing in it when you're in it, how do you come out of it and where are you now?[32]

With that gift of an overview, he proceeded to share his own path to studying film at UCLA, which like many of the first-year Muccers was paved by community activists, not industry insiders.[33]

Born in the South Bronx, Garza made his way west in the mid-'60s, landing in Los Angeles within weeks of the Watts Uprising. He cobbled together a living with odd jobs, an unpaid photography apprenticeship with Sam Kwong (a commercial photographer from Hong Kong who offered him in exchange a place to sleep in his basement), and sporadic work in Hollywood as an extra, cast often as American Indian because he knew how to ride a horse. Ultimately, a social worker friend of Garza's introduced him to community organizer Ed Bonilla, who ran an East L.A. chapter of NAPP, the Neighborhood Adult Participation Program, which Garza explains was one of Lyndon Johnson's Great Society job training programs. Garza describes Bonilla as "a barrel of a man . . . total Raza from East L.A., heavy into the beginnings of the movement . . . the old guard . . . goatee, black sunglasses"—not how the young Garza imagined the director of a government program would look. Apparently, Bonilla was just as confused by Garza, who'd walked into his office with a camera around his neck:

> "So, you're from New York?" I go, "Yeah." "And you're Chicano?" Now, I was not familiar with the term. "If you say so." I was not going to blow the gig. "A Chicano from New York? You're not Puerto Rican." I go, "Well, by osmosis." I'm also Italian, Jewish, Irish, by osmosis, that's the only way I could survive in New York, I had to be a chameleon. So, Ed says, "A Chicano from New York . . . órale! That's different. And you need a job . . . órale! You got the job esé!" I go, "Alright, fantastic man! Um, what is the job?" He says, "You're going to organize." I go, "Organize who, organize what?" He says, "You're going to organize the people." So that was my introduction.

Bonilla took an interest in Garza's camera and introduced him to the editors of *La Raza*.[34] Bonilla also encouraged Garza to go back to school, suggesting that he could get him into UCLA through yet another Great Society program. "This is how Chicano Studies or Black Studies or Asian Studies were recruiting from the various communities . . . getting your foot in the door for those who thought they never had a chance at higher education. So, I got in." Once on campus he met up with Moctesuma Esparza, who he'd known from *La Raza*, and Esparza recruited him into the Media Urban Crisis program. While I'd read about the groups' feisty nickname, this was the first I'd heard it directly from someone involved:

We referred to ourselves as *Mother Muccers*. Oh, we took great pride. After doing some doobies and drinking, you know, we'd be singing, "All praises, all power to the Mother Muccers!" But it was also a reference to journalism, muckraking, and so there was a metaphoric interpretation of it . . . because we raised hell.

The Muccers were a serious presence on campus, according to Moctesuma Esparza. Gregory Nava, who was not a part of the Muccers but was at UCLA at the time, reportedly told Esparza that when he'd see the Muccers walking down the hall, "Everybody would open up and let us cross . . . afraid of us."[35] On a more serious note, Garza explained that the first group of students had real battles with the administration to demand that they be taken seriously and their requests for new and relevant curriculum be implemented. He described the process as a real learning curve, "doing school work and then doing community work," especially "at a time when there was such chaos throughout the country and in our communities." This precarious balance of tackling activist work both on and off campus immediately became a thread in my conversations with each of the first group of Muccers.

Esparza, the student who may have received the most mainstream commercial success later in his career, was also one of the students who was most entrenched in movement activism of the late '60s—from felony conspiracy charges to Emmy award winner and Oscar nominated producer. Esparza was already an organizer when he graduated from Lincoln High School in 1967: "I had been trained by folks that had worked and trained with Cesar Chavez, and so from the age of about fourteen I had already been engaged as an organizer."[36] At UCLA as an undergrad he was one of the founders of UMAS (United Mexican American Students), which later changed its name to MEChA (Movimiento Estudiantil Chicano de Aztlan); he was also one of the founders of the Brown Berets. For orchestrating the 1968 East L.A. Walkouts, Esparza, his Lincoln High teacher and movement mentor Sal Castro, and eleven others were arrested on felony conspiracy charges for "disturbing the peace," and dubbed the "East L.A. 13." Esparza explained to me that around the time he was out on bail, UMAS had decided to take on various departments on the UCLA campus regarding educational and curriculum reform. "And someone suggested to me that maybe I should look at the film school. . . . so I reached out to the film school, and I met Elyseo Taylor and he recruited me."[37] As mentioned in chapter 1, Taylor first saw Esparza at a Black Power Rally in 1968; a year later he hired Esparza to be a student recruiter for the newly conceived Media Urban Crisis program. Esparza remembers strategizing curriculum with Taylor, then recruiting the first twelve "Third World" students: "We went and occupied Colin Young's office . . . and happily he approved . . . this was an incredible, astonishing time. And all of a sudden there was a huge presence in the film school—African Americans, Native Americans, Asians, Chicanos—and there was this sense that we could actually change things."[38] Esparza hadn't initially planned to be part of the program, as he'd started out as a history major at UCLA. But Elyseo Taylor was pivotal in convincing Esparza that he belonged in the film department:

> I was an organizer . . . a hired gun slinger so to speak, went in there and organized and then was going to move on to do something else. . . . [Taylor] said to me, "You don't get it. You're a producer. You've been organizing people, you've been getting people to do things and that's what producers do." He was very instrumental in me ultimately ending up as a producer.[39]

Esparza further explains that after recruiting the initial twelve Latina/o, Native American, Asian American and Black students, he became number thirteen . . . *again.* "I love that number, thirteen. It's a symbolic number of the thirteen levels of heaven in the Nahuatl Aztec cosmology . . . . People thought it was an unlucky number, right? But there was the East L.A. 13, the indictment, but we declared it to be a sacred number."[40]

Full disclosure: when I first came across the names of the African American students admitted to that first class, I did not recognize a single one. I'd expected to see at least one or two names that I'd become familiar with from studies on the L.A. Rebellion. Richard Wells, Cliff Stewart, Rufus Howard, Wendell Handy? They rang no bells. I'd been in conversation with Charles Burnett and Ben Caldwell at this point and asked them about these names. Burnett replied quickly in an email that "Cliff Stewart, Richard Wells and Wendell Handy came into the department under Ethno-Communications. They tended to stick together. There seemed to be two groups. That is something to talk about."[41]

Caldwell, who entered UCLA at the tail end of the Ethno-Communications Program, elaborated on Burnett's assessment of the two groups. He confirmed, "I knew them all, yeah, but they weren't a part of us." I asked, "What do you mean, 'not part of us'—the Rebellion folk?" Caldwell described Wells et al. as "more Hollywood" whereas "we were really students of Haile [Gerima]. It was like an arm of Haile's philosophy and his word that we all liked." Then he singled out Richard Wells by saying that his professional experience, even if "Hollywood" in their eyes, was useful to the Rebellion filmmakers' projects: "Richard worked with us, he helped our quality. He helped the sound quality a lot."[42] So, now I was very curious about this mysterious and "Hollywood" Wells figure. Thanks to Luis Garza's good contacts, by the time I was interviewing Caldwell and asking about Wells, I had a new message in my inbox from Wells himself saying he'd be "happy to help."

On an ethnographic note, one that may support Burnett and Caldwell's ideas about Wells and his cohort's Hollywood leaning, my meetings with Burnett and Caldwell took place in the Crenshaw district of South L.A.—with Burnett at one of his favorite Chinese restaurants in the Crenshaw Shopping Square, with Caldwell at his storefront multimedia/community arts center, Kaos Network, in Leimert Park.[43] Richard Wells, meanwhile, invited me to his home in the Pacific Palisades, just south of Malibu and one of the most expensive areas in the city. As we settled in his living room to speak, I was only mildly distracted by the wall-length window views of the roaring ocean.

Until this moment I'd heard more about Richard Wells's sister than I'd heard about Wells himself. Several of his cohort fondly remembered Twyla, and that she'd been a "Miss Watts" beauty pageant winner. She also ended up marrying Wells's Ethno classmate Cliff Stewart, who was a black belt and martial arts instructor before and after UCLA, so apparently the guys appreciated her respectfully and from afar. Wells began by telling me that it was Twyla, who was working at UCLA in the late '60s, who told him about the Media Urban Crisis program and encouraged him to apply. Richard, who was a Vietnam vet working as a still photographer, jumped at the chance. He grew up in the Compton/Gardena area of South L.A., and when I asked if he grew up thinking he'd work in film, he said, "Of course. Everybody who grows up here does. It wasn't anything I was seriously pursuing, because I didn't really have any access, and certainly I hadn't considered film school," which he imagined would cost a fortune. He remembers this program at UCLA came with some funding: "They got us money, support, and I had the G.I. Bill as well."[44]

While an activist trajectory did not bring Wells to UCLA in a similar way as Garza or Esparza, he remembers activism—both the filming of rallies and protest as well as the spirit of giving back with film training programs for children through Head Start—as central to the film work he was involved in during the MUC program. He mentions shooting footage of the Panthers, shooting Teamsters strikes, and crewing for a shoot at the Chicano Moratorium, a project that became the Muccers collective film *Requiem 29,* "where Salazar the reporter was shot. We were there for that. I remember that was the first time I was ever tear gassed, at least in civilian life." He further emphasizes that his activism was not racially exclusive. "We were all sort of crossing over into whatever the political interests were of the members of the group. So, you were always out and trying to be involved, trying to be relevant at the time . . . trying to use media to expand the political awareness of not only ourselves but the quote unquote community." I ask more about the multiracial aspect of the program, and he remembers that it had an impact:

> It gave you . . . connections and contact with a wide variety of people. I mean Danny [Kwan] and Garza . . . I stayed in contact with those guys probably longest afterward. . . . It made you aware that there were other people struggling through some of the same things. . . . I was with a Brazilian guy . . . Mario who was shooting at that Latino demonstration. We got gassed together [laughs] so there was a sense of coalition. . . . As a learning experience, as a shared thing, everybody wanted to figure out a way to get into media and utilize it, make sure it had an application.

Wells later described his satisfaction at turning young people on to filmmaking via a Super 8 workshop off campus and related it to the spirit of community service inherent in the MUC program: "You know, you try to pass it on and become a resource for those who wanted to also get into the media . . . that was part of the spirit of the program. If Elyseo did anything, I think that was certainly part of the deal."[45] I ask why he thinks Taylor did not continue to receive support for the program, why such a

The Mother Muccers: Danny Kwan, Richard Wells, and Luis Garza, with Betty Chen (sitting on wheelchair holding the camera) and Nancy Dowd holding the microphone. Courtesy of Luis C. Garza.

beneficial program only lasted a few years. Thoughtfully Wells offered: "It's that syndrome of: how long does your guilt hold? How long is that going to play itself out where you feel responsible and feel like you've got to DO something about it?"

I asked if he had a sense of why Taylor was denied tenure or what happened to him. Wells remembered one professor, John Boehm, who was "one of our biggest nemeses. . . . He didn't like the idea of the program and he was a thorn in Elyseo's side and a block for us." But more than the active naysayers, Wells seems convinced the program's demise had more to do with that short-lived guilt or sense of duty: "It's usually one or two voices in the darkness that are yelling about it, there are those who feel guilty and therefore go along, and so you get a bit of momentum and you get something happening. But those voices become silent for any number of reasons, the guilt goes away, and then whatever was built goes away."

Wells credits the program for equipping him with skills that he never would have had access to, skills that prepared him for various employment opportunities straight out of school: "I think I've done every job . . . on set, maybe not makeup and hair, but the point being is that the program gave me that opportunity, so I took that opportunity [and] with a little luck went to work." While still a student, Wells was working on multiple projects both on and off campus. He'd met documentary filmmaker and cinematographer Joan Churchill before UCLA and ultimately worked on several projects as her second assistant cameraman, most notably on *Punishment Park* (1971). Along with MUC program classmates Wendell Handy, Cliff Stewart, and Brian Maeda, Wells also crewed for several productions for the University Extension Media Center, overseen by Peter Schnitzler. Schnitzler produced a series of short educational films grappling with race and gender identity called the "Social Seminar Series" for the National Institute for Mental Health. Wells remembered that Schnitzler was concerned that there were no directors of color hired on the project, so he gave Wells his first big break. "What an incredible opportunity, a door opened!" Not only was he able to use the film as his Project 2, he was "paid to make a film . . . a dream come true!" The short Social Seminar film he made, called *Teddy*, became a "calling card" for Wells. He was able to move from that experience to producing segments for an early West Coast African American public-affairs program for ABC called *I Am Somebody*. This show was paired for broadcasting with a Latino half-hour show called *Unidos*. *Unidos* and *Reflecciones* were two public-affairs shows that allowed UCLA classmates Sylvia Morales, Luis Garza, Susan Racho, José Luis Ruiz, and David Garcia the opportunity to produce and broadcast community-centered documentary films right out of film school.[46]

After these initial conversations with members of that first class, it became clearer that while this group, including the Black Muccers, may not have necessarily become "Hollywood," almost all of them prioritized getting out into the industry as soon as possible to earn income. Beyond the public-affairs realm, a number of Muccers pursued studio or guild apprenticeships that led to well-paid union jobs. Brian Maeda, for example, would become one of the first Asian Americans in the cinematographers' guild. This path was encouraged by Wendell Handy, a fellow Muccer who'd left UCLA to get an entry-level sound department job at Universal and told Maeda: "'B, you gotta come out there, you gotta come out to Universal, you gotta get a gig there.' I said, 'Ah Wendell, that's Hollywood.' 'Brother B, I'm making a lot of money. . . .'"[47] Handy was working on *Marcus Welby, M.D.*, and following his classmate's lead, Maeda eventually found himself apprenticing on the legal drama *Owen Marshall: Counselor at Law*. He remembers seeing his professor Elyseo Taylor on the lot one day at Universal: "He saw me, and I saw him, and he was just tickled. He had a grin from ear to ear. He was really proud."

For Brian Maeda, the most memorable and important aspect of the MUC program was the multiracial element. One of the last children born in the camp at Manzanar, Maeda was introduced to the UCLA program through the important Japanese American community activist and organizer (and future California State Assemblyman) Warren Furutani. He still remembers the day vividly, walking through Little Tokyo circa 1969, "before it became so hip," and meeting up with Furutani in his Japanese American Community Center offices. Furutani, who'd heard about the planning stages for the Ethno program, told him to call Elyseo Taylor. Maeda reverently refers to Elyseo Taylor as "Dr. Taylor," although Taylor almost certainly did not hold a PhD.

> I remember meeting Dr. Taylor in his office and him telling us about . . . what he is putting together, which would be an accredited Third World film crew. The first in the nation. So, we were in control of it, we had the power to put together the curriculum and the biggest thing . . . the second generation, which was Bob Nakamura, we interviewed them. We had the power to say yay or nay. We basically took everybody, Nakamura, Eddie Wong. . . .

The biggest difference, and the thing that upset Maeda the most about the distance between his first class and the "second generation," was that the first class collaborated cross-racially and he viewed the second generation as self-segregating. "They didn't intermingle! And that really pissed us off. We created this curriculum and now we're bringing in two, three times more Third World students, but what happened, like immediately is that they started to segregate themselves. Asians over here, Blacks here, Chicanos here and never the twain to meet."

The crossing between each other's communities was, for Maeda, "what made it so special." The friendship with Wendell Handy seems to have impacted him most. Everyone who mentions Handy remembers that his father was a Black Republican from Compton and that the first-year Muccers went to Compton to film the Handy family as part of Wendell's Project One.

> Our groups would go to different neighborhoods. Most of us, we'd never been in each other's neighborhoods. We went to film Wendell's dad, to Wendell's parents' house, in the patio, it was a Saturday afternoon, really hot. His dad had a suit and tie on, and there were these Black women all dressed up, dresses and high heels. And he gave his pitch, I remember the pitch so clearly, he goes, "You know, I've been up and down this great state of California and I must say, Compton is the place to be. I love Compton!" They owned a liquor store, which was kind of unusual I think and also the fact that he was Republican. . . .

Maeda remembers Handy also visiting the Japanese community on the West Side. "He kinda gravitated to me and would come over to my house and my mother was still alive and active. Wendell would always call her 'Mama Maeda': 'Mama Maeda, how are you today?' Handy . . . he became one of my best friends." Maeda seems to grieve the loss of this multiracial cohesion in the shift from the first to the second group of the UCLA program and in his own shift to the unapologetically racist world of the Hollywood studio system: "I had to listen to the new 'Jap' joke every day from an Irish dolly grip . . . to go from such a relevant situation and then to go to Universal Studios which we affectionately called East Berlin," was trying at best.

In my follow-up meeting with Luis Garza, this time joined by Danny Kwan, we revisited some of these themes of the difference between the first and second group. Kwan stresses that the multiracial make-up and bonding of the first group "led to an exposure that would not have happened otherwise. . . . It led to a much broader diversity of real involvement for me."[48] And regarding the self-segregating impulse of the second generation, Kwan remembered,

> I think the Asians dealt with the Asians. . . . Like I said, I found it much more interesting to hang out with the Blacks than to hang out with the Asians. We were different. We embraced each other; we pursued that embrace. So, it led to, like I would never have otherwise gone to the Chicano

Moratorium. I think to this day, partly because of Media Urban Crisis, I seem to be much more involved with the Mexican American community than I do with the Asian community.

At another moment in the conversation when we were going over the lists of various filmmakers of color at UCLA, names like Betty Chen and Sylvia Morales, and whether or not they were in the MUC program or Ethno or "folded in" (Garza's expression) unofficially, Kwan gave me a sense that whether they were officially Muccers or not, the students of color gravitated toward each other and worked on each other's projects: "At some point there was this sense that we were creating something, so all the minority students all banded together."[49] Garza chimed in: "What Danny was just saying, I think everybody that was recruited comes in from a different trajectory, we're all unknown to each other for the most part . . . and there had to be some form of camaraderie in order to exist." Danny affirmed, "We did have the camaraderie." He gave Elyseo Taylor significant credit for this: "I think it was his vision. He actually had a class called 'Film and Social Change,' so, he had really felt that films were not addressing social problems. I really give credit to Elyseo." He said that while he and Garza are not currently working in the film industry, "we're, to this day, still involved in social change, so our theme is always about social change, social justice, social injustice."

Brian Maeda was sincerely disappointed by what he felt was a lack of multiracial cohesion in the second class, and he further expressed disappointment regarding the way that he feels the second-generation Asian American students in Ethno who founded Visual Communications "poo pooed us who went into the industry. They didn't want any advice, they didn't want any of us working on their 'community' films. I guess maybe they felt that we had sold out to Hollywood or something." On some level Maeda's greatest contention is that he doesn't feel like the Muccers get enough credit for what they started: "My own personal thing with VC is I feel—we never got any credit. The 13 Mother Muccers, the original group that created it . . . if we weren't here they never would have happened."[50]

Danny Kwan described different tensions between the first and later groups around questions of identity and aesthetics. He told me that being involved with the Asian American Studies Center "created an identity and an involvement with that identity for a number of years that I more or less found unfulfilling." He explained that the Asian American movement for him "created a false identity," and "nowadays I say I'm not Asian American, I'm Chinese American. I had more in common with Luis and his mother than I have with Brian Maeda, a Japanese." He felt that the things he was "trying to pursue as an artist were not seen or tolerated by that Asian American . . . the consciousness to accept another way of thinking, it wasn't there. The second generation of Ethno, except for a few people who were involved with Visual Communications, like Duane, were pretty square." Finally, he believed the second generation thought about community involvement in a different way, "The second generation was all school boys who, I think, think about involvement in a much more academic way."

Considering Kwan's statement causes me to rethink the focus of his student film *Homecoming Game,* which features Asian American Hardcore, a movement organization focused on drug rehabilitation and empowerment. The visual of Asian American men with tattoos and long hair (one slightly elder hipster does his best to rock an Afro) and hearing youth interviewed describe how they started smoking weed at age thirteen or fourteen, then progressed to "Bennies and reds" and didn't start dropping acid "heavy" until fifteen—well, this is not your model minority. Kwan's film swings from partying to profound introspection. At one moment we see a group of clearly stoned friends playing Scrabble, where someone gets up to call 4–1–1 (information) to find out if "ting" is a word: "You better call someone with a dictionary!" Laughs turn to abstract reflections on self-hatred. We see a woman with false eyelashes and heavy, clownish makeup. She blinks her eyes in slow motion, while a female voice-over monologue tells of how many Asian American women scotch tape their eyes, "because guys like the white chicks with their pretty eyes." The storyteller says this strategy would get messed up in high school in gym class because they had to take swimming lessons and the scotch tape would come off. The scene is also carefully balanced with a ballad sung by Nobuko Miyamoto with Chris Iijima, "Something About Me Today." Nobuko offers these empowering lines that counter the mask and self-hatred reflected in the image and monologue: "I looked in the mirror, and

I saw me/And I didn't wanna be any other way."[51] The film has quite a bit of alpha-male party and politics energy, and this moment is the film's most quiet, layered, and quite possibly its most radical.

In an interview with Ethno student Mary Uyematsu Kao, she mentioned that another filmmaker who was in Ethno, cinematographer Geraldine Kudaka, ended up marrying one of the founders of Asian American Hardcore, Ray Tasaki. This shifts us to talking about Kwan's film. Kao remembered Kwan as an "oddball among the Asians," but "I love the *Homecoming* film. I was so glad [Kwan] got the Asian American Hardcore, that was just really special. I really like that film." She remembered the scene I describe above in great detail, particularly because she knew the woman in the scene. She struggled with drugs and mental illness well beyond the time of the filming, and ultimately died from an overdose. About the scene Kao says, "That was just so packed with stuff because that's such an Asian woman thing, you know, the eyes."[52] Hearing Kao's memories of the film, which again were crystal clear in 2017, almost fifty years after it was made, tells me that the film clearly mattered to the community, the "community" that Kwan seemed to struggle with, yet served. Still in such polarized times, *Homecoming Game* stands out for its messiness. There is humor and shame, intoxication and recovery, confusion and empowerment, and the revolutionary politics of the time tended to not allow this much space for uncertainty.

Richard Wells's short film *Teddy* presents a young African American man searching for his path as an activist, and in some ways echoes Kwan's film in that it avoids polemical certitudes. Wells shows us the high-school-aged Teddy in choir practice, at home playing dominos with his brother and friends, and at a community rap session with other high school boys and young adult counselors. While we hear bits of diegetic sound, song, and conversations in these scenes, it is Teddy's meditative voice-over that gives the film its depth. Teddy's stream of introspection moves from his experience being kicked out of numerous high schools for organizing a walkout to demand updated books and to protest "teachers who aren't teaching." We hear his thoughts on drug use among his peers, the violence in Vietnam and violence at home, and whether or not a revolutionary is better off using violence or not. In the case of the Watts rebellion, he offers this:

> They have more out in Watts than they had before that riot. I noticed white people were beginning to focus on Watts, wanting to find out what's going on . . . what's the problem . . . what do these people want over there? And they was beginning to do something because they were scared. They didn't want it to happen again. That's why I believe violence worked there.

But after witnessing the overwhelming violence perpetrated against the Black Panther Party headquarters by the LAPD, he reconsiders: "From that incident I realized we can't use the gun. If we pick up the .45, he gonna pick up a rifle. We pick up a rifle, he gonna use a tank." Where Wells ends the piece is with Teddy realizing that while a lot of young Black men want to be like the Panthers or to be like Malcolm X, "I want to be myself, be somebody new." Wells then moves visually from stark archival footage of the shooting victims being pulled out of the Panther headquarters at 41st and Central, bloody and handcuffed, back to the earlier choir practice scene where a soloist sings a hymn about the "Lamb of God." We see Teddy again on the boys' side of the choir, singing, not passionately but in unison. The film closes on a pastor praying about the grace of God and offering a blessing "for each and everyone in the building." What may sound heavy-handed is rendered with such quiet that it comes off as neither evangelizing nor mocking, nor, sadly for the protagonist, ultimately satisfying. We sense that the path to the "somebody new" that Teddy wants to become is not at all clear. This is not the certainty of, say, the Panthers' ten-point program, so perhaps the film might seem less radical than later work by the Black filmmakers associated with the "L.A. Rebellion." Still, the "more Hollywood" label given to the Black filmmakers of MUC does not quite ring true.

Did the nuance, the political ambiguity of these Muccer projects contribute to the later Ethno/Rebellion students' sense that these filmmakers were "more Hollywood," and somehow less rebellious, or worse, less "community" focused? This is an interesting tension, especially considering that it seemed to happen not just with the Black Muccers but the Asian American Muccers too. Maeda complains that this first class did not get enough credit for laying the foundation. Perhaps the space for discovery *and* ambiguity in those earlier MUC projects was a necessary precursor for the bolder statements, the more radical films of the next groups of Ethno filmmakers.

Sandy Johnson and Yasu Osawa were active participants in the first class of the MUC program, and if it had not been for an equipment glitch, they might have continued on with the new recruits of the second generation. They'd hoped to have access to a camera over the summer of 1970 to continue working on projects, but their memory is that it was not available. "Professor Taylor took the camera to Europe for his own film project— this was the word with all the students," the Osawas wrote in an email to me. "This actually led to Yasu and I dropping out and not returning so we could make films [and] we did just that."[53]

Sandra Sunrising Johnson (eventually Osawa), like many other Muccers, came to the program with a background in activism. Most immediately, before she entered the MUC program she taught English in the High Potential Program at UCLA, but earlier, in her Makah community of Washington, she worked with Great Society poverty programs such as the Neighborhood Youth Corps and Head Start. Historian Daniel Cobb writes that in her tribal community of Neah Bay on the Olympic Peninsula, as director of the Community Action Program, "she inaugurated what amounted to revolutionary changes. This included providing incentives for K-12 students to learn Makah language and culture in the context of summer programs and to pay elders to serve as teachers in the Head Start preschool program."[54] Sandra later remembered, "There was never anything to do on the reservation. I tried to have a movie night, but it was difficult with no films about us and particularly nothing about Northwest tribes."[55] Cobb's study of Native American activism, *Say We Are Nations: Documents of Politics and Protest in Indigenous America since 1887*, highlights the Pan-Tribal educational forum "Workshop on American Indian Affairs" convened by Cherokee anthropologist Robert K. Thomas.

> I had graduated from Lewis and Clark, but my main education on Native American issues came from the institute of American Indian Affairs. . . . In those days (1962) there was only, probably thirty or forty . . . a handful of Native Americans going to college, so . . . we had people from all over, from the Southwest, the Plains, California, Oregon, Washington, Alaska. . . . We got to know everything about other tribes. In fact, the ten-part series that I did for NBC . . . Bob Thomas . . . he was such a great mentor that I based a lot of the ten programs around his lectures. . . . The first Indian doctors and attorneys and [laughs] filmmakers came out of this little workshop.[56]

The Native American Series with producer Sandra Osawa, production staff, and singer/songwriter Floyd Westerman circa 1975. Courtesy of Upstream Productions.

While Yasu Osawa was listed as a member of the original thirteen Muccers, Sandra points out that he was actually a TA of the first group: "He had already won some super 8 filmmaking contests."[57] She also repeatedly stressed to me her concern that Yasu's name is "somewhat forgotten."[58] She described to me the commitment he made as far back as the UCLA days to work on projects with her about American Indian issues. According to her, he thought her community needed more urgent attention than his at the time. In an essay their daughter, attorney Saza Osawa, wrote about her parents for the collection *Native Americans on Film: Conversation, Teaching and Theory*, she describes their creative partnership:

> Sandra Osawa has been working as a filmmaker longer than any other American Indian in the country. She is also my mother and I have been lucky enough to travel with her and my father, Yasu Osawa, to many parts of

Indian country since I was eight years old. At a young age, I never thought the work my parents did was special. It was not until later that I realized my mother, and really both of my parents, had unique gifts that they cultivated all of their lives to make them into master story tellers: my mother shaped the stories through words and thematic concepts while my father followed those concepts by finding ways to bring them out visually.[59]

As gently as he can in our first in-person visit, Yasu tells me that Sandy's technical skills with the camera were not so strong, so he shot most of the first student film she directed at UCLA, a one-minute Super 8 film called *Curios*.[60] In this project the camera feels as though it is flying through a museum, a literal fly, not on the wall but buzzing around the walls watching white people stare at Indian curios and even one Indian mummy. Adding to the pace and frenzy, the piece is cut to a menacing rendition of "One Little, Two Little, Three Little Indians," complete with what sounds like white children mocking Indian war cries. Near the end of the song, to the soundscape is added a brief and sharp voice-over of a female patron's voice. Responding to the image of the mummy behind the glass, she shrieks with disgust, "What is that!? Ahh!" Then, with what feels like short ends of eight to ten seconds left of film, we see quick cuts of contemporary 1970s American Indian youth living their lives, going to basketball games, eating breakfast cereal, seen at last by eyes, by a camera that wants to see them upright, breathing, not curios nor curiosities, but whole and out from behind the glass. Considering that the two quarters of the MUC program, the Winter and Spring quarters of 1970, correspond with the occupation of Alcatraz, with a large percentage of the occupiers being recently admitted UCLA High Potential Program students,[61] it is noteworthy that when *Curios* does turn to contemporary images of American Indians there is no obvious gesture toward that historic rebellion. The breezy, quotidian shots of young Indians on campus are still decidedly an act of resistance to mainstream museum and film culture that would keep Indians on display as mummies or otherwise fixed in the past.

It is hard to know what further student films Sandy and Yasu might have made had they stayed in the program, but in the event, several years after leaving UCLA Sandra Osawa was hired by NBC to create and produce *The Native American Series,* a ten-episode series that blended the public-affairs news format with elements of a variety show, including occasional skits and musical guest performances, all written and performed by American Indians. Yasu shot much of the footage used in these episodes and continued to partner with Sandra on award-winning documentaries for the next five decades.

I wish to take a moment here to address the lack of other Native American Ethno students discussed in this text. Aside from Sandra Osawa, the only other two names that came up in my interviews with the Ethno filmmakers were Bernadine "Bunny" Lindquist and Rita Keshena. Sandra Osawa told me that she remembered distinctly that Bunny had a completed film, a kind of music video of her two children set to the popular '60s tune "Get Together" by the Youngbloods, that was "well shot and well edited." Osawa also hired Bunny to help with the NBC series, but later lost track of her.[62] Larry Clark also had strong memories of Rita Keshena, who died in 2008 at the age of eighty-seven, so she would have been in her fifties at the time Clark was in film school. Keshena did not make films but was researching images of Native Americans in media and eventually published a piece in UCLA's *American Indian Culture and Research Journal* on "The Role of American Indians in Motion Pictures." Her obituary says she did get a degree in cinema from UCLA, and at age fifty-seven she went to law school, becoming the first Menominee woman to receive a law degree. She was the Menominee Tribe chief justice when she died.[63] Haile Gerima always says he remembers seeing films by Native American classmates, but he doesn't have the specific names, so this is a loss that warrants further digging.[64]

Did the cross-racial collaborations, friendships—and in one case a marriage—continue into the next generations of the Ethno-Communications program? While some of the Muccers state their disappointment that later generations seemed to self-segregate, there is plenty of evidence just looking at the credits of student films by Rebellion filmmakers Haile Gerima, Larry Clark, and later Carroll Parrott Blue, Don Amis, Bernard Nicolas, Barbara McCullough, and O.Funmilayo Makarah that their Asian American and Latina/o UCLA classmates, from Danny Kwan and Eddie Wong to Luis Ospina, Geraldine Kudaka, Monona Wali, and John Esaki collaborated as crew on a number of their projects. This is not to mention the musical crossings, from Roberto Miranda and Guillermo Loo as musicians on Gerima's *Child of Resistance* (1973), to Benny Yee performing with L.A.

Steve Tatsukawa, Rufus Howard, Eddie Wong (behind camera), and Larry Clark. Photo: Robert Nakamura. Courtesy of Visual Communications Photographic Archive.

Panther Somayah "Peaches" Moore singing her original composition, "Inside Los Angeles," at the close of Carroll Parrott Blue's *Varnette's World* (1979). Perhaps more important than the fact of this cross-racial crewing is the evidence of the broader impact that coming together in the Ethno program had on the content of the films produced. A pivotal moment in Larry Clark's *As Above, So Below* reveals how critical these crossings were to the political storytelling he produced as a member of the second-year recruits.

In a photo by Robert Nakamura we see Steve Tatsukawa, Rufus Howard, Eddie Wong (behind camera), and Larry Clark on a location shooting class trip in 1971. All but Howard, including Nakamura, had come into the Ethno program in its second year. Though this was the first year it was called "Ethno-Communications," the Muccers refer to this group as the "second generation." The *Los Angeles Times* marked the launch of the Ethno program with an article in September of 1970, "New Curriculum Will Develop Ethnic Media: Ethnocommunications at UCLA Intended as a Permanent 2-Year Degree Program." The author of the article is not named, but the principal student voice in the piece is Danny Kwan, listed here as Danny Chung Yen Kwan and described as "a student representative on the Ethnocommunications Committee." The article mentions that the curriculum was developed by students from "Media Urban Crisis (MUC)" which is defined here as a two-quarter, "experimental program" that Kwan found frustrating in its initial short-term stage: "On paper the program was very stimulating, but programs never solve anything because they are short range." The program, designed to stress "minority group management of their media image," according to Kwan would only be effective if it became "a functional and integral part of the Theater Arts Department." For the fall quarter, the article reports, twenty-four new first-year students were to join the thirteen continuing MUC participants. Larry Clark came in at that time, along with Robert Nakamura, Steve Tatsukawa, Duane Kubo, and Eddie Wong, all of whom became instrumental in the formation of the Asian American community media organization Visual Communications.

Robert Nakamura remembered this location shooting class trip as an especially important bonding time: "Essentially we experienced every position on a small documentary crew. But what was really fun was going into different communities. It was good training, but it was a great opportunity to exchange ideas and learn about other people's communities and some of the issues. . . . I think that was the strongest, or one of the strengths of the program. Because we weren't paying lip service to becoming multi-ethnic and learning from each other, we really did! There was some bonding and there were some fights too. But generally, it was a bonding experience."[65] Steve Tatsukawa remembered that the group traveled to the Bay Area and filmed the Black Panthers, agricultural workers in Locke, the Chicano Studies program at UC Berkeley, as well as the Bay Area Native American Center.[66]

Like his earlier MUC classmates, Larry Clark arrived at UCLA with a background in activism. Born in Cleveland, Ohio, Clark spent some of his youth living with his father in Los Angeles. He remembers of his first day at Mount Vernon Junior High School near the Crenshaw district the surprise of seeing such a diverse student body in Los Angeles in contrast to his experience in Cleveland: "It was the first time I had seen white people, my whole world was Black, elementary to junior high was just Black, the street I lived on was Black. Although the teachers were white. . . . I think a third of the class were Japanese Americans, a third of the class were African American, and the other third were white or Latino. It was a whole different world."[67] Clark returned to Cleveland to finish high school and he received his BA from Miami University of Ohio, but he returned to L.A. to pursue his interests in photography and film.

Clark had been the president of the Black Student Union at Miami and began taking photos in the community of militant organizations such as Afro-Set and the Republic of New Libya. "These guys were so tough, they wouldn't allow the Panthers to come to Cleveland, that's how tough they were. I knew them, so I took photographs of them. A lot of social commentary; in fact, those photographs are what got me into UCLA."[68] His impulse as a former BSU president to make his first stop on UCLA's campus the newly formed Center for Afro-American Studies served him well, as he immediately met the center's first permanent director, Dr. Art Smith (later known as Molefi Asante). Dr. Smith directed Clark to speak with Elyseo Taylor in the Film department, and according to Clark by the end of the day he was not only accepted into Ethno-Communications but between Professors Smith and Taylor he received full funding for the program.

Clark explained to me that, as pleased as he was to be entering the program at UCLA, he was determined to keep one foot in on campus and one foot in the community. The community foot landed at the Performing Arts Society of Los Angeles (PASLA), founded by another early African American graduate of UCLA's film school, Vantile Whitfield.[69] According to theater scholar Margaret Wilkerson, after graduating with his MA from UCLA, Whitfield "set out quite consciously to create a mass communication arts center that would reflect the spirit and soul of Black people." For Whitfield the geographic location ("in a ghetto") or the fact of the company being run by Black people did not make it a Black theater. "According to Whitfield, PASLA became 'Black' when it committed its energies to the development and expression of Black art or culture for the liberation of Black People."[70] This ethos of connecting creative production to the needs of the people aligned with Clark's commitments. He managed to balance his coursework at UCLA while offering film workshops at PASLA. The fruit of this effort is seen in his provocative student film, *As Above So Below*

(1973), billed as a "Performing Arts Society of Los Angeles Film Workshop Production" featuring many of the PASLA acting ensemble's strongest talents, including Nathaniel Taylor in the role of the film's protagonist, Jita Hadi.[71] While the impact of Clark putting one foot in the community is clear, the campus foot—due to the multiracial recruitment to that campus by the Muccers and Elyseo Taylor—also benefited from a growing awareness of the liberation politics of his Asian, Chicana/o, and Native American classmates.

The kinds of exchanges across communities and justice issues that Nakamura recalled of those location shoots may have inspired an early scene in Clark's *As Above So Below*. The long short film (52 minutes), described as "one of the more politically radical films of the L.A. Rebellion,"[72] about a group of underground Black militants post-Watts plotting revolution, gives an unexpected and underexplored nod to the struggles of Clark's Japanese American Ethno cohort. Everything, as the title suggests, is turned upside down in this film. The opening credit sequence is shot in black and white, and we meet our comrade protagonist, Jita Hadi, holding a rifle in the woods, in the snow. Jita Hadi seems to be advancing toward some enemy, though the enemy is never revealed. Very quickly the film cuts to a title card reading "1945," and we are now in a flashback, shot in color, zoomed in on a radio broadcasting a report about the release of 110,000 Japanese Americans who have just received permission from the war relocation authority to leave all concentration camps. We see a Black woman sweeping the kitchen floor and a young Jita Hadi, eyes closed, holding his head in his hands at the kitchen table. It is unclear if he has fallen asleep or if the report has saddened the child. When we finally see his eyes they are wet . . . from sleep or tears? The radio continues: "All told some 110,000 Japanese men, women and children were sent inland to relocation centers. There was no recourse to the courts, guilt was assumed, the charge being: they looked like the enemy." The audio track allows us to hear that entire statement before Jita Hadi's mother calls for him to hurry along and get to school.

Clark then shows us the child walk out of the dilapidated house and onto bleak city streets. He wears a stained, holey t-shirt. As he plays with an abandoned tire and throws a few rocks, we hear a different radio commentator, now talking about the Negro ghetto. It's unclear if the off-camera commentator is speaking about 1945 or 1965. These are some of the lines we hear:

> Fear plus overcrowding produces panic, thus creating an explosive awareness of their need for more land. We cannot allow this to happen. . . . Our wisest and most urgent move now is to put them in small ghettos and let them think they have community control, so they will have a false feeling of security—thus creating self-containment and most importantly pacification. Once this is done, our problems will be solved, and the negro will remain in his place.

A fictional riff by screenwriter Clark? No, real lines from a 1968 report, "Guerrilla Warfare Advocates in the United States," prepared by the House of Representatives Committee on Un-American Activities.

When I asked Clark about this section of the film, he described what an impact Robert Nakamura's student film *Manzanar* (1971), shot a year or two prior to *As Above, So Below*, had on him. *Manzanar*, a personal narrative about the Nakamura family's relocation to the concentration camp when he was six years old, is considered one of the first independent films to address the internment of Japanese Americans during World War II. Clark had not been aware of that history until seeing his Ethno classmate's film. Clark also remembered in the early Ethno days that Nakamura and other classmates were organizing to repeal Title II of the "Internal Security Act of 1950," dubbed the "concentration camp law," which granted the government in times of "emergency" the power of "preventive detention." Discussing the impact of this film and his classmates' participation in the anti-Title II campaign, Clark made the point of reminding me that this was the time of Nixon and Hoover, so for him the precedent of what had happened to Japanese Americans thirty years earlier drew urgent parallels to threats against Black insurgents of the 1960s and early '70s.[73] The short "1945" section of *As Above, So Below*, is so visually striking—flashing back to color from black and white—it is possible that one might miss or not fully absorb the radio broadcasts. But having more of a sense of the breadth of the projects, classmates, and activism surrounding Clark during his film school training can empower our eyes and ears, to return to Toni Cade Bambara, to see and hear these relational signs.

Larry Clark's remarkably generative collaboration with composer/community organizer Horace Tapscott began with *As Above, So Below*. Tapscott would later score, perform in, and be the principal inspiration for Clark's narrative feature *Passing Through* (1977). And in 2017 Barbara McCullough released her long-awaited documentary feature, *Horace Tapscott: Musical Griot*. Much has been written about Tapscott's connection to the Rebellion filmmakers,[74] yet once again, considering the wider range of filmmakers who were part of the Ethno program allows us to look at how this practice of community-based musicians scoring and later appearing within the films of the Ethno filmmakers was neither rare nor the exclusive domain of the Black filmmakers at UCLA, especially when we consider the frequency with which the Asian American filmmakers from Ethno collaborated with composers Dan and June Kuramoto from Hiroshima (see chapter 4).[75] From Watts and Little Tokyo to Westwood and back, the program Elyseo Taylor set in motion could not die with his campus departure, because the film students themselves braided the community and campus together in ways that could not be undone. The filmography established by the MUC and Ethno students will forever be proof of the force of these kind of campus/community collaborations, and the following chapter will offer a range of close readings of these activist projects read relationally. First, however, a few remaining reflections on the fate of Professor Taylor.

It is still unclear precisely why Taylor was let go, as even apart from the formation of the groundbreaking/controversial MUC/Ethno programs, he was busy doing so many of the things an untenured faculty member ought to be doing. In the period between 1970 to 1974, Elyseo Taylor helped to host one of the first African Film Festivals in the United States at UCLA, which brought eight filmmakers from the continent (including Ousmane Sembene) to the campus. He directed the short documentary film *Black Art, Black Artists,* which featured an interview with printmaker Van Slater conducted by Taylor.[76] He delivered a paper at the 1972 American Political Science Association in Washington, DC, that was later published as "Film and Social Change in Africa South of the Sahara." Robert Hardgrave, the convener of the panel, described in his editorial notes additional Taylor achievements: "In Africa, he made several films for European television. He is currently engaged in developing private fund-

Elyseo Taylor with teaching assistants Morteza Rezvani and Maria Kodani, special guest Frank Capra, and an unknown young man. Courtesy of Morteza Rezvani.

ing sources for African films and film distribution in the United States."[77] I list all of these activities to suggest that Taylor was a productive film scholar and filmmaker, and he may have had more opportunities to curate and distribute African film from the vantage of his UCLA faculty post if he had not been denied tenure.

Individual reflections about Taylor from the students of his that I communicated with run the gamut. Ben Caldwell considered Taylor a friend and, as discussed above, included a dedication to him at the end of his film *I & I: An African Allegory*. He explained to me that Taylor was "an engaging, smart man and I felt he should have gotten tenure as much as any of the other professors there and probably more so than most of the other professors there because of his training. If he was white, he would have had the job."[78] What Caldwell referred to as his "straightforward style," perhaps a result of his military background, others found too rigid, even referring to him as "Papa Doc."[79] Sylvia Morales was impressed that Taylor got the program started, calling that a "miracle," but as a counselor she remembered him as sexist and unsupportive: "You know what he told me when I first met him? He was counseling me and he said, 'Well what do you want to do?' and I said, 'Well, I want to learn how to shoot the camera.' He says, 'Oh no, no, you don't want to shoot the camera, they're heavy.' So, when he told me no, I went and learned it."[80] Pamela Jones, considered part of the first wave of Rebellion filmmakers and most well-known for her acting roles in Clark's *Passing Through* and Caldwell's *I & I: An African Allegory*, shared deeply ambivalent memories of Taylor in her oral history for the UCLA Film and Television Archive: "Some people liked Elyseo Taylor and some people didn't. Some people found him helpful and some people thought he was a snake. . . . We fought for him because he needed to be fought for, because UCLA was what it was. But was he an obvious Abdias Nascimento? I don't think so."[81] Ethno alum and editor Gail Yasunaga remembers Taylor as "inspirational and awesome . . . [he] showed us films like *La Hora de Los Hornos* and films from Africa," and she added that the class "certainly widened my perspective on the powers of film and art."[82] And director Bobby Roth, who was a co-teaching assistant (TA) with Teshome Gabriel for Elyseo Taylor, could not say enough about what a great teacher he was, claiming that whenever anyone spoke of a UCLA film professor with praise, Roth would say, "not as good as Taylor."[83]

Interestingly, it was a number of the international students—Bernard Nicolas from Haiti, Mario da Silva from Brazil, and Ntongela Masilela, born in South Africa and raised in Kenya—who had the most positive memories of Taylor. Nicolas was deeply impacted by the range of films from India, Brazil, and Senegal that Taylor introduced him to and said he remembered thinking, "Where did this guy come from? How did he know all this? And, of course he was the only one in the entire film school who was covering that area."[84] Da Silva recalled Taylor's generosity and that he even gave him a 16mm Bolex camera at one point. "Elyseo and I used to have long conversations. . . . I visited his office very often. One thing he said one time was: A beautiful thing deserves to be photographed because it is beautiful. An ugly thing deserves to be photographed because it is ugly."[85] Masilela emphasized Taylor's "worldliness" and erudition:

"Definitely without question, he preferred his European experience to his American experience in that he felt fully accepted as a human being. When he came to UCLA, he had a worldly experience much deeper and more extensive than any of the white American professors in the Department. Perhaps some of the resentment against him came from the fact that he could speak German and French. . . . Many of the books in his office were in both French and German." Masilela even wondered if Taylor's white colleagues "thought he had lost touch with the 'Black American experience,' as though their whiteness gave them a privileged understanding of it, thus making themselves its supposed guardians."[86] In a separate email Masilela did suggest that some of Taylor's "African American and African students developed an intense dislike for him which deeply mystified and hurt me."[87]

Taylor's UCLA colleague Molefi Asante, known then as Art Smith, reflected on this range of student responses, suggesting that some of the American students, versus the international students, "did not find . . . they had to find their way with him," and added that Taylor arrived, "at the very pinnacle of UCLA's revolutionary moment. . . . This is when Angela Davis came, they brought us all there that same year, 1969. . . . As I think back to it, I can sort of understand why he didn't want to get too engaged with what we were dealing with, because what we were dealing with was so different than probably what his experiences had been up until that time. He was probably shell shocked."[88] Asante found him to be a very serious person, deeply engaged in his scholarship and perhaps less interested in the kinds of political debates many of the Black faculty and students were engaged with. "He was visible but not necessarily as loquacious as the rest of us . . . but he was very much doing his work and a very hard worker . . . always had his briefcase. . . . So, he brought maybe even a whole European notion through the campus. . . ." Finally, Asante raised an interesting idea about Clyde Taylor's nomenclature of "L.A. Rebellion" and whether or not it quite fit the other Taylor or if it might be "granting to Elyseo more nationalist legitimacy" than he may have wanted or warranted. "But the man was obviously extremely brilliant [and] had an immense vocabulary of filmmaking." Unfortunately for Taylor, this was apparently not as obvious to the rest of the film department faculty or university administration.

There is almost no sign of Elyseo Taylor beyond his UCLA days: no later teaching position, no future films, no academic publications beyond the mid-1970s. Other than one lecture he gave in 1976 at the Bellagio Institute, it seems as if he vanished. Some assumed he must have died young and are astonished to know he lived until 2006. A 1996 clipping of his membership in a Purple Hearts veterans club in a north New Jersey suburb is the final thing I could find before a "find a grave" listing that announced he was buried at Brigadier General William C. Doyle Veterans Memorial Cemetery in Wrightstown, New Jersey. I could not find a published obituary for Elyseo Jose Taylor, Jr. By gathering and guiding a new generation of American Indian, Asian American, Black, and Latina/o film students to Westwood when he did, an unparalleled filmography of the art, music, good living, and good struggle of communities of color in Los Angeles was born . . . and in that sense, Elyseo Taylor lives.

3 Relational Filmographies of Rebellion

The late, great, Harlem-born poet Sekou Sundiata once prophetically warned: *People be droppin' revolution, like it was a pickup line. You wouldn't use that word if you knew what it meant. It ain't pretty. It's bloody. It overturns things.*[1] After an oversaturated season of "solidarity," in the late spring of 2020 when Amazon, Nike, and most major institutions of higher learning were posting "solidarity statements" like they were pickup lines in response to the police killings of George Floyd and Breonna Taylor, that "s" word began to ring as hollow as Sundiata bemoaned *revolution* had years before. Still, like a pastor searching for an amen, I stand firm in the tradition of comparative ethnic studies scholars and coalition-building culture workers before me, hoping somebody will still say "solidarity" and imbue it with the substance and urgency necessary for these times and the next.

Multiracial solidarity, when it is "thick," as writers Roseann Liu and Savannah Shange posit, "layers interpersonal empathy with historical analysis, political acumen, and a willingness to be led by those most directly impacted." Further, they insist that for solidarity to be thick, it must be able to "withstand the tension of critique."[2] While I have described interracial collaborations and rich interpersonal empathy in the relations between MUC and Ethno-trained filmmakers in the previous chapter, I want to make a distinction here. The presentation of the following "relational" aspects of this wider Ethno filmography is not a collection of feel-good or easy scenes of solidarity that aim to suggest false equivalencies of social suffering or histories of exploitation. What I am instead suggesting is that when these films are carefully studied, programmed, and taught in conversation, they have the force to become effective tools to establish thicker solidarity or, in M. Jacqui Alexander's formulation, greater "fluency," between communities of color.

Alexander devotes an entire chapter of *Pedagogies of Crossing* to the iconic women of color anthology *This Bridge Called My Back: Writings by Radical Women of Color* (edited by Gloria Anzaldúa and Cherríe Moraga, with a foreword by Toni Cade Bambara). She charts, with gratitude, the contributors' efforts to create "collective fluency" and to unlearn "an impulse that allows mythologies about each other to replace knowing about one another."[3] The arrangement of the anthology itself, the foreword by Bambara, and the preface by Moraga all shape the organization and focus of my engagement with the Ethno filmography. Bambara's words appear first, and she praises the collection for its "gathering-us-in-ness," its multigenre and multiracial sharing of "letters testimonials poems interviews essays journal entries" by "Sisters of the yam Sisters of the rice Sisters of the corn Sisters of the plantain. . . ." Bambara contends—in language that must have directly influenced Alexander—that the only way to combat diabolical efforts to divide and conquer will be "to know each other better and teach each other our ways, our views." She expresses hope that the anthology "can get us there. Can coax us into the habit of listening to each other and learning each other's ways of seeing and being."[4]

Moraga's "Preface" declares her desire to bridge communities, queer and straight, brown and not so brown ("in my light flesh . . . protected by the gold highlights my hair dares to take on, like an insult"), Black feminist and Chicana feminist (using her own productively challenging sisterhood with Barbara Smith as a case in point). Moraga is urgent about bridging neighborhoods as different as the white suburb of Watertown and the Black community of Roxbury. She describes a subway ride from Harvard Square to Roxbury where a white cop assaults a fourteen-year-old Black boy, just days after another Black boy was shot in the head by another white cop ... and the train moves on and the summer gets hotter:

> I hear there are some women in this town plotting a lesbian revolution. What does that mean about the boy shot in the head is what I want to know. I am a lesbian. I want a movement that helps me make some sense of the trip from Watertown to Roxbury, from white to Black. I love women the entire way, beyond a doubt.

She needs a movement—and ultimately the gathering of writers assembled in the anthology—to make meaning of that journey. She resolves that "the passage is *through,* not over, not by, not around but through. This book, as long as I see it for myself as a passage through, I hope will function for others ... in the same way."[5] The *Bridge* anthology was conceived and first published roughly in the same years as the Ethno filmmakers were producing their thesis films and earliest professional projects, and so this formational women of color text, with its intersectional vision (well before Kimberlé Crenshaw would coin the term) and interdependent insistence is in parallel bloom with the New Los Angeles cinema of the 1970s and '80s analyzed in the pages ahead.

Structurally, I am also inspired by Anzaldúa and Moraga's decision to produce a multigenre anthology (itself a rebellious move in the scheme of "canonical" single-genre literary anthologies of poetry or short stories or essays). Further, Moraga and Anzaldúa organized the sections of the anthology not by genre—and certainly not by racial group—but by "major areas of concern for Third World women."[6] In the following analysis of several selections of films by Ethno directors, I too group films across genre lines, discussing short films alongside features, documentaries with narrative fiction films, because together they shed light on similar "areas of concern" for the communities of color each filmmaker presents.[7]

It is not surprising that when Toni Cade Bambara decided to critically assess two decades of "Black insurgent" filmmaking at UCLA in *Reading the Signs*, she moved with ease across their mixed-genre repertoire, synthesizing and signifying on shared themes, shared casts, "intertextual echoes" and overlapping political concerns. She declared that by 1977, "the insurgents' thematic foci became discernible: family, women, history, and folklore."[8] For Bambara, writing in the early 1990s just after the release of *Daughters of the Dust*, Dash's feature embodies all of these themes, which qualifies the film in Bambara's view as "the maturation of the LA rebellion agenda."[9] It is in this context that Bambara makes the claim I discuss in this book's introduction about *Daughters* honoring *multiple* perspectives rather than the perspective of an *individual hero* that Hollywood industry fare has conditioned us to see. Recall that film viewers who commit to carefully reading multiple perspectives will, in Bambara's formulation, be rewarded with "an empowered eye."[10]

Where Bambara saw four central "thematic foci" for the Black insurgents, I discuss three central areas emerging from the wider Ethno filmography: the protection of sacred and familial land, workplace dignity for fathers, and the cost of activism for women organizers. Three films whose intertextual echoes rang especially loud for centering powerful matriarchs and their protective stewardship of the land were Haile Gerima's narrative feature *Ashes and Embers* (1982), Esperanza Vasquez and Moctesuma Esparza's documentary *Agueda Martinez: Our People, Our Country* (1977), and Sandra Osawa's documentary *In the Heart of Big Mountain* (1988). As a kind of call and response to these three portraits of women protecting the land, I move next to consider three portraits that humanize men of color, fathers, in dehumanizing workplaces. If we could call this a genre—"humanizing fathers in the face of dehumanizing work"—certainly Charles Burnett's *Killer of Sheep* (1977) would be its signature film, but here I look at Burnett's earlier student film *The Horse* (1973) in relation to two even earlier student works by Ethno filmmakers, Eddie Wong's *Wong Sinsaang* (1971) and Jeff Furumura's *I Don't Think I Said Much* (1971). Virtually all of the early Rebellion works and films of the Ethno-trained filmmakers address activist struggles, from the Chicano Moratorium to Black Power and the movement to free Angela Davis, from battles against housing discrimination and gentrification to struggles for Indigenous land and fishing rights. For this activism section, I zero in on the personal and political cost of rebellion for women activists of the 1960s and '70s by exploring two early Ethno-era shorts, Betty Chen's *Portraits of a Young Girl* (1970?) and Laura Ho's *Sleepwalker* (1971), in conversation with Sylvia Morales's more recent feature documentary, *A Crushing Love: Chicanas, Motherhood and Activism* (2009), which features 1960s and '70s movement icons Dolores Huerta, Elizabeth "Betita" Martinez, Alicia Escalante, Martha Cotera, and (emerging a bit later) Cherríe Moraga. While the final set of films features projects that center activist figures in their diegesis, I would say that every film in this chapter is doing a kind of activist work by raising the concerns of the filmmaker's community members with such care and specificity. It is my hope that fresh consideration of these intertextual echoes can have the potential to galvanize greater interracial fluencies, unexpected alliances, and perhaps even transformative collaborations among new generations of BIPOC activists, artists, and filmmakers.

WHO RAISED THEM?

When Haile Gerima set out in 1978 to do a film on the Wilmington 10 case (*Wilmington 10 . . . USA 10,000*), he did not go out to report or prove the activists' case with a *Nightline* or *60 Minutes* approach. Instead, he told Elvis Mitchell in a 2016 interview, he focused on the activists' families: "I want to know who raised them? Who raised them? Because often black people are orphaned by the official literature and cinema. They're orphaned, they don't come from nowhere." Gerima's creative process included seeking out the mothers and grandmothers of the nine Black men in Wilmington, North Carolina, who (with one white woman) were falsely charged with arson and conspiracy in 1971 and jailed for nearly a decade. At a rare screening of *Wilmington 10 . . .*, at Philadelphia's 2017 Black Star Film Festival, I was struck by the opening sequences of elderly African American women on their front porches, in familiar rocking chairs and swings, offering electrifying tales of defiance in the face of Southern racial terror. These women instantly reminded me of the Grandmother character in Gerima's later narrative film *Ashes and Embers*. In the interview with Mitchell, Gerima confirms that he was developing the script for *Ashes* while filming these elder women in Wilmington. These elders, explained Gerima, held "the history of resistance," and wanted to pass it down to the younger generations. The attentive director then wove their vision into the words, walk, and even the squeaky porch swing of Grandma in *Ashes and Embers*.[11]

Grandma (Evelyn Blackwell) in *Ashes and Embers* by Haile Gerima (1982).
Courtesy of Haile Gerima, Shirikiana Aina, and Mypheduh Films.

Though we are in Los Angeles when we initially meet Vietnam vet Nay
Charles, the protagonist of *Ashes and Embers*, within the first nine minutes of the film Gerima sends Nay Charles back to rural Virginia to recon-
nect with his grandmother. Called simply Grandma, and played with mesmerizing conviction by Evelyn A. Blackwell, this matriarch works the
land, passes on the history of Black resistance to Nay Charles and Liza
Jane (Nay's sometimes lover/comrade), and fulfills Gerima's agenda to
foreground the intergenerational connections of his lead characters—
there are no orphans here. This point could not be made more explicit
than in the sequence where we are introduced to Grandma and see her
reunion with her grandson.

Exterior shots of Nay Charles charging down an unpaved country back
road on foot are scored by a haunting ballad sung by Zulema Cusseaux
called "American Fruit." When he arrives within earshot of his ancestral
home, we hear Cusseaux sing: "now that we are aware of our African roots."
The nondiegetic soundtrack continues while diegetic sounds of birds
tweeting and dogs barking rise and meet Nay Charles's own voice, shout-
ing, "Grandma! Grandma!" We move to an interior shot of what must be

Screenshot from *Agueda Martinez* (Esperanza Vasquez, 1977).

Grandma's bedroom, though the camera first shows us only the top of a bedframe and a sepia-toned early twentieth-century photo of a Black man and woman, likely Grandma's parents. As we now hear Nay Charles's shouts through the window of this bedroom, we see a gray-haired woman's head and torso rise to a seated position in her bed; her smiling face becomes a triptych with the couple from the photo. The couple faces forward, while Grandma looks over her right shoulder in the direction of the sound of her grandson. Still image, live woman, and voice through the window connect three generations. There are no orphans here.

In the following scene in Grandma's kitchen, she proceeds to make Nay Charles a ten-course (and counting) meal, including lima beans, cabbage, collard greens, fresh apple juice. "Everything you eatin' came from our garden," she says. "Home grown." She moves back and forth from the kitchen, serving new dishes, telling Nay about the nutritional properties and vitamins inside these dishes made from the land, the family land. In subsequent scenes we see Grandma, Nay Charles, Liza Jane, and her son Kimathi all working the land together. We also see and hear Grandma's grief about having to sell so much of the land to pay the taxes and her rage at the constant harassment from real estate developers: "Vultures! Waiting for me to die, trying to uproot me!" It is clear that she wants Nay Charles to remain with her on the land to help out. But it is also clear that, first, he is still too traumatized from the war to be of much help to anyone, and, second, staying with Grandma comes with the cost of pressure from her to attend her church and believe as she does. Though we witness Nay Charles struggle throughout the film with severe post-traumatic stress that exacerbates his sense of being misunderstood and alone, Gerima ultimately and tenderly returns the harried vet to Grandma's arms by the close of the film, the familiar squeaky porch swing now landing like a lullaby.

The intertextual and intergenerational echoes between *Ashes and Embers*'s Grandma figure and the New Mexican and Navajo matriarchs of Esperanza Vasquez and Sandra Osawa's documentaries are striking. The visual symmetry between Gerima's Grandma and Agueda Martinez alone is so striking that without seeing *Wilmington 10* it would be natural to wonder if part of the inspiration for the character of Grandma had been Vasquez's portrait of Agueda.

Agueda Martinez (1977) is a short documentary, directed and edited by Esperanza Vasquez and produced by Moctesuma Esparza. Vasquez was not an Ethno-Communications student; however, she had been part of an earlier film trainee program in Los Angeles called the New Communicators run by USC Professor Mel Sloan, Jack Dunbar, and Mae Churchill (who secured the US Office of Economic Opportunity grant that funded the initiative).[12] Vasquez was one of two women and sixteen men who were being trained for employment in the film industry. The program, which started in the summer of 1968, lasted less than eight months and by the following year at least two of its Chicana/o recruits, Vasquez and Francisco Martinez, wound up at UCLA.[13] Vasquez worked as a director and editor with Esparza on a six-episode public affairs series for the McGraw Hill Company called *La Raza* (1974). For an episode called "Survival," Esparza tells me he wanted to do something about a great-grandmother, "who lives on the land, who is an artisan and is transmitting culture and is part of New Mexico before the conquest. So, her people go back."[14] Through activist comrades Esparza had known in New Mexico from his organizing work with Reies López Tijerina, he and Vasquez ultimately found Agueda, who was well known for her weaving. Agueda Martinez was so captivating to the filmmakers that they decided to use the outtakes they shot of her for the "Survival" episode and create a stand-alone sixteen-minute documentary, *Agueda Martinez: Our People, Our Country,* which went on to be nominated for a 1978 Academy Award for short subject documentary.

As with Grandma in *Ashes,* we come to understand Agueda's intimacy with the land through filmed footage of the eighty-year-old woman plowing and harvesting (sometimes by herself and other times with her daughter's children) as well as her voice-over reflections.[15] Whereas Gerima scores the scene where we meet Grandma with a song describing African roots and American fruit, in *Agueda Martinez* we meet our protagonist describing her own Indigenous roots; her grandparents on both sides are Navajo. Like Gerima, Vasquez inserts sepia-toned family photos early on to ground and connect her protagonist to her distinct lineage.

Later in the film when Agueda, like Grandma, discusses the healing herbs she uses for her family, she again nods to these roots: "I give herbs to everyone . . . all this comes from my great-grandfather. Indians were better experts with herbs." At least once more in the film she emphasizes, "We may consider ourselves Mexicans or we may consider ourselves Hispanics . . . but we are more Indian." While the portrait of Agueda is mostly lush and somewhat idyllic—we watch her pull water from the well, chop firewood, till the land, and feed her family from its harvest, then work late into the night on her loom weaving original patterned serapes— Agueda describes at least one generational tension that is similar to the tension between Nay Charles and Grandma in *Ashes:* disappointment with the younger generation not attending church. "All the children today seldom go near a church," she explains, commenting how this would never have been accepted in her youth. We briefly see Agueda's warm connection to her church community; however, the deepest spiritual connection we witness and hear about from her is her connection with the land: "The land is a blessed thing because it is what produces our food, it produces the clothes that I have because it produces the cotton, it maintains the sheep that produce the wool, it supports the cow that is the meat and the milk. How can the land not be blessed?"

There is no explicit mention of greedy land developers waiting in the wings to poach the Martinez land. At least twice, though, we hear Agueda adamantly insist, "I shall never sell my ranch in my lifetime . . . not in my lifetime will I sell my ranch." In a follow-up email exchange with Esparza, he confirmed my hunch: "Agueda's words are a reference to the historical forces that caused many to either be pushed off their land or to sell to pay arbitrary taxes created by the European American victors of the U.S. Mexican War of 1848."[16]

Esparza's analysis directly resonates with a moment in Gerima's film, when Grandma responds to Nay Charles's question about why she had to sell so much of their family land: "What? Taxes!" By asking the question, Nay Charles has angered Grandma so powerfully that she says she has to go talk to Grandpa. We see Grandma move through the woods to where her late husband was buried, and she squats low, shrunk in grief, still wearing her wide-brimmed sun hat. Gerima cuts here to a newsreel image of a Vietnamese widow squatting and wearing a wide-brimmed sun hat. She is also looking down in what must be grief. The visual of his grandmother is connected in Nay Charles's mind with the wives and grandmothers he witnessed in Vietnam, bent over dead sons, grandsons, and grieving over land decimated and dispossessed. While Gerima is already connecting the dispossession echoes between this grieving Virginia grandmother and the grieving Vietnamese woman, by including *Agueda Martinez* in this comparison, we can trace multiple threads across the Ethno filmography that expose the threat and devastation of land dispossession for women of color from Southeast Asia to New Mexico to the Southeast United States. Sandra Sunrising Osawa similarly takes up this issue for an Indigenous activist matriarch, this time on the Arizona side of Navajo Nation.

In Osawa's 1988 documentary short *In the Heart of Big Mountain,* we meet Katherine Smith, a Navajo elder who has resisted government orders to move from her land on a disputed Navajo/Hopi borderline for over fifteen years. Katherine's family has lived in this location, at the heart of Arizona's Big Mountain, for four generations. The site is a sacred place in Navajo creation stories; we hear Katherine refer to the mountain itself as her mother. One of her daughters further explains, "Our religion revolves around the land. Our prayers are tied with the earth here." Like Agueda, we hear from Katherine about the healing properties of the plants and herbs growing on her land. We also hear about her determination to never

Katherine Smith, production still from *In the Heart of Big Mountain* (Sandra Osawa, 1988). Photo: Sandra Osawa. Courtesy of Upstream Productions.

leave the land: "My spirit's going to be here forever." In the case of Katherine's spiritual practices, we do not see the same intergenerational conflict portrayed in *Agueda* and *Ashes*. Katherine's grown children return to the land to visit and keep religious traditions alive (one grown son, a Vietnam vet like the fictional Nay Charles, even goes home to live with Katherine). However, Osawa does take time in the film to portray the tragic consequences to one of Katherine's daughters who leaves the area permanently, losing the connection to the land.

The final section of the documentary takes us into Tuba City to meet Nancy, who has obeyed relocation orders by moving there with her family. While we have experienced Katherine in exclusively exterior shots, tending to her land, her sheep, even washing and grooming herself outside, Osawa films Nancy in direct-address interviews from inside her home. The resulting contrast feels effectively claustrophobic. Though Nancy and her family were offered a large home through the relocation program, and she claims there are many conveniences to living in the city, she also admits her "quiet is gone." Nancy describes her work as a translator for

Navajo relocators who do not speak English, and she shares details about her pain and tears in hearing their stories of loss and heartache. Finally, she admits to her own depression, describing how "Public law 93- 531," the 1974 Navajo/Hopi land settlement act, "has ruined me. . . . I notice that I'm losing my memory. . . . I can't sleep at night." She says she does not think anything can help. Sandra Osawa, who has provided voice-over narration, then tells us that not long after filming Nancy, she died of a brain hemorrhage, which was brought on by "massive heartache."

Osawa's film, which is already devastating, becomes much more so in relation to *Ashes and Embers* and *Agueda Martinez,* primarily due to the story of Nancy. While we are invited to dwell in the strength of these elder matriarchs like the fictional Grandma in *Ashes* and the real Agueda and Katherine, Nancy's story forces us to imagine that those other matriarchs may be just one late tax payment, one new arbitrary borderline, or one forced removal away from Nancy's lethal broken heart. The power and cultural legacy of these three matriarchs is presented with a precision that insists we appreciate these women's strength as well as their potential vulnerability. Each director presents this precarity so well, yet the call of these films to bear witness and remain alert to the vulnerability of women like these is even stronger when considering their struggles relationally.

FATHERSONGS

Shifting focus from mostly rural matriarchs to three films about fathers within the Ethno filmography, I look here at three student works by Charles Burnett, Eddie Wong, and Jeff Furumura. Before carefully studying the films of this wider Ethno filmography and keeping close accounts of the timeline of the various films, I admit when I first saw clips from Eddie Wong's film *Wong Sinsaang* in Arthur Dong's documentary about Visual Communications,[17] I figured the grainy black-and-white documentary footage about a father's workplace humiliation must have been inspired by Charles Burnett's *Killer of Sheep.* I was surprised to find that even if we consider production on *Killer of Sheep* as having started as early as 1972, Wong's student film was still made before Burnett's feature. Though stylistically very different than either *Killer of Sheep* or *Wong*

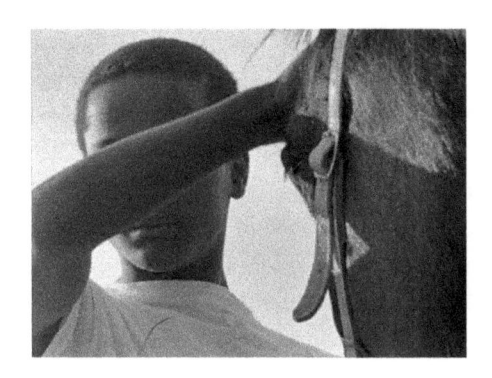

Screenshot from *The Horse* (Charles Burnett, 1973).

Sinsaang, it is Burnett's short film *The Horse,* completed in 1973 (on a hiatus from work on *Killer of Sheep*) that I wish to place in conversation with Wong's short and also one by Wong's Ethno-Communications class-mate Jeff Furumura, *I Don't Think I Said Much.* If the earlier trio of films grouped three grandmothers, this one groups three father figures, work-ing-class men who suffer indignities from white bosses or patrons at times in view or earshot of their children. What both sets share is the require-ment of a supple and empowered eye to read multiple and interlocking signs of oppression and aggression faced by the protagonists at the center of each narrative.

Far outside the realm of Watts, and looking more like the rural land-scapes that might belong to the earlier trio of films, *The Horse,* based on an unpublished short story by Burnett, takes place on a sprawling mountain range in California. We enter a tense, disorienting landscape where three impatient adult white men on the dilapidated porch of an unkempt ranch house wait for something or someone. We wonder if the something they are waiting for has anything to do with the pre-teen Black child twenty yards or so out from the porch, steadily stroking the mane of a dark brown horse. We come to understand that the boy's father has been called to kill the horse. Within earshot of the son, we hear the father referred to as "some damn nigger," and we see how the sound of that verbal assault causes the child's already lowered head to sink even lower. In need of com-fort himself, the child continues to comfort the horse.

When Ray, the boy's father (played by filmmaker Larry Clark) finally arrives, he is wearing a white hat. It is more Kangol cap than cowboy hat, but nevertheless—he wears a white hat. He then extends his heroic stance by actually squatting to greet his son, to be on his level in order to swoop the child up into his arms in a moment of unexpected jubilation. The tenderness is cut short when the head rancher/owner approaches Ray's car to see that Ray has brought a gun, and now the father must complete his day's work. The actual killing of the horse is done off camera. Instead, Burnett keeps the camera on the wincing son while we listen. James Naremore connects this moment to the harrowing work of the father in *Killer of Sheep*, work he describes as "the cruelest, most psychologically damaging work . . . assigned to the poorest and least powerful." In one crucial way, Naremore differentiates the father's work in *The Horse:* Ray "is hired to kill a single animal at a moment when his son happens to be present, but the father [in *Killer of Sheep*] is hired to kill many animals on an almost daily basis, always out of sight of his family."[18] This distinction is why I choose *The Horse* to put in conversation with the films by Wong and Furumura, because all of these films and filmmakers have something to say about the impact of bearing direct witness to the dehumanizing behavior their fathers and/or men of their father's generation had to endure from white employers and patrons.

Jeff Furumura, who entered the Ethno-Communications program in the same class as Larry Clark and Eddie Wong, straddles the realm of documentary and fiction in his short film about Japanese American gardener Elmer Uchida, *I Don't Think I Said Much* (1971). In an email interview with Furumura, I learned that Uchida was not Furumura's father, but at the time of filming Furumura's sister was dating Uchida's son Randy. Also, Furumura worked for Uchida in the summer of '71: "I spent the better part of that summer working alongside Elmer on his route through the Brentwood area, including Debbie Reynolds's house!" The film begins on a black screen, and we only hear voices—young people's voices daring one another to do what sounds like a man-on-the-street interview. The white man that they select is asked by the Interviewer about the man we will come to know as Elmer: "Do you see that guy over there? Well, what do you think of him?" Man: "What do you mean what do I think of him?" Interviewer: "What do you think he is?" Man: "I don't kn—just a gardener." Up from black now we see still, color photos of Elmer around his work van. Furumura cuts from one photo to the next to the sound of a percussive metal rake scraping across concrete. When the camera goes to live action we are in slow motion, as Elmer pulls his rubber garden shoes from the back of his van. The rubber shoes gracefully, almost balletically, fall to the sidewalk and bounce before Elmer wiggles his work shoes into them. Slowing this action down already sets this mundane daily task apart, cueing us to be alert to other poetic aspects of Elmer's labor and his life.

We hear the beginning of a voice-over monologue from one of the homeowners for whom Elmer gardens. The homeowner's sentiments sound innocent enough initially, with the man saying how lucky he feels to have had Elmer working for him for fifteen years or more. He describes Elmer as hardworking, very quiet, and that he keeps to himself. Before this verbal portrait becomes unbearably paternalistic, Furumura fades back to black, then switches gears visually and sonically. We now see black-and-white photos of Elmer's family on a Sacramento farm, and hear a Japanese woman's voice, possibly Elmer's mother or an older sister, tell us in Japanese about Elmer's childhood on the farm in the 1920s. This voice is blended with the sound of a classical Japanese stringed instrument and a low mournful singing voice. We see portraits of a very large family wearing their Sunday best—the men in suits look especially proud—while we hear about how hard all the family, children and adults, had to work on the land. Then we hear about his family's relocation to a concentration camp during World War II and see archival footage of the relocation announcement. We learn that Elmer met his wife "in camp," and that his family had nothing to offer the bride after their marriage "but love." This section ends with Elmer's relative saying how proud she is of the man he has become. Furumura then returns to the present-day story of Elmer as gardener, but also as family man and a practitioner of the Japanese art of Suiseki.

When Elmer's customers talk about their summer vacation plans, Elmer tells us in his own voice-over monologue, "I quite often get [long pause] discouraged, because it's the time of the year when gardening gets long and very tiring." Furumura films this section of Elmer's monologue showing Elmer work around one particular patron's enormous Rolls Royce. From the perspective of the camera, the shadow of the hood ornament of the Rolls looks superimposed onto Elmer's laboring body. Elmer looks as though he is only twice the height of the ornament, which ought

Screenshot of Elmer Uchida from
I Don't Think I Said Much (Jeff
Furumura, 1971).

to fit in his hand. Furumura also shoots Elmer's reflection off the wide, mirror-like front grill of the vehicle. When I asked Furumura about the monologue of the "white man" telling us about Elmer that he intercuts with Elmer's story of himself, Furumura explained that the white patron's monologue was scripted, "paraphrased from a conversation with the attorney who owned the Rolls Royce." Here are the final lines we hear from the attorney's monologue in the film:

> [Elmer] never misses a cheerful, "Hi." He's always smiling. There must be something in the Japanese nature or character that allow them to do this kind of work without complaint. Most of my friends have oriental gardeners and they're all pretty much alike, hardworking, quiet, very simple people.

From these words the film shifts a final time to an exploration of Elmer's "hobby," as he calls it, the Japanese art of rock appreciation called Suiseki. We see Elmer now working the land for his own purposes, on his own time, digging out large rocks and holding them in his gloved hands, considering their shape, color, form. Elmer, still in voice-over, searches for the language to explain his pleasure in this pursuit: "My satisfaction really goes much deeper than looking at rocks. It [long pause] gives me [pause] peace, and, uh, relaxation . . . in addition to what you really enjoy in looking at that particular stone." And after another long pause, he offers his humble self-assessment, which became the film's title: "I don't think I said much." Furumura moves to Elmer's son and wife and their humorous reaction to Elmer's hobby. And then we see Elmer, home now, remove his eyeglasses and, in slow motion once again, observe and touch the rocks as in a meditation. The film closes by cycling back to the opening teaser of voices on the street: "What do you think he is?" Now when we hear the man on the street say, "Just a gardener," we understand the lie, the erasure of Elmer. In a film just shy of sixteen minutes, Elmer and Furumura say so much about this full man. Furumura explained to me, "I made the film hoping to show that individuals like Elmer, who are so easily written off as the help or the Yard Guy, have lives that are full of meaning and beauty even if they themselves don't even recognize it. . . . He remains one of my heroes."[19]

Eddie Wong's short film *Wong Sinsaang*, the only one of the three in this discussion where the filmmaker literally takes direct aim at his own father, is much more conflicted about the man at the center of his film. In a 1990 interview, Wong discussed his first student film as one he "needed to do . . . to try to reconcile my own feelings about my father, who is a, was a Chinese laundryman." He explained that at the time of making the film, he had just finished reading the *Autobiography of Malcolm X* and from it gained insight about "colonial relations" and how "people who are colonized related to their parents in a very stilted manner. They see them through the eyes of their oppressors."[20]

Structured similarly to Furumura's short—from the stereotype you think you know to the nuanced man and father you get to finally meet—the twelve-minute piece begins with shots of Eddie Wong's father in his storefront laundry, layering the harsh sounds of heavy steam machines and industrial irons with the harsh and patronizing sounds of white customers' chatter. From this, we move to another realm where the viewer is invited to the rich inner life of Mr. Wong. What differentiates this shift from the similar move in Furumura's work is the first-person grappling the director/son weaves into the narrative. Eddie Wong's young and urgent voice explains that he couldn't see past what he calls the "chink" mask, or stereotypical docile courteous Chinaman his father revealed to his customers. "I never understood how a man could put up with the daily humiliations from the obnoxious white customers or the deadliness of the twelve-hour grind." Then reflecting even deeper, he admits, "I loved him as son to father, as much as I held him in contempt as brother to brother, man to man. But . . . I really didn't know him."

Mr. Frank Wong takes a break from his laundry business to work on his poetry. Screenshot from *Wong Sinsaang* (Eddie Wong, 1971). Courtesy of Visual Communications Photographic Archive.

For the duration of the film, we move with the son and his camera as he begins the work of getting to know his father on a deeper level. Empowering his own eyes, the son empowers ours as we watch the elder Mr. Wong painting, reading poetry, and moving through an elegant martial arts sequence as if his laundry parking lot were an Olympic auditorium. We are also made aware of Mr. Wong's immigration history, detailed for us in photographs and newspaper clippings. Finally, Eddie Wong ends the film with what sounds like a new beginning, at least the beginning of an interview between son and father:

> SON: How long have you been in the laundry business?
> FATHER: Oh, about twenty-one years.
> SON: What do you think about it?
> FATHER: Can't think about it, just make living. . . .

When we consider these three films in conversation, the concluding interview in *Wong Sinsaang* prompts us to consider what kinds of questions the child in Burnett's short might one day ask of his father, a killer of horses who endures his work with racist white men and still manages to show up to that work with a white hat and a tender embrace for his son. How different, how quiet and spare is Burnett's portrait of Ray, his gun, and this killing compared to the Hollywood portraits of Black men with guns flooding the cinemas at the time Burnett produced this. Also, what did it mean for this early-'70s generation of independent Asian American filmmakers, for these young Asian American UCLA students, to finally interrogate the one-note Japanese gardener and Chinese laundryman stereotypes that dominated the industry fare of their fathers' generation? These fathersongs join the earlier set of films to announce the humanity of both mothers/grandmothers and fathers of color in ways that independent cinema, both narrative and documentary, had seldom achieved. The specificity of their renderings also help to make them cross-racially recognizable and relatable, fostering the potential for the kind of "listening (and) learning each other's ways" that Bambara believed the multiracial anthology *Bridge* would do.

THE *CRUSHING* COST OF ACTIVISM

Two of the most striking discoveries of the early UCLA student filmography come from Betty Chen and Laura Ho.[21] The films of theirs that I will consider here, *Portraits of a Young Girl* (1970?) and *Sleepwalker* (1971), address issues of women and political activism in very different ways. Chen's piece is an animation that does not become overtly "political" until the shocking final frames. *Sleepwalker* is on first viewing not explicitly political but becomes devastatingly so once the circumstances of the filmmaker and filmmaking are revealed. These two early shorts by Ethno-era women directors, in their consideration of political activism, relate to projects by male members of their cohort that have received much more attention, such as *Requiem 29* (David Garcia, 1971) and *Bush Mama* (Haile Gerima, 1975). I take the title for this subsection from Sylvia Morales's 2009 documentary, *A Crushing Love: Chicanas, Motherhood, and Activism*, which incorporates archival footage from *Requiem 29* and, in the figure of welfare rights activist Alicia Escalante, takes up parallel

Betty Chen with microphone.
Photo: Mary Uyematsu Kao.

concerns to Gerima's *Bush Mama* regarding the egregious and predatory violence of the welfare state against women of color. Placing Morales's reverent and rigorous look into the lives of five Chicana activists—raising hell and raising children from the 1960s onward—in conversation with Chen and Ho's work, we see that these films confront sorrow, fear, and unfathomable loss head on, and yet still manage to suggest imaginative and generative recovery strategies and paths to making sense of the distinctive cost for women who prioritize protest.

Betty Chen arrived at UCLA's graduate film program in the pre-Ethno days, and like Charles Burnett and David Garcia, she eventually became one of the teaching assistants to the earliest cohorts of Ethno-Communications students. Robert Nakamura remembers her as his teacher, and in the credits of his landmark student film *Manzanar*, she appears as one of only three members of his production crew. Fellow Visual Communications (VC) cofounder Eddie Wong also thanked her on

Wong Sinsaang. She collaborated with and inspired other women of color from the Ethno program such as Sylvia Morales and Mary Uyematsu Kao, and she also worked on projects by white women directors and writers from UCLA such as Judith Dancoff (*Judy Chicago and the California Girls*, 1971), Yolande du Luart (*Angela Davis: Portrait of a Revolutionary*, 1971), and future Oscar-winning screenwriter Nancy Dowd (*Marguerite*, 1971).[22] At some point, likely just before all of the projects above, Chen created a personal animated piece, *Portraits of a Young Girl*, in response to the May 1970 US invasion of Cambodia. It delivered a one-two punch so stunning that one can easily understand why she would become any young insurgent filmmaker's go-to comrade collaborator.[23]

Portraits of a Young Girl, which begins (and remains) in silence, opens with what looks like a live-action sketch pad. A black marker skates across a blank white canvas, creating the lines of a young girl's face. This face swirls into a series of additional color portraits of young women—some realistic, some psychedelic, in profile or staring full frontal. Some faces rest among the stars and moon, others dreamily gaze at rolling landscapes. These images dance and stream into one another for just over a minute, and then the vivid colors abruptly fade to a smoky gray charcoal image of men wearing gas masks and aiming rifles at an unseen target. With rapid fades to and up from black, Chen achieves a strobe light effect of gun blasts. Again, the piece is silent, but the visual effect conjures the sound of gun fire.

Finally, one portrait remains. This time, the young girl is not illustrated but photographed, a familiar black-and-white yearbook photo. This time, the young girl's portrait does not swirl or dance; it is static and accompanied by a descriptive text:

> Allison Krause.
> B 1951
> D May 3, 1970
> Kent, Ohio.

And, suddenly, the school portrait and the earlier animated image of the armed national guardsmen register. In less than two minutes flat, Betty Chen captured the unspeakable horror of the Kent State University student massacre, where in thirteen seconds, Ohio National Guardsmen fired sixty-seven rounds into a sea of student antiwar protesters, wounding nine and killing four, including nineteen-year-old Krause.[24] Forget trigger warnings, literally—there is absolutely no indication from the benign title of Chen's film, nor the swirling, colorful animated faces of dreaming girls, that we are heading toward a portrait of THAT girl.

Chen notes the date of death as May 3, not May 4; this could be because Krause, the day before she was martyred, is remembered for her statement to a National Guardsman with a lilac sprouting from his rifle (inserted by a fellow protestor): "Flowers are better than guns." She was fatally fired upon the following day, May 4, 1970. To learn, as many press clippings after Krause's death reveal, that she was an art student may have moved Chen, who was a painter, illustrator, and budding animator herself. A later work of Chen's was her illustrations for Bob Miyamoto's short film *Gaman ... to Endure* (1982) of the Japanese American concentration camp experience through a child's eyes.[25] One wonders if Chen's artwork of a young girl with a flower, standing before a barbed-wire fence policed by armed soldiers, bears any connection to the young, flower-praising Krause whom Chen memorialized in *Portraits*. In either case, it is significant that in Chen's work engaging both Japanese Internment and protests against the wars in Southeast Asia she chose to center the lives of young women and girls.

The National Chicano Moratorium Committee against the Vietnam War had been planning protests across the Southwest well before the events at Kent State.[26] Betty Chen's UCLA classmates—led by her fellow Ethno-Communications TA David Garcia and Moctesuma Esparza—convened to film the third and largest rally in East Los Angeles on August 29, 1970. These Ethno students could not have known at the time that their resulting film would come to be called *Requiem 29* in solemn tribute to journalist Ruben Salazar, who was murdered at the march on that day. The film presents vivid color footage of the thousands of Chicanas and Chicanos gathered to make a stand against the war that was killing their men in disproportionate numbers to their percentage of the population. This proud and festive footage is intercut with haunting black-and-white footage of the memorial service for their slain hero, Salazar, as well as tense sequences of the Los Angeles County coroner's inquest into his death.[27] The longest section of the coroner's inquest features the testimony of Chicano activist and *La Raza* photographer Raul Ruiz. Footage of Ruiz's analysis of the inquest is also featured prominently. There is ample footage of the participation of women of all ages at the rally and at the inquest hearing, but we are not introduced by name to a single Chicana in the film. Two brief "portraits" of young, unnamed Chicanas in *Requiem* are worthy of more consideration here in connection to the figure of Krause at Kent State memorialized in Chen's *Portraits*.

In what is presented as an unwarranted invasion of riot-gear-clad police, we see the gathered community frantically attempt to flee the formerly peaceful scene. Some protesters try to defend themselves from the siege of batons and tear gas, and one camera captures a young woman (perhaps a teenager) throwing something that looks like a rock, or perhaps she is returning a canister of tear gas. We then see a policeman charge her, bashing the back of her head with a billy club, and she falls to the ground. Eventually we see another woman attempt to help her to her feet, but within seconds there is a cut to a wider shot of more tear gas, and we never return to this brutalized victim. What became of her? Is it too cynical to say that if she had died from this blow we might have known her name?

There is only one brief man-on-the-street interview that bridges this riot footage to the first inquest interview with Ruiz; significantly, this interview is with a *woman*-on-the-street, who appears to be about twenty years old. She is not named, yet she provides this critical witness:

> I was gassed along with thousands of other Chicanos, Chicanas. I was in the restroom with little children that were there. They were very scared. They were crying. The mother had never seen such a thing, she didn't know something like that would occur. She thought she would be safe being that it was made clear that it was going to be a legal and peaceful demonstration. The tear gas pellet went into the restroom and the children were gassed along with the adults and other people that were there.

The woman is clearly shaken, and then she is gone. Who was she? Did she, like the mothers and children she described, just show up to the demonstration? Or was she a known organizer and therefore a voice sought out to be included in the film? The roughly fifteen minutes of screen time devoted to Ruiz's testimony and follow-up interview suggests that the Ethno crew who produced and edited the film made the decision to prioritize the

Screenshot from *Requiem 29* (David Garcia, 1970).

charismatic male activist's voice over these two unnamed female participants, whose combined screen time is less than two minutes.

When I spoke with Moctesuma Esparza about his memories of the day
and of making the film, he spoke about his role as producer, securing
money and equipment from three particular men in the community he
respected and to whom he wanted to be sure to pay tribute:

> I remember David Garcia said to me, "You're the producer! Go get it! Go get
> the equipment and go get the money!" We got the equipment free from Jack
> Pill. He had a rental house on Santa Monica Boulevard, and he was helping
> young Black and Latino and Asian filmmakers. Jewish guy. So, I want to
> remember him. . . . Esteban Torres, who became a congressman and was the
> executive director of TELACU, gave me five grand. TELACU stood for The
> East Los Angeles Community Union, a community action and antipoverty
> program Torres founded in 1968. . . . Raul Yzaguirre, who was then a con-
> sultant for the Southwestern Council of La Raza—he became the executive
> director of the Southwestern Council of La Raza which then became the
> National Council of La Raza—he gave me five grand, and that's how we
> financed buying the film and processing the film.[28]

Elsewhere it has been noted that Esparza also met his longtime collaborator and future wife, filmmaker/editor Esperanza Vasquez, at the Moratorium. A *Los Angeles Times* piece about their Oscar-nominated documentary *Agueda Martinez* describes the union as follows: "They met in 1970 at the Chicano Moratorium. Each was there to make a film, Esparza with a student collective and Ms. Vasquez alone. They joined resources and the result was 'Requiem 29'. . . ."[29] There is no crew listed in the credits, so the contributions of the vast number of UCLA students who may have worked on the film is unclear, but we know from this *Times* piece there was at least one Chicana filmmaker crewing that day. In this, my first interview with Esparza, he did not mention meeting Vasquez on that day, nor did he mention her participation on the film. He highlighted instead the generous and supportive men who made this Chicano movement film possible. Yet Chicanas are irrefutably part of this film and this historic moment, both on and behind the cameras. The women's range of activities captured on camera is wide—from dancing and marching to being on the receiving end of police batons and tear gas—but the slim space they occupy in contrast with the "important" male activist's screen time must be questioned. Considering the two Chicanas—one clubbed, one gassed, both disappeared—in conversation with Laura Ho's *Sleepwalker*, we are given the space to wonder what happened to the women of color activists who we catch only glimpses of in histories of resistance movements and in critically received, often male-directed documentaries of those movements. Where did these women go when they were ushered off camera and off the pages of activist discourse?

"I did experience discrimination as a woman and as an Asian," explained Laura Ho, reflecting on her time as a political organizer and UCLA film student, "but what really held me back was the male chauvinism that I had grown up with and internalized. I never believed I could make it."[30] Ho was instrumental in the founding of critical and transformational Asian American organizations such as the movement journal *Gidra,* and also ARM, the Asian Radical Movement; it is remarkable to consider that this was all achieved *in spite of* Ho's sense of doubt and the burden of internalized chauvinism. The honesty and vulnerability of the statement match the tender interiority of the central character of her short student film from 1971. Even if, retrospectively, she assesses her work as the work of someone lacking belief in herself, there is a confidence in her storytelling and framing here that suggests otherwise. This is the work of a director who insists that we dwell in the dialogue-less world of a young, Asian American woman/worker/dreamer who is suffering *and* seeks something new. Ho insists that her protagonist belongs at the center of an art-house-style dramatic short, and that we should take the time to get to know her world, take the time to walk, even *sleep*walk, in her shoes.

Sleepwalker follows several days in the life of a typist played by Suzi Wong, sister of Eddie Wong. She waits for a city bus, she arrives at her workplace, she types all day, she rubs her sore hands, she waits for the bus to return home—and, repeat. One day, she decides to skip the bus to work and take a meandering walk instead. She trembles at a barking dog. She looks longingly through a chain-link fence at a young girl bouncing a ball in an empty schoolyard. She dares to join this girl and to play.

Through superimposition of the two faces, the viewer experiences the feeling that this girl is a version of the woman.[31] The girl easily looks into the camera, but the woman avoids any direct gaze. The two play catch, bouncing this ball and flinging their arms high in the sky, exchanging wide smiles . . . until the ball bounces into the street and the young girl chases after it. There is a crash. The camera stays on the terror-struck face of the protagonist and never returns to the young girl. The typist moves on.

She walks through a park, weaving through trees, and there is another curious superimposition. This time it is not of the young girl's face blended with the typist's face but of something that looks more like their limbs or arms. The arms formerly raised high to play ball in the school yard, now float like ghosts among the trees. The typist moves on again, now to a windy field of grass.

The strong breeze presses against the typist, and she leans into it tenderly, almost erotically, resting in its embrace. She floats her own arms out to the side to ride this wind. Here, Ho superimposes shots of a seagull (whose "caw, caw" has been heard off and on among other amplified nature squawks and squeals) matched as closely to the typist's flying body as her face had been earlier matched to the young girl's. There is a sense that these camera movements and floating superimpositions fulfill the lonely typist's profound hunger to connect. From leaning into the wind, the typist now lays on a bed of grass and sensuously combs her fingers through its

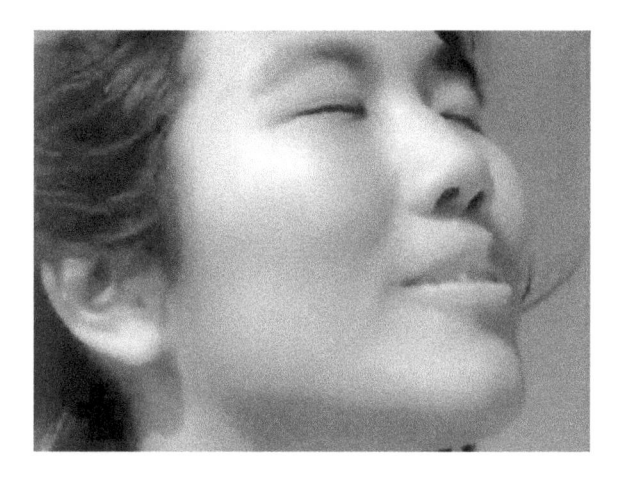

Screenshot from *Sleepwalker* (Laura Ho, 1971).

blades. Then, abruptly, the typist is back at the bus stop. Has this all been a dream? Or is this simply a new workday, now made more bearable by the prior "mental health day" off? Fade to the end title card: *Sleepwalker.*

For the twentieth anniversary of Visual Communications (VC) in 1990, Abraham Ferrer, VC's Archives & Distribution Manager, curated a program called "Asian American Ethnos" for the Los Angeles Asian Pacific Film Festival that included *Sleepwalker* with other student works by Ethno-Communications alum including Robert Nakamura, Eddie Wong, Jeff Furumura, Danny Kwan, and Brian Maeda.[32] On my first viewing of this collection on Ferrer's computer at the VC offices, especially after so many images of concentration camps, testimonies of drug addiction, racist humiliation faced by Japanese gardeners and Chinese laundry men, it was hard to make sense of Ho's film, which felt much more *Meshes of the Afternoon* than *Manzanar.* It may contain a mild anticapitalist critique, with its penetrating city soundscape of squealing bus brakes and rapid-fire typewriters. These sounds cover shots of our overworked protagonist massaging her aching hands at a bus stop, while her white male "boss" skips out of work with a stack of fresh typed papers made possible by the labor of this miserable woman of color. But what, if any, additional political message was there?

The filmmaker, now Laura Ho Fineman, who had not seen *Sleepwalker* in many years, attended the 1990 screening and shared that she was "just

Screenshot from *A Crushing Love: Chicanas, Motherhood and Activism* (Sylvia Morales, 2009), featuring Dolores Huerta (*left*) and Alicia Escalante (*center*).

shocked at how . . . wounded it seemed." Her initial reaction was: "Whoa, something's really wrong with the person who made this movie." Struggling to respond to her film decades after its completion, she recounted the story of an arrest in 1969: "I don't know if Eddie [Wong] told you, but we were all arrested."[33]

Ho, who had also been an SDS organizer, was one of the leaders of the Asian Radical Movement (ARM). An ARM "sit-in" in support of an unjustly fired African American food worker led to nineteen arrests and charges of felony kidnapping and conspiracy to kidnap.[34] "They later dropped it down," Ho explains. "It was a very difficult time for people. It changed everybody."

Offering a major insight into the sense of isolation of her *Sleepwalker* protagonist, Ho further details that, "Part of the terms of my probation were not to associate with anybody . . . [with] those people that I essentially got in trouble with . . . and not to be political . . . for five years. So, I just kind of hibernated and kept to myself." After a couple years of dead-end jobs, including writing copy for a department store and working for the IRS (until they found out she had an arrest record), she went back to school and made *Sleepwalker* as her "Project 2." Suddenly the film's place alongside the more overtly political projects of Ho's UCLA cohort made perfect sense, and given this context, *Sleepwalker*—as a meditation on the aftermath of political organizing—can and ought to take its place along-side a number of contemporary fiction and nonfiction films about women of color organizers.[35]

To think in terms of *after*maths of activism might be met with resistance from the five women featured in Sylvia Morales's feature documentary *A Crushing Love: Chicanas, Motherhood and Activism* (2009), as their organizing, their creative and political work, never ceased. The same can be said for the filmmaker herself, who appears in the film along with her children. Morales had briefly introduced two of the organizers from *A Crushing Love*, Dolores Huerta and Alicia Escalante, three decades earlier in her UCLA MFA thesis film *Chicana* (1979).[36] *A Crushing Love* is in many respects a sequel to *Chicana*, which, in Morales's own words, went "beyond the stereotype of the Chicana as a nurturing woman" and instead presented "a pantheon of images that stimulate a new vitality in the history of the Chicana," moving from pre-Columbian feminine deities to the story of La Malinche and the conquest of Mexico, up to twentieth-century labor rights activist Francisca Flores.[37] *Chicana* offers a sweeping history, which Rosa Linda Fregoso suggests was a frequent impulse of early Chicanx film: "The tendency to tell all of our history in one filmic statement—five hundred years in roughly twenty minutes."[38] But Morales's follow-up feature-length documentary delivers intimate and rigorous interviews of five Chicana activists who are also mothers: Dolores Huerta, Alicia Escalante, Elizabeth "Betita" Martinez, Martha Cotera, and Cherríe Moraga. The interviews are framed by Morales's own autobiographical sketches of life as an activist filmmaker, as she takes her teenage daughter on the road with her to film these extraordinary women. Whereas Betty Chen, Laura Ho, and the Ethno students who shot *Requiem 29* in 1970 were addressing the lives and losses of activists of the period *directly* in the moment those losses occurred, the decades between *Chicana* and *A Crushing Love* allow Sylvia Morales and her subjects the space of self-reflection and the wisdom of hindsight not yet possible in the earlier films. With that self-reflection comes brutal honesty from the *Crushing* protagonists about the ways they straddled organizing and mothering. Morales's move to include interviews with several of the adult children of these activist icons additionally creates the space in her film to confront and reckon with moments when the children suffered from their mothers' political actions. A particular sequence between Betita Martinez and her daughter Tess, as they separately remember the 1970 Chicano Moratorium, illustrates one such reckoning.

Born in 1925, historian, publisher, and organizer Betita Martinez had been working nationally and internationally on justice issues for over two decades when she arrived in Los Angeles from New Mexico for the great Chicano antiwar rally on August 29, 1970.[39] Instead of a direct-address interview with Martinez recalling the day's events, Morales includes footage of Martinez giving a talk about the Moratorium to a group of Latina/o youth, where she offers a playful and humorous recounting of the chaos of the rally. Martinez explains that she was with her teenage daughter, Tess, and they were handing out copies of the latest edition of the bilingual movement newspaper she cofounded, *El Grito del Norte,* just before the riot police stormed the crowd. Somewhat casually, she describes losing her daughter in the mayhem and looking for her in all the places the scattered activists were being arrested. Finally, she reports, at 11 p.m. she found Tess. Martinez laughs and slaps her podium several times as she delivers the punchline of the story: "I found her at a party! [She was] fine, having a great time. . . ."

With the help of footage shot that day by Sylvia Morales's Ethno-Communications classmates, Morales intercuts Martinez's lighthearted storytelling with the scene from *Requiem 29* detailed earlier, where we see tear-gassed crowds in a panic, as a policeman bashes the back of the skull of a young Chicana. As if this ironic intercutting of the humorous recounting with the brutal images was not sharp enough, Morales also includes an interview with Tess recalling her own fear that something bad was about to happen at the rally:

> Tess Koning-Martinez: I do remember one of our last little exchanges before the police riots started was . . . I must have been standing near her . . . and I said something, I was concerned that something was gonna happen. And I think she said, no, she didn't think anything was gonna, anything was gonna happen.

Morales moves immediately from the two separate tales of the Moratorium by mother and daughter to a stunningly vulnerable interview with Martinez, shot in close-up, where she admits her difficulty with parenting-while-organizing:

Betita Martinez: It's very hard for me to talk about how I combined my life as an activist with my life as a mother, because I think I did not do well at all as a mother, okay. I was completely absorbed by the struggles going on and I just . . . I involved my daughter in them sometimes, but I certainly didn't mother her very well, at all.

Morales does include a second interview clip with Tess where she characterizes the moment where her mother found her at the party as a "typical mother-teenage daughter kind of thing . . . we just happened to be at the big Chicano Moratorium." But by intercutting this sequence with the scene of a teenage Chicana knocked to the ground by a police baton, we have graphic evidence that Martinez's decision to include her daughter in her activist work on that particular day was potentially life-threatening.

The sequence insists that we confront the central, *Crushing* question: what is the cost of prioritizing activism for these Chicana mothers? The earlier projects that bear witness to the Vietnam-era killings of Allison Krause and Ruben Salazar represent one kind of loss. Morales, in her 2009 project, bears witness to the daily and decades-long losses experienced by mothers (and their children) when the path of activism keeps them from the intimacy of home *and* when the role of mother prevents them from committing to their justice work and creative work at the level of concentration and productivity to which they aspire. In other words, these Chicana icons may be sheroes to the world and to their communities, but given the opportunity to weigh in, their adult children's assessment is not so clear cut. Very few films deal with this tension so directly and honestly.

When I asked Morales how the project came about, she explained that she initially set out to do a series on Chicana feminism and she began with the interview with Betita Martinez, whose social justice work since the 1940s had inspired Morales. At some point, she finally asked Martinez,

"How did you manage?" And she looked at me and she goes, "You ask hard questions." Then she says, "Well . . . I wasn't a very good mother." I was shocked. And then I thought, oh my god, she feels the same guilt that I feel when I'm not with the kids. . . . So, I realized that that was the question that I had wanted to ask. I really did think, how did they do it? Maybe they know, and they can tell me, so I won't feel so fucked up.[40]

Morales also explained that the footage between her and her own daughter began as a playful experiment of how to keep her daughter engaged when, because of a lack of available childcare, she had to take her on the road for a film shoot. Her editor fell in love with the footage, and they realized it offered not only levity but also an immediacy regarding the activism/parenting challenge: "It made it more real because that was happening right now, whereas everything that happened to them, [with] the older ones, was in the past."

Connecting the challenges of working mothers in the present with the past is one of many offerings to Chicana feminist history and media Morales provides with *A Crushing Love*. And while the central drive of the film is to engage and reflect upon the decades-long struggles and sacrifices these Chicana icons and their children experienced, Morales also connects these chronicles of Chicana activism to other communities of color working for justice. She does this with her keen selection of archival photos and moving images. Dolores Huerta is seen standing next to Bobby Kennedy *and* Filipino labor organizer and UFW cofounder Larry Itliong.

Betita Martinez's daughter Tess discusses her mother's letters from Mississippi in 1964, and tells of the time she recruited her mother's friend Stokely Carmichael for a junior high homework assignment; Morales grounds these tales by editing in images of Carmichael and of the Freedom Schools that Martinez and her SNCC comrades organized. With both still and moving images, Morales shows a young Alicia Escalante picketing and organizing in solidarity with African American women leaders in the welfare rights movement.[41] This leads me to my final point about the impact of engaging the wider Ethno filmography cross-racially.

In a critical sequence of the *Crushing Love* documentary, Alicia Escalante details the aggressive and dehumanizing raids conducted by the welfare state, raids that sound more like predatory police seeking out violent drug lords than licensed social workers "checking in" on mothers of color who have requested assistance. "Usually, a worker would come through the back door, and another one would come through the front door, unannounced, as early as five in the morning," Escalante recounts, as Morales shoots a suspenseful sequence of black and white images of a housing project yard, her camera racing toward a front door. This sequence sheds light on Haile Gerima's related scene in his scripted feature *Bush Mama*, where his protagonist Dorothy is harassed and threatened in her home by an invasive welfare worker. Gerima presents a fantasy sequence here, where the demoralized Dorothy leaps up out of her defeated position on the couch and breaks a bottle over the head of the welfare worker, knocking her from her chair. I had never quite made sense of why, when we see Dorothy jump up to hit the welfare worker, her dress is unfastened in the back. Now that I have heard Escalante's testimony about the absurd hours in which these raids would occur, it makes sense that this subtle choice in Gerima's film alerts us that this visit was likely unannounced, causing Dorothy to rush from sleep to pull something on to answer the door without having time to fasten her dress. Reading these analogous moments across two films shot decades apart by UCLA classmates empowers our eyes to see the signs of shared struggle of women of color in Los Angeles in the 1970s.

In *Bush Mama*, Gerima concludes his welfare-worker visit with the agent demanding that Dorothy get an abortion so that she can continue to receive assistance. As described earlier in the introduction of this book, when Gerima shows the agonized Dorothy walk into an abortion clinic later in the film, Gerima casts the clinic with a room full of Latina, Asian American, and Black women. Prior to this scene, the cast of this film, with the exception of one white policeman, has been predominantly Black. This clinic casting infers that these women, across racial communities, have been subject to similar forms of harassment and intimidation experienced by Dorothy. Beyond this suggested parallel suffering in Gerima's scripted work, Morales's documentary, with the activist figure of Escalante, provides evidence of hope, evidence of the path out of suffering for these women made possible by the burgeoning welfare rights organizing by women of color throughout Los Angeles.

Morales's film compels one to research more about each of the women she profiles, including mother and daughter feminist scholars Martha and Maria Cotera as well as the one and only Cherríe Moraga, whose foundational women of color feminism/queer of color critique guides this very chapter.[42] Finding out more about Alicia Escalante's work not only in the Chicana community but in collaboration with African American welfare rights activists such as Johnnie Tillmon and Catherine Jermany, produced in me a kind of retroactive longing for a fictional character like *Bush Mama*'s Dorothy to encounter these real women who were fighting for justice for mothers like her well before, during, and after the filming of Gerima's feature.[43] Gerima's film effectively reminds us that the injustices of the welfare state were impacting more than just Black women in Los Angeles; Morales's film expands upon this inclusive vision to remind us that the response to these injustices was indeed cross-racial and collective. This cross-racial response is in keeping with Gerima's activist character Angie in *Bush Mama*, who, again, prophetically proclaims: "If all us mad folks unite—like the Indians, Chicanos, blacks, Asians—we'd shape up them white folks and they'd have to act differently."

From protection of the land, to exposure of workplace indignities, to a re-centering of the efforts of women organizers in social justice movements of the '60s and '70s, a relational look at the wider filmography of the Ethno-Communications filmmakers draws attention to the parallel struggles and often collective and cross-racial nature of the liberation movements of that time. Individual mono-racial studies of this work in effect do the immensely valuable labor of reminding activist filmmakers of color today (a la Gerima) that they are not orphans, that there are models of inspiring, independent, social justice media-making by each of these communities of filmmakers from which BIPOC filmmakers today can draw strength. It is my hope that fresh comparative and relational consideration of these intertextual echoes can galvanize greater cross-racial fluencies, unexpected alliances, and encourage generative collaborations among new generations of BIPOC activists, artists, and filmmakers.

This filmography has power. Above I considered its organizing power and potential; in the next and final chapter I will speak specifically about its pedagogical power, especially in the realm of both jazz studies and film studies of the 1970s. In other words, I put this bursting archive to work, to expose and fill gaps in jazz studies and jazz documentary studies, in particular where West Coast contributions are concerned (or shamefully overlooked). Then, inspired by the music, I stage a determined call and response between several iconic "New Hollywood" films of the early '70s with projects produced contemporaneously and just miles away by the "New Los Angeles" filmmakers of the Ethno program, raising sharp questions about just how cutting-edge or progressive the Hollywood directors were regarding matters of class, race, sexuality, politics, and history. With this wider comparative move, I offer tangible and ample evidence of the extraordinary value of this collective Ethno archive, demonstrating how much richer our understanding of both jazz and film culture of this period becomes when we study these works relationally.

4 Uses of Ethno

THE ETHNO FILMOGRAPHY AS PEDAGOGICAL POWER

> There are many kinds of power, used and unused, acknowl-
> edged or otherwise. The erotic is a resource within each of
> us that lies in a deeply female and spiritual plane, firmly
> rooted in the power of our unexpressed or unrecognized
> feeling. In order to perpetuate itself, every oppression must
> corrupt or distort those various sources of power within the
> culture of the oppressed that can provide energy for
> change.
>
> Audre Lorde, "Uses of the Erotic: The Erotic as Power"

There is power in the multiracial, cumulative filmography of the filmmakers of UCLA associated with the Ethno-Communications program, power that I argue can provide energy for change. The films themselves provided energy for change as they were being made and shared; they provide pedagogical power now as tools to inspire, challenge, and disrupt outdated paradigms and fill gaps in histories of music, politics, and filmmaking in Los Angeles and beyond. The first-generation ("O.G.") Mother Muccers might say the Ethno filmography lets this generation's rebel filmmakers and activists know what time it is and what time it can be.

This chapter will not substantively dive into Audre Lorde's endlessly generative essay, "Uses of the Erotic: the Erotic as Power"; still I am inspired here by many of its lines, its inherent practicality, and of course its title, which I repurpose to give focus to the power and usefulness of this visual archive. Lorde writes that the power of the erotic underlines her "capacity for joy . . . whether it is dancing, building a bookcase, writing a poem, examining an idea."[1] While I happen to share Lorde's joy in building bookcases, writing poems, and examining ideas, in this chapter it is my aim and my joy to put the Ethno-Communications filmography to work, by building useful frameworks for relational analysis in order to open up narrow or fixed canons in both jazz studies and American film history. By "American film history" I am speaking pointedly to the period of the late 1960s and '70s that saw the rise of the "New Hollywood" filmmakers who came to prominence in roughly the same period as the Ethno filmmakers trained, created, and shared their earliest work.

CENTRAL AVE, KOTO STRINGS, AND PEYOTE CHANTS THAT SWING: JAZZ ON FILM *WAY* OUT WEST

To encounter a filmography so dense with jazz scoring, soundtrack, and on-camera performance remains for me one of the more significant aspects of this body of work. If the wider Ethno filmography were a radio, we could turn its dial to well-known artists such as Ella Fitzgerald (Julie Dash's *Illusions*, 1982) and Nina Simone (Dash's *Four Women*, 1975, and Bernard Nicolas's *Daydream Therapy*, 1977) and the inimitable Dinah Washington (Charles Burnett's *Killer of Sheep*, 1977) in one direction. John Coltrane (in Melvonna Ballenger's *Rain*, 1978), Miles Davis (Larry Clark's *Tamu*, 1970), and Herbie Hancock (Elyseo Taylor's *Black Art, Black Artists*, 1971) with a spin in the other direction. We'd actually encounter a range of Miles Davis recordings, from *Sketches of Spain* to *In a Silent Way*, in works by Chicano and Asian American directors José Luis Ruiz (*Cinco Vidas*, 1973, written by Moctesuma Esparza) and Eddie Wong (*Wong Sinsaang*, 1971) as well. And at the far (out) end of the dial, we could hear Archie Shepp (*Daydream Therapy*, Billy Woodberry's *Bless Their Little Hearts*, 1984), Keith Jarrett (with Jim Pepper in Sandra Osawa's *Pepper's Pow Wow*, 1997), The World Saxophone Quartet (in Barbara McCullough's documentary *World Saxophone Quartet*, 1980), and Don Cherry (McCullough's *Water Ritual #1: An Urban Rite of Purification*, 1979, and again in *Pepper's Pow Wow*). Hearing these artists on the soundtrack of these projects is one thing, but this filmography presents us with something even more important, especially as it pertains to West Coast jazz: on-camera performances and interviews with the region's innovators.

Anthony Macías has questioned the tendency of jazz critics to suggest that "other than 1950s white cool jazz, nothing of real importance happened in California," and I have argued elsewhere that popular jazz documentary has gone a long way to fortify this false assumption.[2] Two culprits (there are more) are Bruce Weber's Oscar-nominated documentary *Let's Get Lost* (1988) with its seductive shots of Chet Baker cruising along the Santa Monica coastline, and Ken Burns's ten-episode series for PBS, *Jazz* (2001), in which very little of the nineteen hours of footage went west of Kansas City. Macías suggests a repair strategy of creating a California Composer Laureate position; he nominated Gerald Wilson to be its first recipient, because Wilson's "fusion of African American, Mexican, and other Latin musical traditions links us to the history of our racially rich, ethnically diverse state." Gerald Wilson happens to appear on camera in Zeinabu irene Davis's *Trumpetistically Clora Bryant* (2005) waxing poetic about Central Avenue with his comrade and coeditor of *Central Avenue Sounds*, Ms. Bryant—and, so I would add to Macías's repair strategy that greater attention also be paid to the West Coast titans featured in the music-focused films of the Ethno filmography.[3]

When I began to encounter pianist Eddie Cano, percussionist Munyungo Jackson, kotoist June Kuramoto, and trumpetiste Clora Bryant, not to mention the one and only Horace Tapscott, in the work of the Ethno filmmakers, it occurred to me that all of this extraordinary footage was captured well before 2001, which in theory meant it was available for Burns's "definitive" portrait of the music. Not one frame of it is there. This would come as no surprise to many of the series's critics, including pianist Keith Jarrett, who vehemently railed:

> Now that we've been put through the socioeconomic racial forensics of a jazz-illiterate historian and a self-imposed jazz expert prone to sophomoric generalizations and ultraconservative politically correct (for now) utterances— *can we have some films about jazz by people who actually know and understand the music itself and are willing to deal comprehensively with the last 40 years of this richest of American treasures?*[4]

What Jarrett did not know, nor did I until encountering this archive, is that there were multiple films dealing with great West Coast innovators of the music of the last forty years (and beyond), but not one of them was ever given the platform or publicity budget of a Ken Burns or managed to create the Oscar buzz of a Bruce Weber.

Burns, who is praised for his extensive research and ability to find the rarest archival footage, did not seek this material out, presumably because it did not fit his "official story" of the music. This story was not invented by Burns, but already firmly entrenched by the early 1990s by a handful of white music critics who characterized the tradition as follows:

> After an obligatory nod to African origins and ragtime antecedents, the music is shown to move through a succession of styles and periods, each with a conveniently distinctive label and time period: New Orleans jazz up through the 1920s, swing in the 1930s, bebop in the 1940s, cool jazz and hard bop in the 1950s, free jazz and fusion in the 1960s.[5]

The end. This quote from Scott DeVeaux's critical work on jazz historiography fits Burns's outline to a T, though the series barely touches the 1960s and even then only in the final segment. Amiri Baraka must have revised his classic essay "Jazz and the White Critic" in part to admonish the continuation of the "white critic, black musician apartheid" carried out in the PBS series, beginning with his distress at its name: "The title *Ken Burns Jazz* is disheartening up front. Whether there is an apostrophe or not!" The film spent so much time on the critics, instead of the players, that Baraka found it "maddening, in the extreme, not to hear them speak for themselves!"[6]

Music scholar Sherrie Tucker, admittedly suffering from her own "personal *Jazz* flashbacks" in her field-changing essay "Big Ears: Listening for Gender in Jazz Studies," charges readers to grow "bigger ears" (a call not unlike Toni Cade Bambara's call to "empower our eyes to read the signs"). To have "big ears" in jazz means that one has "the ability to hear and make meaning out of complex music. . . . Big ears are needed to hear dissonances and silences . . . needed to follow nuanced conversations between soloists; between soloists and rhythm sections; between music and other social realms. . . ."[7] In the realm of jazz studies, Tucker advocates for the kind of "ear training" that can enable jazz researchers to better listen for gender, for without this, "jazz studies risks overlooking a category of analysis that closely follows race (and is, in fact, intertwined with it) as the social category most capable of deconstructing this dominant discourse."[8]

Tucker delineates the "predictable riffs" ("great men, sudden style changes, colorful anecdotes about eccentric individuals") and "easy listening histories" that she argues permeate the series in "harmful" ways. She stresses that her critique is not meant as a "beef with Burns":

> I am not simply calling for inclusion of women as musicians into the existing narrative. The narrative itself is shaped by notions of gender and sexuality and race that I find problematic. . . . Burns did not invent these privileged narratives of jazz discourse, nor is he responsible for the longevity of dominant desires that make them marketable to major funding agencies. He is responsible, however, for skillfully fulfilling these desires for familiar representations and stories.[9]

The desire for familiar representations and stories . . . is that what "viewers like us" really wish to see—predictable riffs of jazz musicians as junkies, as tragic geniuses?[10] And what do we make of Wynton Marsalis in episode 1 declaring that jazz "objectifies America," when the series leaves out so many of the Americans (read women, read Asian, Latina/o, American Indian) who play this music? Even the category of genius, with its emphasis on the individual versus the collective, can be problematic and forgetful of the structure of collaboration, call and response, and deep listening that the music requires too; not to mention how "geniuses" in Burns become genius when they can be elevated to the stature of European classical musicians. David Hajdu, Billy Strayhorn's biographer, is particularly dismayed by the series's framing of Ellington:

> Burns's distortion of the way Ellington composed his music is defensive and patronizing. To ignore the collaborative aspect of Ellington's method is to demean the culture he devoted his life to celebrating, and to remake him in the mold of Western classical icons is to propagate their sovereignty. Why do we need to think of Ellington as another Mozart or Stravinsky? He is the first Ellington, and that is quite enough.[11]

This "collaborative aspect" of jazz between musicians and especially between the musicians and the communities of listeners: these relationships are at the center of the music films that come out of the Ethno archive. Social ethicist Peter Paris has written of improvisation as "a moral virtue" that "embraces and enhances the whole and thus serves to promote and preserve the goal of community."[12] For Paris the converse of the virtue of improvisation is "rigidity, fixity, legalism, dogmatism, all of which connote an incapacity for creativity and an insensitivity to the psychic needs of oppressed peoples."[13] Daniel Fischlin, Ajay Heble, and George Lipsitz emphasize the element of listening as one of the core components of musical improvisation and community justice work. Listening to the work of John Coltrane, Sun Ra, or Horace Tapscott, they write, "we are encouraged to hear a compelling and, indeed, an urgent story about the need to learn how to listen, a story about the need, especially in the context of aggrieved populations struggling for access to resources, for rights, and for justice, to cultivate resources for curious, critical, active (and perhaps even radical) listening."[14] In the examples that follow, we experience a number of documentaries in the wider Ethno filmography that move against the fixity of old and rigid "official narratives" of this music, and instead do the work of promoting and preserving community and in the process assist viewers/listeners in growing bigger ears and empowering eyes.

> You know, he's a river . . . endless river of knowledge, flowing through life, giving his charging, rolling waters to the driest parts of brothers' minds.
> Warmack on Poppa Harris in *Passing Through*

> He told me once, "Horace, I'll give you this knowledge if you promise to pass it on." There's so much knowledge that he has and he gave it all to this community.
> Horace Tapscott on Samuel Browne in *Musical Griot*

In 2023, Larry Clark's thesis film *Passing Through* was named to the Library of Congress National Film Board Registry. The film has long been hailed one of the most important and authentic representations of Black jazz musicians in a narrative feature film, inspiring one French critic to describe it as "the only jazz film in the history of cinema."[15] The fictional narrative (in a screenplay coauthored by Ted Lange) follows saxophonist/bandleader Warmack (Nathaniel Taylor), just out of prison and returned to Los Angeles in search of his grandfather and musical guru Poppa Harris (Clarence Muse). The real Los Angeles musician who inspired, provided original music for, and performs in *Passing Through* is also the subject of Barbara McCullough's feature-length documentary *Musical Griot—* Horace Tapscott. And he is *not for sale*.[16] The founder of UGMA/UGMAA (Underground Musicians Association/Union of God's Musicians and Artists Ascension) and PAPA (Pan Afrikan People's Arkestra or "The Ark"), died in 1999, yet I write of him in the present tense here because his presence in the L.A. Rebellion filmography is alive and still singing *Songs of the Unsung*.[17] Haile Gerima's use of Tapscott's musical collaboration with L.A. Black Panther Party member Elaine Brown, *Seize the Time*, in his 1971 Project One film *Hour Glass*, may be the earliest sonic presence of Tapscott's music in the L.A. Rebellion filmography.[18] The Arkestra recorded two projects with Elaine Brown and supported many other Panther endeavors, to the point where one Arkestra member, David Bryant (who is a featured bassist in *Passing Through*) said that they became "like the musical arm" of the Panthers.[19] One could argue that Tapscott and his Arkestra became a musical arm of the L.A. Rebellion filmography as well, as Tapscott moved to composing original music for Larry Clark's *As Above, So Below,* and then the multiple duties of composing and performing in *Passing Through*. Finally, his own life and musical legacy is at the center of McCullough's feature-length documentary.

As the *Musical Griot* title suggests, McCullough structures her film around a West African tradition of the griot/storyteller/holder of history offering oral praise to his community, in this case an extended lecture offered in conjunction with one of Tapscott's early 1990s solo piano concerts. McCullough had been filming Tapscott for two decades by that point, so she is able to move out and back from the lecture to allow us to witness extraordinary footage of outdoor concert happenings with the Pan Afrikan People's Arkestra in Watts, intimate club dates with trio stalwarts Roberto Miranda and Andrew Cyrille in Manhattan, and even a one-on-one rap session between Tapscott and *Flyboy*-era Village Voice critic Greg Tate. Yet, almost like the structure of a ring shout, all of that footage forms a circle around the center soloist, "the lean Griot" Tapscott himself, dressed in a dashing cream-colored tuxedo jacket, sharing the story of his family and his teachers and his Los Angeles. The camera moves and rhythmic

Horace Tapscott from *Horace Tapscott: Musical Griot* (Barbara McCullough, 2017). Photo by Scott Brock, from the collection of Barbara McCullough.

editing of this scene place director McCullough in the role of accompanist for Tapscott's virtuosic solo.

In this solo/story, Tapscott sets the scene of South Los Angeles along Central Avenue in the 1940s and '50s. Tapscott's family, part of the Great Migration west from Houston, Texas, arrived in 1943, and we learn that music was so important to his musician mother that she took her son from Union Station directly to the home of Tapscott's first trombone teacher. He laughs that he didn't even know where he would be living, but he knew who he was going to report to for lessons the next day.[20] We also share in Tapscott's celebration of his most beloved high school teacher, Jefferson High School's bandleader, Mr. Samuel Browne. Under Browne's stellar leadership, the celebrated jazz program at Jefferson, along with its rival band at neighboring Jordan High School, trained generations of some of the most renowned Black and Brown musicians in the city, such as Dexter Gordon, Buddy Colette, Anthony Ortega, and Chico Hamilton. Tapscott lovingly recounts Browne's commitment to intergenerational transmission: "He told me once, 'Horace, *I'll give you this knowledge if you promise to pass it on.*' There's so much knowledge that he has and he gave it all to this community." Haile Gerima's earlier question resonates here too; when preparing the Wilmington 10 project he said he wanted to know "who raised these activists" so that they would not appear as orphans. Barbara McCullough, by pointing her camera at a figure like Samuel Browne, provides a kind of answer to *who raised these improvisers?* When later in the film we hear from Tapscott about the constant harassment and threats he and his musicians faced in the 1960s and '70s, primarily from the LAPD, we understand that Tapscott's Arkestra members formed "bands of healing" fortified by these teachers, elders, and ancestors that made backing down from these threats unthinkable. As longtime Arkestra member and poet Kamau Daáood wrote in his poem "PAPA, the Lean Griot," dedicated to his mentor, "we did what we had to do, with what we had to do it with . . . ."[21] McCullough's documentary, like Daáood's poem, offers testimony and archival evidence of "sources of power within the culture" that can, as Audre Lorde wrote, "provide energy for change."

Like her L.A. Rebellion elders Clark and McCullough, Zeinabu irene Davis's work consistently reflects the importance of teachers and knowledge transmission, and her documentary on Central Avenue's grand dame, trumpetiste, vocalist, composer, and educator Ms. Clora Bryant is no exception.[22] Davis was fortunate enough to collaborate with Bryant on two projects at the same time while she was still in film school—while the feature biographical documentary, *Trumpetistically Clora Bryant* (1989/2005) was in progress, Davis asked Bryant to improvise some original music for her beloved short film *Cycles* (1989).[23] I want to briefly describe the "duet" in *Cycles* between the film's dancing protagonist Rasheeda (Stephanie Ingram) and Bryant's playful (though off-camera) musical riffing, before more substantively addressing *Trumpetistically*.

Cycles is a story about a woman, Rasheeda, waiting for her menstrual cycle to arrive. We watch her carry out her own womanish rituals of preparation, which include doing laundry, making her bed, and meticulously cleaning her bathroom in preparation for a good soak in the tub. Davis uses stop-motion photography to capture Rasheeda's cycles of emotions from desire to restlessness, from yearning to a deep blues, as she considers what it will mean and what she will do if her period does not come. Clora Bryant's trumpet and her Louis-Armstrong-style scatting are there to underscore these blues. Rasheeda contracts and releases her body, squeezing the sponge, scouring her white tiles as Bryant's horn growls, then Bryant performs her own call and response between her vocals and her horn. Rasheeda's body moves like Judith Jameson's in Alvin Ailey's "Cry," though here it is director Zeinabu irene Davis who is masterfully choreographing sound/body/image, with humor and precision—all in preparation for a self-care soak in what is surely the most sparkling bathtub in film history.

The presence of Bryant's trumpet and vocal improvisations in *Cycles* serve as a kind of voice/breath support for Rasheeda's efforts to care for her body and soul. Considering the power of her sound in *Cycles,* especially the trumpet, it is with both awe and bittersweet eyes and ears that we watch Davis's documentary about Bryant's life unfold. Davis takes us on a journey with Bryant from her childhood days in Texas, to becoming a lead trumpet soloist in the 1940s all-female band the *International Sweethearts of Rhythm.* She developed a solo career, was mentored and adored by Dizzy Gillespie, released just one solo album at the height of her career (1957's *Gal with Horn*), and went to the Soviet Union in 1988. Bryant became the first female jazz instrumentalist to tour the USSR and in one of the film's most joyous sequences Davis films her there in her full jazz diplomacy glory, performing at that time with two of her musician sons and with adoring Russian musicians eager to jam with her. It is heartbreaking when Bryant, several years after the trip, has to have quadruple bypass surgery and is told she can't ever play the trumpet again.

The emotional and professional toll of Bryant's health challenge initially devastates the entire family, and director Davis insists that we fully take this in. Davis gives us closeups of Bryant's sons in tears, speaking honestly about how their mother's ability to make a living with her horn made their lives possible. Still, we see the determined Bryant carry on. Her dear friend and teacher, the esteemed folklorist and UCLA theater professor Dr. Beverly Robinson, suggests on camera that "as a replacement" for her ability to play the trumpet, "She's using her memory, her

Screenshot of Zeinabu irene Davis, Clora Bryant, and Dr. Beverly Robinson from *Trumpetistically Clora Bryant* (Zeinabu irene Davis, 2005).

eloquence with words to still blow out some truths!" Davis then films Bryant singing and teaching, devoting her life to coaching women jazz instrumentalists. We see that through writing and lecturing about the history of Central Avenue, Bryant remains committed to keeping Los Angeles at the center and not the periphery of jazz history. That the Ken Burns series makes reference to two women instrumentalists in nineteen hours is not the entire issue. He could and certainly ought to have shown more. What he utterly failed to take on, however, is the level of gender analysis that Davis unpacks with such insight and care for Bryant in *Trumpetistically*.

Just a few miles west of Clora Bryant's Central Avenue, June Kuramoto, one of the cofounders of the jazz fusion group Hiroshima, grew up in the Crenshaw district, studying classical Japanese koto with renowned teacher Kazue Kudo while grooving to doo wop at Dorsey High School.[24] Her daring to improvise on the ancient instrument and blend the Black and Latin musical sounds she and her future bandmates Dan Kuramoto and Johnny Mori were steeped in is a central focus of Duane Kubo's *Cruisin' J-Town* (1975).[25] In *Cruisin'* we see performance footage of the Hiroshima musicians before they even settled on that as the name for their band.

June Kuramoto and Dan Kuramoto. Photo: Mary Uyematsu Kao.

Rehearsals and gigs in Little Tokyo are intercut with deeply moving and intimate interviews with the three young musicians about identity, musical crossings, and community activism. The film concludes with visible as well as audio evidence of these literal crossings by showing a casual conversation between Dan Kuramoto and actor/musician (and future leading man of *Zoot Suit* [dir. Luis Valdez, 1981]) Danny Valdez that segues to a riveting joint performance between Teatro Campesino musicians and Hiroshima in San Juan Bautista.[26]

Kubo aims his camera at June Kuramoto stringing her koto, as she tells us how she got "stuck" with the instrument in junior high when her grandmother died and no one else wanted it. As we watch June tune and set up her koto (pulling strings with gloves that look more like a falconer's than a musician's), we listen to her musical and political journey, from receiving her instrument from her grandmother to the first time she was invited to improvise or "jam":

> I think it's a reflection of my personal search. . . . I've come from a long life of confusion, identity crisis. I didn't know what I really was . . . and then at

the same time the Asian American movement began happening. And I knew that the Japanese music is a large part of me, but yet, it didn't express the true experiences of here. In the beginning it was just . . . I was invited to jam, "Just bring down the koto and let's jam." And I was very uptight because I never improvised before and I was very inhibited. But then once we started working then it just fit in. I guess everyone was kind of excited 'cause it was something different and then it was definitely something Asian.

With the adjustments of her koto complete, just at the moment when she speaks of this musical (and) identity synthesis, she strums a fully in-tune scale. Amiri Baraka's earlier critique of *Jazz* comes to mind here again when we consider how little of that nineteen hours was focused on musicians telling their own stories of musical development rooted in community and movement building. In the case of June and her then-husband Dan Kuramoto, their music and movement building intersected multiple times with the filmmakers of the Ethno program. The Kuramotos scored so many of the early Asian American projects, from *I Told You So* to *Hito Hata,* that like Tapscott and his Arkestra, they virtually became "house musicians" for the early Ethno filmography. The two bands also coheadlined one of the first Watts Towers Jazz Festivals in 1978. The Arkestra and Hiroshima on the same stage?[27] No meaningful jazz west of Kansas City?

Within the Ethno filmography there is more than ample evidence of meaningful jazz innovation all along the West Coast, from J-Town to the Pacific Northwest. While Sandra Osawa showcased a range of Native musicians and music on her 1975 ten-episode series for NBC, in the early 1990s she and her husband Yasu Osawa focused their attention on Oregon-born Kaw/Creek saxophonist Jim Pepper, and made a feature-length documentary called *Pepper's Pow Wow* (1997). Pepper is perhaps most well-known for his rock/jazz inflected "pop" hit "Witchi Tai To." Of the many iterations of the tune, the Osawas begin their film with quick shots of Pepper performing the song in concert with Amina Claudine Myers (of Chicago's legendary AACM). The opening teaser, where Pepper offers the peyote chant taught to him by his grandfather and Myers offers her gospel-inflected harmonies, visually and sonically establishes the meeting of Indigenous and African music traditions at the core of Pepper's improvisation practice. The intergenerational transmission from his grandfather and father echoes McCullough's Tapscott documentary, and Osawa, like McCullough and Kubo, allows us to hear these stories directly from the musicians' mouths. Along with the remarkable array of Pepper's musical collaborators—from the great pianist Mal Waldron (Billie Holiday's last pianist) to the eulogizing love at Pepper's memorial from Don Cherry (who is also in McCullough's doc)—Osawa's film includes critical insights from Native American writers Simon Ortiz and Joy Harjo. Ortiz reflects on all the ways "the American public wants a certain version of Indian. . . . [I]t's not 'Indian' to be a poet, it's not 'Indian' to be a jazz musician."

Osawa herself has said these are the stories she most wants to tell, to create a wider portrait of who Indians are:

> I like to do stories where I feel we are omitted and erased from the picture. That makes me feel that we are more complete. When I tell stories about an American Indian ballerina or an American Indian jazz musician or an American Indian stand-up comedian, I feel like we are doing a fuller portrait of American Indian people than what you would normally see in a more traditional story about our lives. I think this sets me apart because I deliberately seek out stories that are not known or not told or not fully discovered.[28]

This "fuller portrait" of American Indian people in turn contributes to a more expansive understanding of the music known as jazz. In *Pepper's Pow Wow* Harjo speaks on Pepper's fusion of Indigenous music and jazz, arguing, "It's always been my contention that jazz has something to do with Creek people too, that we were there when jazz was invented. . . . [S]o in a way what Jim was doing was a very natural evolution. Especially with jazz, mixing it, say, with stomp dance and tribal music. Because there is a relationship that really no one has talked much about."

Harjo's prompt in Osawa's documentary, "we were there," elicits the best kind of curiosity regarding the history of Native American musics and jazz, and set me off on a search that came full circle back to *Jazz*. Figures like Mildred Bailey and Big Chief Russell Moore emerged in my initial research, and I realized I had in fact seen their images in Burns's *Jazz*.[29] Moore was a Pima trombonist who played with giants of the music like Louis Armstrong and Lionel Hampton; I remembered his face in a photo that is shown in the Burns series. This is an iconic photo of Sidney Bechet, Charlie Parker, Max Roach, and Miles Davis on an airstrip in France in 1949. Standing behind Bechet's right shoulder was his then-trombonist, Big Chief Russell Moore. Moore is never mentioned by name in the series, but an empowered eye can spot him and ask questions about the silence regarding his contributions.[30]

Burns's narration does make space for swing vocalist Mildred Bailey, though he never mentions her Coeur d'Alene ancestry. Music historian Chad Hamill describes the predicament of the erasure of her Indianness: "Mildred Bailey was 'white' because she was cast that way within a jazz narrative that had left no room for Indian jazz musicians."[31] In episode 4, white jazz critic James Maher tells a story about Benny Goodman, whose band was good but not yet distinctive. Maher retells an exchange between Mildred Bailey and Goodman, where Bailey suggests he go up to Harlem and get a better "book," meaning new charts by Black arrangers, in this case Fletcher Henderson. Burns's reliable narrator, Keith David, concludes: "Without Fletcher Henderson, Goodman said, he would have had a pretty good band, but something quite different from what it turned out to be." This significant shift for Goodman's band, the result of the suggestion by a Native American woman, the vocalist and swing icon Mildred Bailey, is noted but not marked for its disruption of the Black/white binary he insists on in his narrative of America's music. The story of this music form is incomplete in this moment and many others like it throughout the series; yet, some of the pieces are there to begin to tell a more perfect story of this music in critical conversation and cooperation with the stories of Jim Pepper, Clora Bryant, June and Dan Kuramoto, and Horace Tapscott so voluptuously offered in the Ethno filmography.

NEW LOS ANGELES FILMMAKING BETWEEN THE FIRES (1965–1992)

The "more perfect" argument I am making throughout this book works nowhere better than in the rethinking of the American New Wave or New Hollywood period of filmmaking in the United States in the 1970s and in newly assessing a number of that period's iconic works in dialogue with a range of fiction and nonfiction works from the Ethno filmography. In Hollywood's Last Golden Age, Jonathan Kirshner periodizes "the seventies film" as roughly a decade that includes the late '60s but excludes the late '70s.[32] Others suggest this rigid periodization is "misleading, as a number of filmmakers with whom the New Wave and New Hollywood are most closely associated would continue to work in the subsequent decades. . . . Robert Altman endured a lengthy spell of marginalization and stasis, before reemerging as a significant creative force with The Player (1992), Short Cuts (1993)."[33] When I teach this period of Hollywood filmmaking and put these directors in conversation with the New Los Angeles filmmakers, I have taken to calling it the period "between the fires," referring to the two rebellions in 1965 and 1992, in part to similarly create a more flexible periodization. In order to zero in on just a few works here, I look most closely at two of the works that Kirshner himself spends a good time on in his Golden Age: Roman Polanski's Chinatown (1974) and Paul Mazursky's Bob & Carol & Ted & Alice (1969). Although I briefly begin this New Hollywood/New Los Angeles call and response in Brooklyn with Hal Ashby's The Landlord (1970), I intentionally focus on "seventies pictures" whose stories are set in Southern California, to invite a new assessment of the wide variety of filmmaking practices taking place in the same metro area in this period. Kirshner writes that the white-male-directed "seventies films" defied traditional industry conventions and "reflected a shift away from the pristine exposition of linear stories with unambiguous moral grounding, and toward self-consciously gritty exploration of complex episodes that challenged the received normative structure of society."[34] The Ethno filmography, made between the fires, challenges the conventions and limitations of the "seventies film" by exposing the lack of complexity many of these films present, particularly in the ways that race, class, and gender play themselves out in the city of Los Angeles.[35]

Hal Ashby and Paul Mazursky each had a string of hits in the seventies, but much of their work is itself on the fringe of the New Hollywood. Some would say this is because they produced comedies, while others cite the very reason I am most interested in their work: they were not afraid to look thoughtfully at issues of race and class. Christopher Sieving says of Ashby's directorial debut (said to be a gift to the Oscar-winning editor from his frequent collaborator Norman Jewison, who produced the film and was originally set to direct it), "*The Landlord* is both a typical and an outstanding 1970 Black-themed Hollywood film." It is typical for presenting what he views as a "stalemate" in terms of race relations between Blacks and whites, yet outstanding because it was "the product of a nearly unprecedented close collaboration between leading film talent of both races," talent pools, he emphasizes, that "rarely commingled."[36]

In the 1970s and 1980s many Black women working in film and television (as directors, writers, or producers) began to source Black women's literature for their film projects, including for example Julie Dash's adaptation of Alice Walker's short story "Diary of an African Nun" while at UCLA. Similarly, Jewison hired Bill Gunn (several years before he was to direct *Ganja and Hess*) to adapt Kristin Hunter's satirical novel. Hunter, who is Black, wrote *The Landlord* in the first-person voice of a white man, Elgar, who purchases an apartment building in a Black neighborhood in Philadelphia. For the film, the location of the tenement building was Park Slope, the pre-gentrified "ghetto" Park Slope of Brooklyn in the late 1960s. The good-looking Elgar Enders (Beau Bridges) is able to charm the rifle toting/ham-hock frying tenant Marge (Pearl Bailey), and he sleeps with his married tenant Fanny (Diana Sands) while her husband Copee (Louis Gossett Jr.) is briefly in jail. Fanny becomes pregnant and tells Elgar she is unwilling to raise their child. She insists that Elgar raise him "white," so that he can be "casual" like his father. No critical race theorist of white privilege could deliver a thesis as damning as Diana Sands's delivery of that word, "casual." The film ends with Elgar driving the newborn baby to the home of his biracial girlfriend Lanie (Marki Bey), after we learn he has given up his role as landlord and transferred ownership of the building to Fanny.

The discovery of the affair with Fanny provokes her husband to attack Elgar, and ultimately Copee is carried off to a mental facility. However, before the revelation of this affair, we actually see Copee convening a meeting with fellow tenants—Fanny, Marge, and Professor DuBoise—in what could be seen as a moment of tenant organizing against the outrageous and self-serving actions of their new landlord. Copee points out that there are poor people out in the street while the wealthy Elgar busies himself improving his own apartment. There are two other humorous yet very short moments that can be read as political critiques of gentrification. In one, we see a Black female real estate agent tour Elgar through one of his new white neighbors' homes. This neighbor, who is remodeling, is thrilled that his new, hideous glass sconces have arrived. He is equally thrilled to meet a fellow white owner and tells Elgar: "This neighborhood is going to be very chic, very chic. Let's hope this influx of the beautiful people is the beginning of an inclination—" and interrupting his thought, a bag of yellow powder is thrown into the front window from the street. It is a surreal moment for the viewer and for Elgar himself, who turns to the real estate agent and asks for an explanation of the powder. She says calmly, "Eviction powder." Elgar, exasperated, demands a better explanation, and she responds, perhaps holding back some delight, "Oh it's nothing, Mr. Enders, just a little voodoo." In another vignette, Marge cooks breakfast for Elgar, and just as he gets comfortable with what seems like an act of generosity and welcome on Marge's part, she hints about the possibility of a rent strike. The two moments are played for humor, and this is a comedy with a "happy" ending, as the naïve and reckless white landlord, transformed by the kindness and humanity of his eccentric Black tenants, returns their kindness by transferring ownership of the building to them.

I love a happy ending. However, in the same period I rediscovered this film and started to include it and other works by Ashby in my course syllabi, I was discovering more and more of the UCLA filmmakers' documentaries addressing gentrification head on, beginning with L.A. Rebellion member Shirikiana Aina's *Brick by Brick*, about gentrification in Washington, DC, in the 1970s. Watching this film, we are immediately confronted with neighborhood blocks that are visually comparable to, though even more run down than, the Brooklyn "slums" of *Landlord*. Further we are confronted with real stakes for poor Black mothers who have been repeatedly displaced by greedy landlords. We hear Black tenants' rights activists tell stories of senior citizens living on $300 a month, who then suffer arbitrary $68 rent increases, meaning that they will have to decide whether to eat or pay their rent. Or, as one activist describes, these same residents will soon have to hop on the "chicken bone" express back to North Carolina or Texas or wherever they might have family that can house them. Confronted with these realities of women who could just as easily be Fanny or Marge from Ashby's film, the good humor and happy ending become much more difficult to casually enjoy.

Back in Los Angeles in the mid-1970s, Duane Kubo and Eddie Wong began to film community protests against the corporate redevelopment agencies trying to force low-income residents and Japanese American community organizations out of Little Tokyo. This footage became a documentary short, *Something's Rotten in Little Tokyo* (1977). The elderly Japanese bachelors in the film had found refuge in the now dilapidated SROs after having been forcibly removed to concentration camps during World War II. In 1980, codirector Kubo, now partnering with Robert Nakamura, retold aspects of this story of intergenerational displacement in *Hito Hata: Raise the Banner*. In the final scene of that film the banners the Issei men and their families raise declare: "Stop the Evictions," "Stop the Destruction," "Little Tokyo is our Home!" while Hiroshima's triumphant score supports the grassroots protest. As the credits scroll on *Hito Hata*, which is the first feature-length narrative film written, directed and produced by Asian Americans, one can see that this historic venture was supported and indeed crewed by a number of L.A. Rebellion filmmakers, including John Rier, Bernard Nicolas, Carroll Parrott Blue, and Orin Mitchell, which is yet another example of the cross-racial/crosstown solidarity among the wider group of Ethno filmmakers working on similar concerns.

As I mention in chapter 3 with my discussion of Betty Chen's cross-racial collaborations with Judith Dancoff, Yolande du Luart, and Nancy Dowd, collaborations with white women directors from UCLA in the 1970s present additional examples of solidarity over shared concerns. Francisco Martinez, one of the original Mother Muccers, worked with director Marsha Goodman as an associate producer and cameraperson on her MFA thesis project *Not Gone, Not Forgotten*.[37] This insurgent documentary, which aired on KCET in 1982 and was produced in association with UCLA's Chicano Studies Department with a grant from the Institute for American Cultures, follows two generations of housing precarity in historic Mexican American communities in Los Angeles. Goodman carefully traces the line of activism in 1979—when residents of Pico-Union who were served eviction notices by the Community Redevelopment Agency (the same agency serving eviction notices in Little Tokyo) in order to expand a Pep Boys facility fought to protect their communities—directly back to the heartbreaking testimonies of the families who were displaced in 1949 from their Chavez Ravine community. At a reunion of the Chavez Ravine families filmed here, one woman bitterly reports that her family's house was located between first and second base at Dodger Stadium, and she won't ever attend a game in that ballpark. A multiracial grassroots organization, Coalition for Economic Survival—whose African American director, Midge Purcell, is featured throughout the documentary—strategizes to stop the bulldozers from repeating history. We hear again testimonies from Chicana mothers that echo precisely the women in *Brick by Brick*, stating that eviction would mean that they'd have to leave the area because there were no affordable housing alternatives. *Brick by Brick, Something's Rotten in Little Tokyo, Hito Hata*, and *Not Gone, Not Forgotten*, when considered alongside Ashby's feature, remind us that urban poor communities of color did not sit idly by hoping for the arrival of Beau Bridges.[38] We see here what it means for the subaltern to get ahold of cameras to begin to prioritize the tenants' stories instead of the landlord's. Thinking about the way that race and class and especially the history of Los Angeles are treated in the Ethno filmography, as opposed to the Hollywood New Wave, attunes our eyes in new ways to many of the iconic films from that wave, perhaps none more obvious than Polanski's *Chinatown* (1974).

The star, the heart and soul of Robert Nakamura and Duane Kubo's feature *Hito Hata*, is the lead actor, Mako. Having worked in Hollywood since the late 1950s, he received an Oscar nomination for Best Supporting Actor for his role in *The Sand Pebbles* (a film that also earned Steve McQueen his one and only Oscar nod for Best Actor) in 1966. The previous year, 1965, out of frustration for the limited and stereotypical roles he and other talented Asian American actors perpetually received, if they received work at all, he cofounded the nation's first professional Asian American theater company, The East West Players. Two of the theater's cofounders, Chinese American actors James Hong and Beulah Quo, would nine years later play "Evelyn's Butler" and "Maid" in Roman Polanski's *Chinatown*. Hong's character does at least have a name within the diegesis of the film: Khan. Jerry Fujikawa, the California-born Japanese American actor, plays the unnamed gardener with a heavy accent, so heavy his mispronunciation of "glass" and "grass" provides a major clue for protagonist/detective, Jake Gittes, played by Jack Nicholson, whom Fujikawa had recently appeared with in Bob Rafelson's *The King of Marvin Gardens* (1972).[39]

It would be easy to dismiss these characters and their small, stereotypical roles, especially if a viewer is consumed in the plot or spellbound by the hypnotic trumpet of the iconic theme song, but when I look at the miles of grass surrounding the compound that we see the first time Gittes visits Evelyn Mulwray at her home unannounced, I can't help but think about the labor of the unnamed gardener to keep it so shimmering. A year or two before the production of Polanski's retro noir, Jeff Furumura had filmed an intimate snapshot of the life of Elmer Uchida, who worked at Brentwood homes very similar to the Mulwrays' (see chapter 3). In fact, shots of the Rolls Royce in Furumura's film resemble the luxury vehicle being waxed by another unnamed and uncredited servant in *Chinatown*. From the light, sweat, iced tea, and banter between Gittes and Escobar about summer colds, we know this is the hottest time of the year for yard workers, so again the visual magnificence of a lawn like the Mulwrays' must make us consider Mr. Uchida, now that we know more of the stories of men like him from the Ethno filmography. Robert Nakamura's UCLA thesis film *Wataridori: Birds of Passage* (1976) also captures the director's own father at work as a gardener, and we hear a tale about when he first came to Los Angeles and started working, he didn't have a car, so he used to bicycle to his workplace, balancing a lawnmower tied to the back. These humanizing scenarios are unforgettable and arouse a world of wonder when we compare them to the shallow formation of a character like Fujikawa's in *Chinatown*.

Not long after Polanski's film was released, Lilian Wu completed her UCLA thesis documentary *In Transit: The Chinese in California* (1977), featuring camera work by three Asian American women, classmates Geraldine Kudaka, Marie Kodani and Wu herself.[40] She weaves together animation, live-action footage, and poetic monologues covering over one hundred years of Chinese American history, dramatically narrated to us by none other than James Hong and Beulah Quo.[41] Given that history and also short personal narratives such as Eddie Wong's 1971 film *Wong Sinsaang*, about his father who worked as a laundryman by day and calligrapher/martial artist by night, it becomes unsettling to confront the limited portrayals of artist/community activists Hong and Quo as "Khan" and "Maid." The Asian American Ethno filmmakers repeatedly give praise to the actors from The East West Players, who like the Black actors from PASLA consistently appeared in and otherwise supported their work.[42]

Several final points about *Chinatown* are relevant here. As limited as the characterizations of the Asian characters are, and as racist as the humor and the persistent Chinatown-equals-evil metaphor is, there is a backhanded way in which the film does at least remember that Los Angeles is not a white-only city. The power struggle over water will also impact poor white farmers and—as we are apt to consider when we see the lone Mexican boy on horseback traipsing through the dried-up riverbank—Mexican farmers too. Thom Andersen's *Los Angeles Plays Itself* narration goes as far as asking: "Isn't the notion of Chinatown as the forsaken hellhole of civic negligence a displaced vision of Watts?" I don't go that far, but there's something about the figure of Jake Gittes learning to speak a few words of Spanish here, a few Chinese phrases there, that suggests the necessity for even a white, Italian-suit-wearing private eye to understand the multiracial nature of his city.

And what about the figure of Escobar? Though performed by Puerto Rican actor Perry Lopez, in the context of 1930s Los Angeles he certainly presents as Mexican American. With his promotion to Lieutenant, he has raised himself out of the muck of the Chinatown post, by his own boot-straps, the film seems to say, further spotlighting the racial hierarchy of the city in the late 1930s, where a Latino male could reach a position of power (power over) that the perpetually foreign Asian residents of the city would not achieve for some time. Finally, while pages and pages of film history and criticism on *Chinatown* spill their ink on the fab four of Polanski, Nicholson, screenwriter Robert Towne, and producer Robert Evans, less frequently do those pages highlight that the spectacular period look of the film was guided by one of the first Mexican American cinema-tographers to join the American Society of Cinematographers (ASC), John A. Alonzo, who happened at one time to be mentored by James Wong Howe (the first person of color in the ASC). This is Hollywood too; Hollywood and Los Angeles come together more often than we think. Alonzo, who shot Hal Ashby's second feature *Harold and Maude* (1971), then *Sounder* (Martin Ritt, 1972), then *Lady Sings the Blues* (Sidney Furie, 1972), would also work as the director of photography for the live concert footage of *Wattstax* (1973), the documentary commemorating seven years since the Watts uprising of 1965, whose crew included Ethno filmmakers Richard Wells (sound) and Larry Clark (camera) as well as Clark's collaborators Ted Lange (cowriter on *Passing Through,* appears as himself in *Wattstax*) and Roderick Young (camera on *Wattstax, Passing Through, As Above So Below,* and *Bush Mama*).

It is well documented in studies of the L.A. Rebellion filmmakers that their filmmaking aesthetics were heavily influenced by the cinemas of Latin America and Africa they were exposed to in Elyseo Taylor's courses. Documentary filmmaking informed the approach to narrative filmmaking as well, especially for Burnett who consistently mentions the impact of Basil Wright, who also taught at UCLA in the late 1960s. Less is discussed about the aesthetics of a film like Julie Dash's *Illusions,* whose faithful adherence to classic Hollywood noir mise-en-scène is in sharp contrast to the film's searing indictment of the period's exclusion of Black women in front of and especially behind the camera. To briefly review, the short narrative follows a Black woman, Mignon Dupree (Lonette McKee), who passes as white in order to rise in the ranks of the Hollywood studio executive hierarchy. The black-and-white film, shot on reversal stock,[43] contributes to the classic noir look as well as the thematic layers of racial passing: there is both the character Mignon, passing for white, as well as her effort to solve a sync-sound failure by hiring a Black singer, Ester Jeeter (Rosanne Katon), to dub a white musical theater performer's voice. While *Illusions* has no hardboiled detective, it shares with *Chinatown* a narrative critique of economic power structures in Los Angeles (Water and Power in the 1930s, Hollywood in the 1940s), and it shares the figure of a mysterious woman who must maintain her secrets in order to combat the corrupt systems that would keep her powerless.[44] If one studies closely the period costuming of the two women, it looks as if the actresses may have also shared the same veil.[45] Yet, Dash insists her choice to costume Mignon in a veil is deeply rooted in African American thought; she is "the veiled women of an African past. A visual metaphor of our Duboisian Double-Consciousness."[46]

The overwhelming difference between Evelyn and Mignon is of course that Dash has given Mignon ambition *and* a career to go with it. Her goals for changing the system are worth the gamble of passing. And her goals are

Lonette McKee as Mignon Dupree in *Illusions* (Julie Dash). From the collection of Julie Dash.

not just for her own career, her own family, or her own race. Mignon repeatedly pitches that her studio should produce a major motion picture about Navajo code talkers. The revelation of Mignon's identity threatens her job security near the end of the film; yet the character's closing internal monologue demonstrates her determination to carry on, "to take action without fearing. Yes, I wanted to use the power of the motion picture, for there are many stories to be told and many battles to begin." Her veiled counterpart in Polanski's picture ends up dead, with the one family member she hoped to protect now more vulnerable than ever. "Did the New Hollywood Hate Women?" asks Kirshner in his chapter named after a key feminist slogan, "The Personal is Political." The next and final section of this chapter will grapple with that question and close with a comparative and intersectional look at gender, class, race, and marriage in the narrative features *Bob & Carol & Ted & Alice* (Mazursky), *Woman Under the Influence* (Cassavetes), and *Bless Their Little Hearts* (Woodberry), with important nods to two additional Ethno works, *Cinco Vidas* (a documentary directed by José Luis Ruiz, written by Moctesuma Esparza, 1973) and *A Different Image* (a longer, scripted short by Alile Sharon Larkin, 1982).

Two decades into the twenty-first century, the iconic production still of *Bob & Carol & Ted & Alice (BCTA)*—featuring both couples, Bob (Robert Culp) and Carol (Natalie Wood), Ted (Elliot Gould) and Alice (Dyan Cannon), naked and not in that order, between the sheets in one very wide hotel bed—looks about as far as possible from the hard-hitting political critique or shocking aesthetic disruption the films of the new Hollywood were said to be delivering one after the next. The Production Code waned in 1966, the shocking violence of *Bonnie and Clyde* struck in 1967, and, as Stephen Farber writes in his sardonic review of *BCTA,* the social problem films of 1969 (*Midnight Cowboy, Easy Rider, Medium Cool*) "tell the young, liberal, intelligent audience *what it already knows*—the contemporary city is squalid and inhuman, Southerners are bigoted and hostile to free-living hippies, the Chicago police are fascist pigs." Farber found *BCTA* "genuinely contemporary and deeply disturbing," because it asks its adult characters, and audience members, to "expose themselves by searching into social changes that no one fully understands yet."[47] In "The Personal is Political," Kirshner also emphasizes that the lead characters confronting the new rules of the sexual revolution in the film are "not kids," but rather four adults who "came of age under the old rules but were still young enough to wonder if they were missing out on something special."[48] Bob and Carol attend a new-age utopian retreat center in California modeled on Esalen. They experience an overnight "encounter session" where they are encouraged to dig into their authentic selves and stop "copping out" by conforming to old gender roles and sexual inhibitions. When they return to their luxurious Beverly Hills or Brentwood community, they try to convert or at least "awaken" their best friends, Ted and Alice, "the squares who seem to have slept through the sixties" quips Farber. The two couples spend the rest of the film sorting out whether or not the "real world"[49] can handle the urgency, ecstasy, and freedoms introduced at the Esalen escape. Ah . . . whose real world?

Even before Bob and Carol arrive at the retreat center, their drive takes place along rolling hills with the sunshine dancing on their faces and expensive protective eyewear, as their convertible mint-green Jaguar hugs each curve in time to Quincy Jones's funky remixed orchestration of Handel's "Messiah." The Jones choir repeats "hallelujah," as I repeat, whose real world? And in order to contrast this world with a different one, I pause here briefly to consider and compare the opening sequence of Alile Sharon Larkin's *A Different Image,* her 1982 thesis film which also centers a free-thinking woman whose journey includes issues of sexual liberation from "old ways." Larkin's Los Angeles story begins on a winding urban street in West Los Angeles, with a Black woman walking. The music, provided by percussionist Munyungo Jackson, is funkier than the Jones piece, and the sun is shining, though the color is muted by the smog and city bus exhaust. Instead of heading to a hilltop retreat, this woman looks to be walking to work—some people walk in L.A.[50] Her bliss is only mildly interrupted as she notices a young Black man staring at a massive billboard of a white woman with long red hair wearing a tiny green bikini, who then turns his head to gaze at her. She keeps walking, now reading her folded newspaper, but once she has passed him and passed the sound of a car honking (at her? we're not sure) she smiles slightly. Has her perfect short Afro, form-hugging leotard top and flowing, floral skirt been appreciated and elicited a flirty smile from the young man or a discomforting, predatory gaze? The Hollywood and the Los Angeles openings of *BCTA* and *A Different Image* both feature bright sunshine, percussive soundtrack, and characters in motion, but the stakes for the solo woman in Larkin's opening include the possibility that the "everyday" walk to work comes with the potential threat of violation (which introduces a theme that will become central to the film), whereas Natalie Wood's Carol is driven, protected by headscarf, sunglasses, and husband, on her way to the hilltop getaway.

Carol does not work outside of the home, and inside her home she has a maid, a Latina maid who does have a name, Maria, and with whom she does speak a few words of Spanish. Carol leaves the house for tennis lessons during the daytime and dinners and dancing with her husband at night, when they are not on vacation. This is Carol's real world. It's not the real world of any of the women of color in the Ethno filmography, whether in fiction or nonfiction works. There are many domestic workers in the Ethno filmography, but unlike Maria in *BCTA,* or Beulah Quo's character in *Chinatown,* these workers have three-dimensional stories (Andais *in*

Bless Their Little Hearts), they have dreams (a hotel maid fantasizes about both killing her predator white boss AND becoming a revolutionary film-maker in Bernard Nicolas's *Daydream Therapy,* 1977), and they face nightmares (a young mother/domestic worker is carried away in a straightjacket after burning her child's head trying to straighten her hair, an act that takes place after we watch this woman obsess over her white employer's straight hair in Larkin's *The Kitchen,* 1975). The Maria character in *BCTA* must have a story, but Mazursky opts not to tell it here.

Maria appears only twice in *BCTA*. Both times, Mazursky frames her as far away from the camera as he can. The first time we see her at the end of a long hallway behind the main action of the two couples lounging around Bob and Carol's living room after a dinner party they've hosted, relaxing with marijuana, a dried fruit plate, and swinging diegetic music that both Carol and Ted dance to. This is the first time in the film a potential "spouse swap" is hinted at, because Bob has collapsed on the couch next to Alice, his head in her lap, and Ted and Carol are admiring each other's dance moves. The maid—who we assume is Maria, although we have no way of knowing because Mazursky does not show us her face nor do we hear her voice until her second scene—is walking across a rear corridor; her body pauses and squares itself full frontal to the scene before her. The headless help must assess, given the pot smoking and couple swap, whether or not she should enter the room to clear the drinks and dried fruit; she decides against it. The second time we see Maria, she does speak; she responds to a request from Carol, in Spanish, to bring out the ice cream for her guests (gathered in their backyard/pool area for their son's birthday party). Carol and Maria speak through the guests, and a couple who has been bickering frame Maria on either side. She is in the literal and metaphoric deep space between them, standing back from them, but she is in focus and the couple is blurred. Maria smiles as she speaks, patient with Carol's strained Spanish. And all at once Maria exits to retrieve the *helados.*

I take time with these interactions because I am attuned in general to how the "help" of color appear and function in the New Hollywood pictures, and specifically because there are multiple and fascinating portraits of Chicana women in the Ethno filmography from this same period, in this same city, that arouse in me a curiosity to know more about Maria, especially the contrast between her life as a woman differently classed and raced from either Carol or Alice. As discussed earlier in this book, Sylvia Morales's short documentary *Chicana* (1979) gives a historic record of five hundred years of cultural and political contributions of Mexican and Mexican American women right up to the 1960s Chicana union organizer Dolores Huerta and welfare rights organizer Alicia Escalante. *Requiem 29* (1970) features young Chicana activists protesting the Vietnam War and in one case being clubbed by police for doing so. We can wonder if a figure like *BCTA*'s Maria marched along with any of these women, or if she lost family members in Vietnam; we can wonder what the effort to smile and cheerfully serve the affluent across town may actually involve. A documentary that is ripe for conversation with *BCTA* is *Cinco Vidas*, a public-affairs-style portrait of five East Los Angeles lives expressing "what is natural, good, and beautiful in the Barrio."[51]

One of the five lives featured is a mother and community activist, Delia Cardenas, whose anger about injustice has sent her both to become a local leader in community issues and to psychological counseling. We are briefly brought inside one of her sessions with her Chicano male therapist. What sent Delia to therapy may be different than what sends Dyan Cannon's fictional Alice to therapy, but these (along with Fonda in *Klute*) are both early scenes of women in therapy where it is not stigmatized or problematized. In fact, in both *BCTA* and *Cinco Vidas*, we hear Delia and Alice testify to how helpful therapy has been. In both projects, these women say repeatedly how much hostility they feel. For Alice it is at least initially prompted by learning that Bob has "cheated" on her best friend Carol. Delia is angry about the racism in the culture that has caused her to feel ashamed of "my family, music, culture." She laments how hard her mother and mother-in-law worked in laundries and sweatshops, but she says her activism with the schools is informed by her determination that "this is not going to happen to my daughters. Their future will be one of college or whatever they want to do in life. . . . Things are changing." To consider these intertextual echoes of one white and one Chicana mother from very different backgrounds asserting their right to be angry and seeking insight about their lives with a mental health worker does indeed signal that things were changing in the culture for women, even across class differences, and that male media makers in Hollywood and in Los Angeles were starting to take note.

The "orgy," or almost "orgy," scene in the Vegas hotel bedroom in *Bob &*
Carol & Ted & Alice is the most anticipated scene of the film; yet one of
the scenes that is most discussed in writing on Mazursky is an earlier
twelve-minute bedroom fight between Alice and Ted, after the dinner
party when they find out Bob has had an extramarital affair that post-
Esalen Carol bafflingly describes as "beautiful." Farber refers to it as "the
painfully long bedroom scene" that "caustically accentuates the sexual
anxiety that is one of the 'normal' problems of long-term marriage, in
order to make us sympathetic to Bob and Carol's frantic search for kicks
outside of marriage."[52] Kirshner calls it the "torturous bedroom scene"
whose unsettling lack of resolve still manages to reveal "deeper truths."[53]
Sam Wasson highlights the Alice and Ted fight as an example of Mazursky's
impulse to write long scenes that are "wholly disproportionate to the
amount of exposition they exposit," yet that "create arenas for different,
often conflicting emotional states to coexist. What results is a depth of
feeling as comprehensive as it is complex . . . an emotional patina that
belongs to all of us in life, but in Hollywood, to Mazursky's films alone."[54]
Outside of Hollywood, if one understands a filmmaker like John Cassavetes
to be working outside of the studio system, surely the even longer fight
scene between Mabel (Gena Rowlands) and Nick (Peter Falk) in *Woman
Under the Influence* (1974), which ends with Mabel being committed to a
psychiatric hospital, demonstrates a "depth of feeling" as complex as
Mazursky achieved. Rowlands's devastatingly vulnerable performance as
Mabel earned her the first of her two Academy Award nominations for
Best Actress.

The two directors, also actors and writers, have a storied connection,
from Cassavetes's reportedly nudging Mazursky to the audition that
landed the latter his first film role in *Blackboard Jungle* (1955), to
Cassavetes and Rowlands starring in Mazursky's *Tempest* (1982).
However, it is the shift in the class status of Nick and Mabel (blue-collar
vs. Beverly Hills) that heightens the stakes of terror and vulnerability of
their extended marriage battle royale. James Monaco has said that

> if Cassavetes is the American Bergman . . . then Mazursky is our Fellini. I've
> often thought, only half-jokingly, that the main problem with Bergman's
> characters was their environment—if only they'd take a vacation, go visit

Fellini's people. Likewise, there are very few characters of American films of the seventies, from Travis Bickle (*Taxi Driver*) to Nick and Mabel Longhetti (*A Woman Under the Influence*), who wouldn't benefit greatly from a visit to a Mazursky movie.[55]

And sure enough the final scene of *Bob & Carol & Ted & Alice* is a fanciful Fellini homage in a Vegas hotel parking lot; yet, this is precisely the kind of luxurious vacation Cassavetes's Nick and Mabel could never afford. Mazursky's zany finale seems to suggest there is no screaming match nor infidelity between either of the *BCTA* couples that a well-dressed parade to a Tony Bennett concert won't cure. Burt Bacharach's "What the World Needs Now is Love" swells as the credits roll, and all is well. Cassavetes's couple will not get off as "casually" as Bob and Carol or Ted and Alice, and neither will the leads in *Bless Their Little Hearts* (dir. Billy Woodberry, written and shot by Charles Burnett, 1983).

In the pantheon of marriage fight scenes, the nine-minute-long single take of Andais (Kaycee Moore) and Charlie Banks (Nate Hardman) in *Bless Their Little Hearts* could and does go as many rounds as any Mazursky or Cassavetes row; both the scenes mentioned above are longer, but include multiple cuts.[56] The three couples tell us a great deal about narrative feature filmmaking in Hollywood and Los Angeles in this period. The Mazursky and Cassavetes couples are both white, and in both cases the family is supported by the husband's full-time job. Ted is a lawyer, while Nick fixes broken water mains in the middle of the night and does other dangerous jobs. In *Bless Their Little Hearts,* Andais is a domestic who takes long bus rides to her job, while her husband Charlie has been mostly unemployed for the past decade. She is as physically exhausted as Cassavetes's Nick, but she is also responsible for cooking, grocery shopping, cleaning—though she has trained her three very young children to help with these tasks. Her biggest job may be bolstering her frustrated and depleted husband. When Charlie steps out on Andais, reconnecting with an old lover, there is nothing "beautiful" about it; it is emotionally humiliating and financially threatening. As hard and dangerous as Nick's job is, Charlie would kill for it.

Cassavetes is demographically sensitive in his casting of Nick's coworkers in the film; a good number of them are in fact Black, and playing

Kaycee Moore and Nate Hardman in *Bless Their Little Hearts* (Billy Woodberry, 1984). Courtesy of Billy Woodberry and Milestone Films.

against race and class stereotypes, Cassavetes has one of Nick's Black co-workers sing Italian opera, much to Mabel's delight. Mabel is exhausted in her own right. Her labor is different than Nick's or Andais's—the exhaustion of waiting for Nick to come home and comfort her nerves or pacing in anticipation of her children's school bus—yet it is ever so subtly also marked by her color, class, gender. Mabel, unsure if she has the right time for her children's school bus, asks two other white, blond women, both well-dressed (they could have walked out of Carol and Alice's world) what time it is, and they literally will not give her the time of day. This "eccentric," maybe homeless or mentally ill woman, the other women's body language seems to say, is one to be avoided. Her whiteness and blond hair do not read as privilege alongside these other white Angelenos. These three couples, especially these three women—Alice who is always a passenger in her husband's convertible Cadillac, Mabel who paces, unkempt, Andais who must take long rides on public transportation—perfectly illustrate the benefit of comparative and intersectional analysis. Woodberry and Burnett belong in conversation with Mazursky and Cassavetes, and certainly Kaycee Moore's performance here belongs in the company of any of Rowlands's great roles. Samantha Sheppard's writing on Moore insists that we read her as a "cocreator" of the project, alongside Woodberry who, Sheppard writes, "develops . . . a protofeminist, anti-auteurist method with Moore's performance acting as an anchor and motor of the film."[57]

I began this book with the notion of crosscutting, a film term, and here have performed more of a musical call and response. A call and response between New Hollywood and New Los Angeles; a call and response between a narrow paradigm of jazz (or *Jazz*) itself and the expansive possibilities of all that improvisation can contain in the portraits of the music on the New Los Angeles side. I return now to Peter Paris's idea of improvisation as a moral virtue, to get at my final thoughts about these comparative readings. The longer Paris passage reads:

> [Improvisation] brings novelty to bear on the familiar, not for the sake of destroying the latter but for the purpose of heightening the individuality and uniqueness of the agent and his or her creative ability. Improvisation expresses not only the agent's creativity and spontaneity but also his or her spirit of perceptive wholeness. By keeping the old and new close at hand, the virtue of improvisation embraces and enhances the whole and thus serves to promote and preserve the goal of community.[58]

This reading is more generous (Paris is calling it a virtue, after all) than I can bear most days in the face of erasure, or in Audre Lorde's language, in the face of the oppressor's acts of corruption and distortion of the histories and creative offerings of communities of color, whether audio or visual or both. On good days, this passage does guide my thinking as a practical strategy for how to move forward as an educator. To refrain from trashing all ten episodes of Burns's *Jazz* may have merit ("not for the sake of destroying the latter"); yet that does not preclude viewers like us from engaging our empowered eyes and bigger ears to hold the series accountable for what it insufficiently frames, obscures, or silences. And this Ethno filmography provides counternarratives that swing so hard, that swing so inclusively. Little by little, for more and more people interested in this music and the place of this music on film, the jazz narratives on the Ethno side will become irresistible, to borrow again from Toni Cade Bambara, who famously said that her job as a culture worker was to make revolution irresistible. Clora Bryant, June Kuramoto, Jim Pepper, and Horace Tapscott? These films and these musicians make that work so much easier . . . if they are seen. And imagine if the hundreds of courses that center "New Hollywood" films across the country (and the world) would begin to tease in more and more of the work of their less-well-funded county cousins on the New Los Angeles side. And, so, I improvise on the Peter Paris line above with this twist: by keeping the *New Hollywood* and the *New Los Angeles* close at hand, the virtue of improvisation embraces and enhances the whole and thus serves to promote and preserve the goal of a *more perfect* cinematic rebellion.

Conclusion

Lights, camera . . . affirmative action . . . is no more.

The excitement captured in Renee Tajima's 1984 essay about the Ethno-Communications Program, "Lights, Camera . . . Affirmative Action," may have been the key that unlocked my desire to take on this research. Though published nearly fifteen years before Peter Biskind's *Easy Riders, Raging Bulls: How the Sex-Drugs-and-Rock 'n Roll Generation Saved Hollywood* (1998), I experienced the essay as a corrective by a woman of color feminist re-writing my favorite era of cinema and finally centering the filmmakers I wanted to hear about. Certainly, I knew that Tajima, now Tajima-Peña, had also codirected the landmark documentary *Who Killed Vincent Chin* (1987), which I'd seen in Loni Ding's class as an undergrad at Berkeley; yet when I first sat down with her in 2016, I had to hold back from saying, "You had me at Lights, Camera, *Affirmative* Action!" It was a busy day for her as her latest documentary, about the forced sterilization of Mexican American women in Los Angeles in the 1970s, *No Más Bebés*, was premiering on PBS that very night. That she took the time to meet with me gave me the idea that she had something serious to say, and she did. She wanted to let me know just how critical the archival footage that the Ethno-Communications filmmakers shot in the 1970s was for *No Más Bebés*.

> Just daily life in Boyle Heights, in East L.A.? That community was not pictured ... but all this footage by people like ... Sylvia (Morales) and Moctesuma Esparza and David Garcia, they were actually filming people. They were filming the community. They were filming beautiful stuff, the streets, people at home, a wedding. I saw that footage and ... the only way I was able to picture the community in the 1970s was through these young independent filmmakers who came out of Ethno-Communications. So, without that archive, it's one thing to talk about the filmmakers who began their careers and who mentored others, but just the actual images are ... if they weren't around? Oh my god, there wouldn't be shit.[1]

With that mic drop, she was out and off to her premiere.

An affirmative action program did that. But now affirmative action, like Joe Turner, come and gone.

Later in 2016, I happened to catch a screening of Damani Baker's *The House on Coco Road* at the L.A. Film Festival, and I heard a story about his filmmaking process that reminded me of Tajima-Peña's. The documentary is about Baker's family, especially his mother, Fannie, who packed up her two children in Oakland, California in the early 1980s and moved them to Grenada to be a part of the island's New Jewel Movement. There is remarkable footage in the film of Prime Minister Maurice Bishop on a speaking tour in the United States, footage that shows a leader so clear, so firm in his commitment to loving justice and moving his people "forward ever, backward never"—come to find out this footage was shot by Haile Gerima. Baker relayed the story in the post-screening Q&A. He told he us had visited Gerima at Sankofa Books in DC and told him about the project; Gerima directed him to a storage room, opened a big case with cans of film, and according to Baker, Gerima said: "Have at it!"[2]

It seemed I was seeing footage I recognized from the Ethno filmography everywhere, including Peter Bratt's documentary on Dolores Huerta, *Dolores* (2017), Tadashi Nakamura's (Robert Nakamura's son) portrait of Chris Iijima *A Song for Ourselves* (2009), Phillip Rodriguez's *Ruben Salazar: Man in the Middle* (2014), and Kate Trumbull-LaValle and Johanna Sokolowski's *Ovarian Psycos* (2016) about a women of color antiviolence bicycle brigade in East Los Angeles, and of course in Zeinabu irene Davis's reverent gathering of the Black insurgents' archive, *Spirits of Rebellion: Black Independent Cinema from Los Angeles* (2016). Each one of the films is about activists of color, powered not only by the archival footage assembled but by an activist filmmaking ethos carried over from the Ethno-Communications days.

Like the gifts of archival footage from which these twenty-first century filmmakers benefited, my research benefited from a fascinating moment in Southern California arts curation in 2011, when it seemed that all of Los Angeles was looking back at the Ethno days because of *Pacific Standard Time: Art in L.A. 1945–1980*, a collaboration of over sixty cultural institutions that ran for six months beginning in the fall of 2011. As part of Pacific Standard Time, art historian Kellie Jones curated the groundbreaking exhibition *Now Dig This!: Art and Black Los Angeles 1960–1980*, at the same time that Allyson Nadia Field, Jacqueline Stewart, and company at the UCLA Film and Television Archive launched their groundbreaking symposium and screening series *L.A. Rebellion: Creating a New Black Cinema*. The projects were interconnected in a number of ways beyond their Pacific Standard Time umbrella and Hammer Museum address (making Wilshire and Westwood the hippest corner in the city that fall). Stewart's essay "Defending Black Imagination" appears in the *Now Dig This!* catalogue edited by Jones, and does the bridge work of linking the creative practices and industrial challenges of the L.A. Rebellion filmmakers with those of their visual artist comrades across the city.[3] Stewart shines an especially important light on Barbara McCullough's connections/crossings with featured Dig artists Betye Saar, David Hammons, and Senga Nengudi, all of whom appeared in McCullough's 1981 documentary *Shopping Bag Spirits and Freeway Fetishes: Reflections on Ritual Space* speaking about their creative practice.

One of the most striking and inspiring aspects of Jones's strategy for the *Now Dig This!* exhibit (and catalogue) was her insistence on acknowledging the multiracial constellation of artists who in some cases worked together with the African American artists featured in the show. In her remarks for the catalogue, Jones writes of the permeability and reach of Black visual artist communities in the city: "Even as African Americans were founding their own institutions and hewing their own path in the national and international art worlds, they had a network of friends who helped and championed them, and who were not always African Americans." She includes the artwork and biographies of other artists of color, especially Asian American and Chicano "friends," in the catalogue; as these connections, she argues, "move artists and art worlds forward."[4]

To further support her exploration of these cross-racial networks in L.A.'s visual art world, Jones includes an essay by art historian Karen Higa about a series of photos of several of the featured *Now Dig This!* artists that were taken by Robert Nakamura in 1970—the same year he decided to leave his professional photography career due to "an early midlife crisis," and enroll in the Ethno-Communications Program at UCLA.[5] Higa's essay details an earlier exhibit her father, Kazuo Higa, and Alonzo Davis of Brockman Gallery partnered on in 1970 at the Da Vinci Gallery of Los Angeles City College's campus: *Black Art in L.A.* Kazuo Higa was then director of the gallery and had been teaching art history at the college since 1968, a period when (his daughter writes) "black art became a key source of identification not just for African Americans but in the broader Third World sense of people-of-color coalitions."

Kazuo Higa called on his former Marshall High School classmate Robert Nakamura to create photographic portraits of the artists selected by Davis for the LACC show. For two days Nakamura and Kazuo—former schoolmates who had both spent earlier years of their childhood at, respectively, the Manzanar and Heart Mountain concentration camps—drove across the city to photograph thirteen African American artists, including Betye Saar, Charles White, David Hammons, and Noah Purifoy, in their studios. Karen Higa sees the collaboration between Alonzo Davis, Robert Nakamura, and her father as providing "a brief view into the relatedness of Asian American and African American communities in the activism of the 1960s and 1970s." She further suggests that the physical movement and meetings of these artists,

> demonstrate a crucial, if little understood aspect of the city's cultural terrain. Theorists of Los Angeles have characterized it as a dispersed, disintegrated, and fragmented metropolis, deeply divided socially and too disjointed to generate a vital public life. Even if one accepts this dystopic vision of the city, there are moments of cross-cultural flowering, often in modest places such as the Da Vinci Gallery at LACC. My father understood this and so did Nakamura. In his photographs of Saar, Outterbridge, and others, the

artists are portrayed as commanding their creative space and image, claiming a place for themselves and their art.[6]

As is evident from the testimonies of the first classes of the MUC and Ethno program, this group of young Asian American, Black, Latina/o, and Native American film students similarly accompanied one another across the city (and beyond) armed with Eclairs, Nagras, hope, and hellfire, claiming a place for themselves and their stories. Committed to an ethos of film and social change, they created—and continue to create—projects that indisputably changed the face of independent media for people of color forever. Communities of color in L.A. (and beyond) with stories to tell and traditions to pass on—the families, artists, musicians, activists—raised those students. For a brief period of time, an affirmative action program in a public university opened its doors, its sound stages, its equipment room and editing facilities for these freedom dreamers to give back to those communities by richly and respectfully telling their stories on film for the first time. For a brief period of time. And now, affirmative action is gone.

When I looked back over the transcription from my interview with one of the original Mother Muccers, Richard Wells, I remembered how haunted I was by his thoughts about short-term guilt. I'd asked him about Elyseo Taylor and why he thought the Ethno program didn't last, and without missing a beat he said, "It's that syndrome of: how long does your guilt hold? How long is that going to play itself out where you feel responsible and feel like you've got to DO something about it?" Guilt only lasts but so long. For much of the past decade, when considering the short yet profoundly generative tenure of the Ethno-Communications Program, that line has haunted me. This is also a refrain that circled in my mind after every "urgent" faculty meeting or campus DEI "special event" in the wake of the deaths of Breonna Taylor and George Floyd in 2020 and the multitude of crises impacting our campuses in the years since. Guilt only lasts but so long.

But sometimes there's a different voice. Twice in the past several years I found myself giving talks about the Ethno-Communications Program, and twice the same person, a current professor at UCLA, has challenged me: "Every time I hear about the L.A. Rebellion or the Ethno-Communications Program, I think, why can't we do that again?"[7] The despair of the guilt refrain gets me nowhere; the energy inside this question provocatively challenges me.

The improvisation studies book I turn to and teach from often, *The Fierce Urgency of Now: Improvisation, Rights, and the Ethics of Cocreation*, borrows its title from a monumental address Dr. King gave one year before he was assassinated. On April 4, 1967, he delivered "Beyond Vietnam: Time to Break Silence" (written with Vincent Harding) to the congregation at Riverside Church in New York, where those gathered were challenged to rededicate themselves to the "long and bitter, but beautiful struggle for a new world." King continued: "Shall we say the odds are too great . . . the struggle is too hard . . . and we send our deepest regrets? Or will there be another message?" Fischlin, Heble, and Lipsitz remind us of those lines at the start of their book, and at the end, in their coda, they offer short writings on key elements of improvisation. It is in their description of "surprise" that I find energy, enough energy to not walk away from King's challenge. Surprise, the collaborative authors write, is

> registered in how people and communities use improvisatory practices to meet (and adapt to) the needs of the moment, to create a way out of no way, to cultivate profound resources of hope out of seemingly dead-end situations. Improvisation is thus something of a leap of faith, a bet on the future, on the possibility that the unforeseen, the emergent, the adaptive, and the unpredictable might be more vital, more important, more resilient, than certainty, familiarity or security.[8]

Affirmative action in higher education has now been declared unconstitutional. Ethnic studies programs have been widely banned. Could a multiracial media training program responding to the crises of these times happen again, happen . . . and last . . . at UCLA or at any university? Shall we say the odds are too great? Or will there be another message? A way— as the womanist theologians preach and the improvisation scholars teach—out of no way? When the film industry seemed impenetrable, the New Los Angeles filmmakers made a way out of no way; they made a collective filmography that tells a story of their Los Angeles that had never been seen before. Even a decade ago when I started this research, I would not have imagined that the university would now seem more impenetrable, and dangerous, than the film industry. Where will the next generation of filmmakers of color as courageous and determined as the Ethno film-makers find accessible and affordable training and support? And will the multiracial crossings have a chance to flourish . . . or even return?

One of the greatest joys of this research was that for a time I was "trad-ing eights" with jazz poet Lawson Inada via an old-school snail mail cor-respondence. In one of my letters asking him about his involvement with the Visual Communications (VC) film project *I Told You So* (dir. Alan Kondo, 1973), as well as the multiracial aspects of the "Ethno days," he returned this bluesy reflection:

> Hard to imagine now, but about the time of VC, most younger writers of color worked together in affiliation, staging gatherings, readings, publica-tions, so much so, it looked like the coalition/solidarity would last forever. . . . Man those were some heavy, heady times; male/female, many of us became "firsts" most became "names" won awards, and besides our bon-afide "degrees" of authenticity (barrio/ghetto/'hood/reservation) we had also begun to infiltrate arts agencies, cultural institutions, campuses . . . looking back, those decades seem like a "phase" because although there were achievements, changes, developments, establishment—things seem to have become static, or diluted, and we've gone our separate ways.[9]

Still, I take this note from Mr. Inada as yet another source of rich and rooted archival material, in line with the raw footage sourced by recent documentary filmmakers like Renee Tajima-Peña and Damani Baker or paintings and photographs curated by Kellie Jones and Karen Higa. All of that material is evidence of the crossings, evidence of fluency building that this Ethno filmography exhibits over and over again. Even if the program didn't last, look at its enduring and nourishing filmic fruit.

O.Funmilayo Makarah was one of the L.A. Rebellion filmmakers I did not get a chance to meet until very late in the writing of this book. I have the organizers of the Sojourner Truth Festival of the Arts Symposium at the University of Chicago in 2023 to thank.[10] Meeting her, revisiting her work—especially her much beloved short on her sister Rebellion film-maker, *Creating a Different Image: Portrait of Alile Sharon Larkin* (1989), as well as her *L.A. in My Mind,* 2006—and then arranging a time to Zoom post symposium with her, I got to thinking about her own empow-ered and empowering eye. The centering of the eyes—Larkin's eyes cap-tured in *Creating a Different Image* and Makarah's close-up of her own

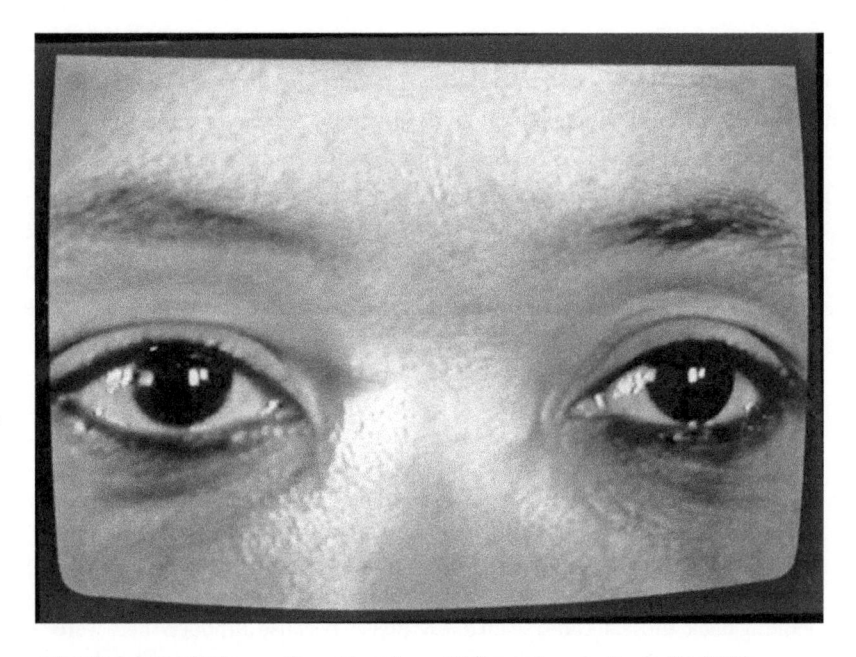

Alile Sharon Larkin's eyes from *Creating a Different Image: Portrait of Alile Sharon Larkin* by O.Funmilayo Makarah.

eyes in *L.A. in My Mind* (2006)—insists we engage their gaze and all it beholds. Makarah's work, especially of the late 1980s, consistently included multiracial crossings and concerns. Her short *Define* (1988) features artists Yreina Cervantez and Kelly Hashimoto speaking about identity/self-definition, and her short *Diversity* (1989) shows a multiracial campus protest at UCLA focused on the tenure battle of Don Nakanishi. Makarah also wrote a piece for Jacqueline Bobo's *Black Women Film and Video Artists* where she speaks about what she learned from meeting Eddie Wong in Shirley Clark's class at UCLA, and adapting what she called the "VC model" for working in the community. This model involved the process of setting up a video monitor at the end of the day when the crew was packing up equipment, so the neighborhood residents could "watch themselves and their neighbors on screen."[11] The lasting impact of these crossings and what they inspired is not contingent on whether an affirmative action media program lasted forever. It matters that the wheels were set in motion; Makarah's eyes were empowered enough to continue to empower others. She continues this work by running the Heritage Film Festival in Maryland. Duane Kubo started his own Asian Pacific film festival in Silicon Valley. The legacies of so many of the filmmakers who committed to long careers as educators of K-12 to community college and university level (Alile Sharon Larkin, Laura Ho Fineman, Duane Kubo, Haile Gerima, Billy Woodberry, Julie Dash, Sylvia Morales, Robert Nakamura, Zeinabu irene Davis, Barbara McCullough, Gay Abel-Bey, and more) is further evidence of generations of empowered eyes empowering future generations.

To not attempt to create similar circumstances or opportunities for new generations of filmmakers because the circumstances might be controversial or might not last—that would be the real failure. In the preface to *Freedom Dreams,* Robin D. G. Kelley makes this point about social movements: that our standards for evaluating them "too often . . . pivot around whether or not they 'succeeded' in realizing their visions rather than on the merits or power of the visions themselves." Yet, it is "these alternative visions and dreams that inspire new generations to continue to struggle for change."[12]

The wider Ethno filmography—made possible in part by Elyseo Taylor's vision for college students of color to have access to the tools of filmmaking so that the "good things" of their communities could be known by others—provides a feast of alternative visions by freedom-dreaming, community-serving filmmakers. Let this filmography itself be a tool kit. Let there be greater access to these materials, more preservation of these materials, more cross-racial, fluency-building curation of these materials, more teaching of these materials cross-racially on campuses (while we can) and certainly in community spaces. It is my first goal, as and after this book goes out, to work on creating digital and DVD packages similar to the brilliant three-disc *L.A. Rebellion* collection the UCLA Film and Television Archive team put together for the Black insurgents. Let us get all the multiracial insurgents' work out there to establish a more perfect cinematic rebellion. This needs to happen now, because these stories— their wisdom, power, tenderness, and organizing capacity—are urgent like a Mother Muccer!

Notes

INTRODUCTION

1. On various reactions to the film and the importance of the preproduction negotiations and collaboration between the Osage Nation and director Scorsese see Jacob Floyd, "History Lives in the Present," *Film Comment,* October 30, 2023.

2. "Story of the L.A. Rebellion," UCLA Film and Television Archive, May 11, 2014, https://www.cinema.ucla.edu/la-rebellion/story-la-rebellion.

3. Toni Cade Bambara included roll calls of black women filmmakers at the end of at least two of her significant writings on Julie Dash's film *Daughters of the Dust*: "Reading the Signs, Empowering the Eye: Daughters of the Dust and the Black Independent Cinema Movement," in *Black American Cinema*, ed. Manthia Diawara (New York: Routledge: 1993), and "Preface," in *Daughters of the Dust: the Making of an African American Women's Film* (New York: New Press, 1992). I also nod here to O.Funmilayo Makarah's short video, *L.A. in My Mind*, 2006, itself a visual roll call of beloved places and people in the city of Los Angeles.

4. See Josh Kun and Laura Pulido's edited collection, *Black and Brown in Los Angeles: Beyond Conflict and Coalition* (Berkeley: University of California Press, 2014) which includes Denise Sandoval's essay, "The Politics of Low and Slow/ *Bajito y Suavecito*" (176–200) and Nery Gabriel Lemus's essay and artwork, "On Fallen Nature and the Two Cities" (341–45). See also Luis Alvarez's "From Zoot

Suits to Hip Hop: Towards a Relational Chicana/o Studies," in *Latino Studies* 5 (2007): 53–75. The work of the other authors listed here— Kurashige, Macías, Widener, and Isoardi—will be addressed directly later in the text.

5. "UCLA Students Will Film Aspects of Ghetto Life as Means to Dialog," *Los Angeles Times,* January 4, 1970, italics mine.

6. See Clyde Taylor, "The L.A. Rebellion: A Turning Point in Black Cinema," *The New American Filmmakers Series* 26 (New York: Whitney Museum of American Art, 1986); Bambara, "Reading the Signs"; and Ntongela Masilela, "The Los Angeles School of Black Filmmakers," in Diawara, *Black American Cinema.*

7. Taylor, "The L.A. Rebellion." See also Clyde Taylor, "Once upon a Time in the West . . . L.A. Rebellion," in *L.A. Rebellion: Creating a New Black Cinema,* ed. Allyson Nadia Field, Jan-Christopher Horak, and Jacqueline Najuma Stewart (Oakland: University of California Press, 2015). Before he referred to the filmmakers as the L.A. Rebellion, he profiled their work in the *Black Collegian* as early as 1980. See for example, Taylor, "The Next Wave: Women Film Artists at UCLA," *Black Collegian*, April/May 1980.

8. Allyson Nadia Field, Jan-Christopher Horak and Jacqueline Najuma Stewart, "Emancipating the Image: The L.A. Rebellion of Black Filmmakers," in Field, Horak, and Stewart, *L.A. Rebellion,* 1. This title was used for their symposium and exhibition series in 2011, the edited volume above, and a 2016 DVD anthology of mostly student work by the Rebellion directors.

9. Bambara, "Reading the Signs," 119. Renee Tajima, now Tajima-Peña, was not a student in the program at UCLA, but she published articles about the film program in several media journals including her important March 1984 piece for *The Independent,* "Lights Camera . . . Affirmative Action." Clyde Taylor did write about the black filmmakers from UCLA earlier than this, and in two pieces for the *Black Collegian* mentions the term Third World and even specifically the training of Chicano filmmakers at UCLA. He also acknowledges that Larry Clark entered UCLA as "one of a group of special admittees to UCLA's film department following the death of Martin Luther King" ("Passing Through. An Underground Film About Black Music Underground," *Black Collegian* February/March 1980). This must be the Ethno-Communications Program, which was considered a response to the so called "urban crisis" at least partly associated with the urban uprisings after King's assassination.

10. Bambara, "Reading the Signs," 132–33.

11. Chon Noriega, *Shot in America: Television, the State, and the Rise of Chicano Cinema* (Minneapolis: University of Minnesota Press, 2000); Glen Mimura, *Ghostlife of Third Cinema: Asian American Film and Video* (Minneapolis: University of Minnesota Press, 2009); and Jun Okada, *Making Asian American Film and Video: History, Institutions, Movements* (New Brunswick: Rutgers University Press: 2015).

12. Field, Horak, and Stewart, *L.A. Rebellion*, 19.

13. Haile Gerima, oral history interview by Zeinabu irene Davis and Jacqueline Stewart, L.A. Rebellion Oral Histories, September 13, 2010.

14. See Clyde Taylor, "New U.S. Black Cinema," *Jump Cut* 28 (April 1983): 46–48, and "The L.A. Rebellion: A Turning Point in Black Cinema"; Masilela, "The Los Angeles School of Black Filmmakers"; Mark Reid, *Redefining Black Film* (Berkeley: University of California Press, 1993); Mike Murashige, "Haile Gerima and the Political Economy of Cinematic Resistance," in *Representing Blackness: Issues in Film and Video*, ed. Valerie Smith (New Brunswick: Rutgers University Press, 1997); Paula Massood, *Black City Cinema: African American Urban Experiences in Film* (Philadelphia: Temple University Press, 2003); Cynthia Young, *Soul Power: Culture, Radicalism, and the Making of a U.S. Third World Left* (Durham: Duke University Press, 2006); and Frank Wilderson III, *Red, White & Black: Cinema and the Structure of U.S. Antagonisms* (Durham: Duke University Press, 2010). Ntongela Masilela differentiated the Black filmmakers who arrived at UCLA in the late 1960s and early 1970s—the "first wave"—and those, like Dash, Larkin, Nicolas, who came in the second.

15. I use "Third World" throughout this book primarily to be in alignment with the way in which the artists, activists and scholars of the Ethno era (1969–1973) and beyond framed themselves in relation to and in solidarity with liberation movements of Africa, Asia, and Latin America, as well as considering themselves, as oppressed people of color in the United States, as "internally colonized." It is not used as a pejorative term to describe poverty or underdevelopment. Vijay Prashad, in *The Darker Nations: A People's History of the Third World*, succinctly suggests that the Third World was a "project" not a place, built by the collective dreaming of new worlds during "the seemingly interminable battles against colonialism"(xv). See also C. Young, *Soul Power*, and M. Jacqui Alexander's extended discussions of the term and its fraught relationship to the term "women of color" in *Pedagogies of Crossing: Mediations on Feminism, Sexual Politics, Memory, and the Sacred* (Durham: Duke University Press, 2005).

16. Ralph Ellison, *Shadow and Act* (New York: Random House, 1964). See also Donald Bogle, *Toms, Coons, Mulattoes, Mammies and Bucks: An Interpretive History*, 4th ed. (New York: Bloomsbury, 2001), on "problem pictures."

17. Bambara, "Reading the Signs," 120–21.

18. Clyde Taylor, interview with Josslyn Luckett, *Society for Cinema and Media Studies Fieldnotes*, October 19, 2019, https://www.cmstudies/page/fieldnotes.

19. See Mark Olsen, "Haile Gerima Rejected Racist Hollywood. How Ava DuVernay Is Helping Pay Tribute," *Los Angeles Times*, September 24, 2021.

20. Clyde Taylor, interview for *Paul Robeson: Here I Stand*, September 30, 1998, PBS.

21. Alexander, *Pedagogies of Crossing*, 269.

22. See for example Jacqueline Bobo's tremendous reading of the influence of what she calls the Spencer Williams homages in Julie Dash's *Daughters of the Dust,* in *Black Women as Cultural Readers* (New York: Columbia University Press, 1995), 140–42.

23. Since this film focuses on the Chinese in Hollywood, it does not cover the recent exciting revelation of even earlier works by a Japanese American film production company who produced a racial uplift film in 1914, *The Oath of the Sword.* See Denise Khor's important work on this film, *Transpacific Convergences: Race, Migration, and Japanese American Film Culture before World War II* (Chapel Hill: UNC Press, 2022).

24. See more on Jurado's life and roles in Anthony Macías, *Chicano Chicana Americana* (Tucson: University of Arizona Press, 2023).

25. See Nobuko Miyamoto's memoir *Not Yo' Butterfly: My Long Song of Relocation, Race, Love, and Revolution*, ed. Deborah Wong (Oakland: University of California Press, 2021). Nobuko and Chris Iijima were songwriting partners/performers who were considered the troubadours of the Asian American movement. Their songs are featured in multiple films by the Asian American alums of Ethno.

26. Moore's screen daughter Sarah Jane was played by Susan Kohner, the daughter of famous Mexican actress Lupita Tovar. The mixed race Mexican/white actress playing the tragic mulatta is a detail often overlooked in reports on that film.

27. Daniel Widener, *Black Arts West: Culture and Struggle in Postwar Los Angeles* (Durham: Duke University Press, 2010), 73–81. Widener remarks that Stewart was born in Harlem in 1910 to Barbadian parents who were Garveyites.

28. Joan Weibel-Orlando, *Indian Country, L.A.: Maintaining Ethnic Community in Complex Society* (Urbana: University of Illinois Press, 1999), 105.

29. This model, both then and now, of successful actors of color supporting financially or creating institutions to support low-budget independent film for filmmakers of color warrants more attention. Tanisha Ford's recent work *Our Secret Society: Mollie Moon and the Glamour, Money, and Power Behind the Civil Rights Movement* (Amistad, 2023) puts a spotlight on black fundraising in the civil rights movement that offers a resonant and critically important counternarrative to the way that "African Americans and other people of color are cast as the pathologically poor recipients of charity, never as institution (re)builders" (310).

30. Zeinabu irene Davis, who enrolled in the film program in 1985, has been called "the last flame" of the L.A. Rebellion by Clyde Taylor ("Once Upon a Time in the West," in Field, Horak, and Stewart, *L.A. Rebellion*, 19). Of all the filmmakers whose work I analyze as part of the "wider filmography" her start date is the furthest from the first semester of the Media Urban Crisis program that officially launched in 1970. Most of the filmmakers whose work I discuss arrived

between 1967 and 1976. I will address a handful of works in this wider filmography made after 1992.

31. The "Last Golden Age" is part of Jonathan Kirshner's title *Hollywood's Last Golden Age: Politics, Society, and the Seventies Film in America* (Ithaca: Cornell University Press, 2012). The quotes about unmotivated heroes and shifting genres are from Thomas Elsaesser's often cited essay "The Pathos of Failure: American Films of the 1970s, Notes on the Unmotivated Hero," in *The Last Great American Picture Show: New Hollywood Cinema in the 1970s*, ed. Thomas Elsaesser, Alexander Horwath, and Noel King (Amsterdam: Amsterdam University Press, 2004).

32. Peter Krämer, "Afterword: New Wave, New Hollywood, New Research," in *New Wave, New Hollywood: Reassessment, Recovery, and Legacy*, ed. Nathan Abrams and Gregory Frame (New York: Bloomsbury Academic, 2021), 224–25.

33. Joy Harjo, "The Path to the Milky Way Leads Through Los Angeles," from *A Map to the Next World: Poems and Tales* by Joy Harjo. Copyright © 2000 by Joy Harjo. Used by permission of W.W. Norton & Company, Inc. The former U.S. Poet Laureate, Harjo herself appears in Ethno filmmaker Sandra Osawa's documentary *Pepper's Pow Wow*.

34. Nicolas G. Rosenthal, *Reimagining Indian Country: Native American Migration and Identity in Twentieth-Century Los Angeles* (Chapel Hill: University of North Carolina Press, 2012), 2. Rosenthal explains that from 1948 to the 1970s, Bureau of Indian Affairs officials "at both the federal and local levels implemented policies designed to break down tribal ties and to assimilate Indian people into the nation's industrial and domestic economy," and the BIA "understood relocation as a way to move Indians off tribal lands and to assimilate them into the larger society" (51–52).

35. Gerald Horne, *Fire This Time: The Watts Uprising and the 1960s* (New York: Da Capo Press, 1997), 31.

36. Gaye Theresa Johnson, *Spaces of Conflict, Sounds of Solidarity: Music, Race, and Spatial Entitlement in Los Angeles* (Berkeley: University of California Press, 2013), 14.

37. George Sanchez, "Why Are Multiracial Communities So Dangerous? A Comparative Look at Hawai'i; Cape Town, South Africa; and Boyle Heights, California," *Pacific Historical Review* 86, no. 1 (2017): 158.

38. Elizabeth R. Escobedo, *From Coveralls to Zoot Suits: The Lives of Mexican American Women on the World War II Home Front* (Chapel Hill: University of North Carolina Press, 2013), 5–7. See also George Sanchez, *Becoming Mexican American: Ethnicity, Culture, and Identity in Chicano Los Angeles 1900–1945* (New York: Oxford University Press, 1993) and "Why Are Multiracial Communities So Dangerous?," where he notes, "The issue of forced removal is critical. . . . (In) 1931, the Los Angeles County Board of Supervisors put together the largest organized repatriation campaign in U.S. history, ironically targeting

Mexican immigrants in a city that their ancestors had founded 150 years prior" (165).

39. Chon Noriega, "City of Dreams," *Aztlan: A Journal of Chicano Studies* 37, no. 1 (2012).

40. Scott Kurashige, *The Shifting Grounds of Race: Black and Japanese Americans in the Making of Multiethnic Los Angeles* (Princeton: Princeton University Press, 2008), 165. Kurashige quotes here various articles from the *California Eagle* dated from November of 1943 to January of 1945.

41. The film featuring Inada, *I Told You So*, was directed by Alan Kondo, who was not a UCLA student but rather a Canadian editor who moved south to collaborate with Visual Communications (VC) in its earliest years, joining founders Robert Nakamura, Duane Kubo, Eddie Wong, Alan Ohashi, and others. The first group of films they produced (while simultaneously finishing their UCLA degrees) were produced as "Visual Communications Productions" and individual directing credit was not identified. Kondo also crewed for Carroll Parrott Blue's *Varnette's World* (1979) and Billy Woodberry's *Bless Their Little Hearts* (1984). For more on VC's collective authorship see Okada, *Making Asian American Film and Video*, 22–23.

42. Lawson Fusao Inada, *Legends from Camp* (Minneapolis: Coffee House Press, 1993), 55–57.

43. Inada, *Legends from Camp*, vi.

44. Rosenthal, *Reimagining Indian Country*, 52.

45. Rosenthal, *Reimagining Indian Country*, 52. For more on Dillon Myer see also Richard Drinnon, *Keeper of Concentration Camps: Dillon S. Myer and American Racism* (Berkeley: University of California Press, 1987).

46. Rosenthal, *Reimagining Indian Country*, 51.

47. Fred Zinnemann, John Houseman, Irvin Kershner, Kent Mackenzie, Pauline Kael, and Colin Young, "Personal Creation in Hollywood: Can it be Done?," *Film Quarterly* 15, no. 3, Special Issue on Hollywood (Spring 1962): 16–34. Young was the Los Angeles editor for *Film Quarterly* while he was head of the film division at UCLA. For more on *The Exiles* and this *Film Quarterly* roundtable see Joshua Glick, *Los Angeles Documentary and the Production of Public History, 1958–1977* (Oakland: University of California Press, 2018).

48. These references to three films by Ethno-Communications students are as follows: the koto player is June Kuramoto, who is featured in Duane Kubo's film, *Cruisin' J-Town* (1975); the SNCC worker is Maria "Betita" Benitez, featured in Sylvia Morales's *A Crushing Love: Chicanas, Motherhood, and Activism* (2009); and the saxophonist is the late Jim Pepper, the subject of Sandra Osawa's *Pepper's Pow Wow* (1997).

49. The *L.A. Rebellion* editors note, after mentioning the gay characters at the "margins" of the *Penitentiary* films by Jamaa Fanaka, that "the L.A. Rebellion filmmakers almost never explored lesbian, gay, bisexual, transgender (LGBT)

issues, a glaring omission that deserves further consideration" (52). Robert Nakamura shared in an interview with me that the filmmaking of his Asian American students at UCLA became more and more expansive in the late 90s into the 2000s, including films on the "gay and lesbian community" (June 1, 2016). Another continuum can be seen in recent work on the New Negress Film Society, a self-defined collective of Black women and non-binary filmmakers who consistently suggest that they see themselves as twenty-first century inheritors of the L.A. Rebellion filmmakers' spirit of "collaboration, experimentation, and community organizing"; see Samantha Sheppard, "A Profound Edge: Collectivism and The New Negress Film Society," *Film Quarterly* 77 (2023): 1. Sheppard describes the collective as producing "formally and narratively challenging works that radically center black sociality, with particular emphasis on Black girls, women, and genderqueer communities" (27).

50. There were some queer and people of color crossings and collaborations happening between the UCLA filmmakers of the 1960s and 1970s that warrant much more research. Some examples include a pre-Ethno short, *Behind Every Good Man* (1967) by white queer filmmaker Nikolai Ursin about a Black trans woman, added to the National Film Registry in 2022. UCLA alum Donna Deitch (director of LGBT classic *Desert Hearts*, 1985) acted in Charles Burnett's *Several Friends* and was visual effects consultant with Duane Kubo on *City, City* (1974). Betty Chen collaborated with Judith Dancoff on *Judy Chicago and the California Girls* (1971), a film that includes heated debate between lesbian and straight white feminists.

51. Peter Sagal, "'52 Words,' an essay on the Preamble to the United States Constitution," 2021, https://www.arionpress.com/preamble-media.

1. THE "URBAN CRISIS" IN WESTWOOD?

Epigraphs: Gilman quoted in Claudia Mitchell-Kernan, ed., *40 Years of Ethnic Studies at UCLA* (Los Angeles: UCLA Graduate Division, 2010); Charles J. Hitch, "President Hitch's Inaugural Address at UCLA," *University Bulletin* 16, no. 34 (May 27, 1968); Renee Tajima, "Lights, Camera . . . Affirmative Action," *The Independent*, March 1984, 16.

1. Barbara A. Rhodes, "UCLA High Potential Program 1968–1969," Academic Support Program Files, UCLA, page 7. The High Potential Program was a minority recruitment program that originally focused on "underprivileged Afro-American and Chicano" students and eventually opened up to Asian American and Native American students. Kenwood Jung, a recruit of Asian American "Hi Pot" in 1970, reflects that the program gave "access for those historically kept out of universities. . . . We were young, brave and ready to change the world." Jung is quoted in Mary Uyematsu Kao, *Rockin' the Boat: Flashbacks of the 1970s*

Asian Movement (Los Angeles: UCLA Asian American Studies Center, 2020), 30.

2. National Advisory Commission on Civil Disorders Report, 1967, available at https://www.ojp.gov/ncjrs/virtual-library/abstracts/national-advisory-commission-civil-disorders-report, quotes from pp. 1, 201–2, 210–12. See also Gayle Wald's excellent discussion of the Kerner Report in *It's Been Beautiful: Soul! and Black Power Television* (Durham: Duke University Press, 2015), 44–49.

3. Budd Schulberg, ed., *From the Ashes: Voices of Watts* (New York: Meridian Books, 1969), 8 and 5. See the bios for Guadalupe de Saavedra and Sonora McKeller.

4. Tajima, "Lights, Camera," 16; Nicolas G. Rosenthal, *Reimagining Indian Country: Native American Migration and Identity in Twentieth-Century Los Angeles* (Chapel Hill: University of North Carolina Press, 2012), 2.

5. David James, *The Most Typical Avant-Garde: History and Geography of Minor Cinemas in Los Angeles* (Berkeley: University of California Press, 2005), 305.

6. *Evergreen* was named to the Library of Congress Film Registry list in 2021.

7. Ray Manzarek, *Light My Fire: My Life with the Doors* (New York: Putnam, 1998), 20. His two younger brothers, Rick and Jim Manczarek, his bandmates from Rick and the Ravens, kept the "c" in their name.

8. Hank Olguin, email, December 10, 2016. Though Olguin did not pursue a professional career in acting, he explained to me that he did later become a member of Nosotros, founded in 1970 by Ricardo Montalbán and other Latina/o actors to combat racial stereotypes in the film industry.

9. Elizabeth R. Escobedo, *From Coveralls to Zoot Suits: The Lives of Mexican American Women on the World War II Home Front* (Chapel Hill: University of North Carolina Press, 2013), 141–42.

10. The *Star Trek* kiss happened in 1968. There had been earlier Hollywood films where Asian actresses were "allowed" to kiss white leading men: *Sayonara* (1957) and *The World of Suzie Wong* (1960). The black and white photography in *Evergreen* is most reminiscent of Resnais's *Hiroshima Mon Amour* (1959), which featured an Asian male actor and white woman kissing in a way that was erotically framed.

11. Anthony Macías, *Mexican American Mojo: Popular Music, Dance, and Urban Culture in Los Angeles* (Durham: Duke University Press, 2008), 25.

12. Manzarek, *Light My Fire*, 91.

13. In an informal interview conducted by Joan Churchill, when discussing the famous bandmates as filmmakers, Colin Young described Morrison's work as "rubbish," then quickly followed up: "Whereas Manzarek was a filmmaker. *Evergreen* . . . is wonderful!" Private *Vimeo* recording, 2021.

14. Tajima, "Lights, Camera," 16; see the full quote in the epigraph of this chapter.

15. Duncan Petrie, "Colin Young: Interview," *Journal of British Cinema and Television* 7, no. 2 (August 1, 2010), 314.

16. Michael Sragow, "Godfatherhood," in *Francis Ford Coppola: Interviews*, ed. Gene D. Phillips and Rodney Hill (Jackson: University Press of Mississippi, 2004), 167. The article was originally published in *The New Yorker*, March 24, 1997.

17. Joseph Gelmis, "Francis Ford Coppola: Free Agent within the System," in Phillips and Hill, *Francis Ford Coppola*, 12. Gelmis conducted the interview in 1968 and originally published it in his collection *The Film Director as Superstar* (Garden City, NY: Doubleday, 1970).

18. Gelmis, "Francis Ford Coppola," 3.

19. Manzarek, *Light My Fire*, 63.

20. Manzarek, *Light My Fire*, 80.

21. Manzarek, *Light My Fire*, 8

22. "Colin Young" for Scottish Television, a tribute on the occasion of his 1992 retirement from the National Film and Television School (NFTS), produced and directed by Alistair Scott, an alum of NFTS.

23. Colin Young, "Teaching Film at UCLA," *Journal of the University Film Producers Association* 16, no. 4 (1964): 14.

24. The project system was set to begin at UCLA in the fall quarter of the 1966/67 school year; see Kevin Thomas, "Hollywood's 'Help Wanted' Sign," *Los Angeles Times*, July 3, 1966.

25. Colin Young, personal interview, February 27, 2017. The "Project One" films become very important in the work on the L.A. Rebellion filmmakers. Allyson Nadia Field comments on how the Project One films allowed for an "open exploration of the medium of film" where the "rebellion" film students "experimented with different strategies for articulating notions of Black 'authenticity'"; see "Rebellious Unlearning: UCLA Project One Films (1967–1978)," in *L.A. Rebellion: Creating a New Black Cinema*, ed. Allyson Nadia Field, Jan-Christopher Horak, and Jacqueline Najuma Stewart (Oakland: University of California Press, 2015), 84.

26. Colin Young, "Teaching Film at UCLA," 20.

27. Colin Young, personal interview.

28. See David MacDougall, "Colin Young, Ethnographic Film, and the Film Culture of the 1960s," *Visual Anthropology Review* 17, no. 2 (2001–2002), 83.

29. Colin Young, personal interview. See also his 1975 essay "Observational Cinema," in *Principles of Visual Anthropology*, ed. Paul Hockings (New York: De Gruyter, 1995).

30. MacDougall, "Colin Young."

31. Joan Churchill and Alan Barker, personal interview, August 10, 2016.

32. MacDougall, "Colin Young," 83–84.

33. MacDougall, "Colin Young," 87.

34. See Colin Young, "Teaching Film at UCLA," 19, where he discusses the advantages and disadvantages of being housed in a theater arts department.

35. Colin Young, personal interview.

36. Petrie, "Colin Young," 315.

37. Colin Young, personal interview. Along with support for the Ethnographic Film Program, Chancellor Murphy supported Young's urging that the university create a film archive. This effort began when Young "persuaded" Murphy to put in a bid for a massive collection of films on nitrate that Paramount announced it would soon destroy. For more on this and the origins of UCLA's film archive see Anthony Slide, *Nitrate Won't Wait: Film Preservation in the United States* (Jefferson, NC: McFarland, 1992), 68–69.

38. Charles J. Hitch, "What We Must Do: The University and The Urban Crisis," A Special Urban Crisis Report of the President of the University of California, May 17, 1968, quoted in Charles Z. Wilson, *Crossing Learning Boundaries by Choice, Black People Must Save Themselves: A Memoir* (Bloomington, IN: Authorhouse, 2008), 288–91.

39. Hitch, "Inaugural Address."

40. In a 1969 article, Colin Young hints at plans for a community film program: "emerging slowly is a cinema of the ethnic minorities. . . . At least one film school hopes to recruit black and brown students to help this process along." See "Film and Social Change," *The Journal of Aesthetic Education* 3, no. 3 (1969): 26. The editors of *L.A. Rebellion* write that Young recruited Elyseo Taylor (7). In my interview with Colin Young he could not remember the circumstances of his hiring Taylor, though he confirmed that when he left UCLA in 1970 he was happy to leave the project in Taylor's capable hands.

41. Vijay Prashad, *The Darker Nations: A People's History of the Third World* (New York: The New Press, 2007), xv–xvii.

42. Here I am invoking Cynthia Young's use of the "U.S. Third World Left" in *Soul Power: Culture, Radicalism, and the Making of a U.S. Third World Left* (Durham: Duke University Press, 2006). Clarifying her use of the term, she writes that her study is "about how the literature, films, political movements, ideologies, agendas, and wars understood to originate in the Third World impacted people of color living in the United States . . . about how the relationship between the global and the local came to be understood and made new cultural and political possibilities available to a group I call U.S. Third World Leftists."

43. Craig Collisson, "The Fight to Legitimize Blackness: How Black Students Changed the University" (PhD diss., University of Washington, 2008), 4. Collisson's quote about the spark that set black studies in motion comes from Fabio Rojas, *From Black Power to Black Studies: How a Radical Social Movement became an Academic Discipline* (Baltimore: The Johns Hopkins University Press, 2007), 20.

44. See Wilson, *Crossing Learning Boundaries*, 295–97; see also "Program at UCLA Promises to Assist Minority Students," *Los Angeles Times*, July 14, 1968.

45. Jacqueline Tasch, "The Long Road Home: Forty Years of Ethnic Studies at UCLA," in Mitchell-Kernan, *Forty Years of Ethnic Studies at UCLA*, 16.

46. Collisson, "The Fight to Legitimize Blackness," 131.

47. Rosenthal, *Reimagining Indian Country*.

48. Tasch, "The Long Road Home," 16.

49. Martha Biondi, *The Black Revolution on Campus* (Berkeley: University of California Press, 2012), 69.

50. San Francisco State established the first Third World College in 1969, now known as the College of Ethnic Studies. In 2019 Cal State University, Los Angeles became only the second College of Ethnic Studies, fifty years later.

51. Mike Murase, "Ethnic Studies and Higher Education for Asian Americans," in *Counterpoint: Perspectives on Asian America*, ed. Emma Gee (Los Angeles: Asian American Studies Center, University of California, 1976).

52. Irene Miyagawa, "UCLA Sells Out," *Gidra* 1, no. 6 (September 1969).

53. Eddie Wong, "Opinion: Shuck 'n Jive," *Gidra* 1, no. 6 (September 1969).

54. Quote from Collisson, "The Fight to Legitimize Blackness," 155. See Noliwe M. Rooks, *White Money, Black Power: The Surprising History of African American Studies and the Crisis of Race in Higher Education* (Boston: Beacon Press, 2006).

55. Collisson, "The Fight to Legitimize Blackness," 155–56.

56. Collisson, "The Fight to Legitimize Blackness," 157–58.

57. Critical Ethnic Studies Editorial Collective, "Introduction: A Sightline," in *Critical Ethnic Studies: A Reader*, ed. Nadia Ellis et al. (Durham: Duke University Press, 2016), 3.

58. All of these journals except for *Amerasia* were started at UCLA. Don T. Nakanishi and Lowell Chun-Hoon created *Amerasia* while they were students at Yale and later moved it to UCLA after first Chun-Hoon and later Nakanishi were hired by the Asian American Studies Center; see Mitchell-Kernan, *Forty Years of Ethnic Studies at UCLA*, 25. The *Journal of Black Studies*, founded by one of the first directors for the Center of Afro-American Studies at UCLA, Art Smith (before he changed his name to Molefi Asante), is now published at Temple University.

59. Rooks, *White Money, Black Power*, 61–62.

60. Rooks, *White Money, Black Power*, 4–5.

61. For example, four of the six scholars who edited the *Critical Ethnic Studies Reader*—Dylan Rodriquez, Jodi Kim, David Hernandez, and Sarita Echavez See—all have PhDs or undergraduate degrees from UC Berkeley. I mention this to emphasize my strong sense that West Coast, especially California, university-trained scholars have generally *not* forgotten this history, yet this history often goes unacknowledged or surprises scholars trained elsewhere.

62. Rooks, *White Money, Black Power*, 9–11.

63. Elaine Brown, *A Taste of Power: A Black Woman's Story* (New York: Anchor Books, 1992), 155.

64. See Scot Brown, *Fighting for US: Maulana Karenga, the US Organiza-tion, and Black Cultural Nationalism* (New York: New York University Press, 2003), 96–97.

65. Moctesuma Esparza, personal interview, June 7, 2016.

66. Moctesuma Esparza, "Black Power Rally," February 18, 1968, Pacifica Radio Archives.

67. Quoted in Tajima, "Lights, Camera."

2. ELYSEO TAYLOR AND THE ETHNO ETHOS

1. Taylor is mentioned in the remarkable war correspondent Trezzvant Ander-son's 1945 account, *Come Out Fighting: The Epic Tale of the 761st Tank Battal-ion 1942–1945* (Salzburg: Salzburger Druckerei und Verlag, 1945), as well as Gina M. DiNicolo's more recent study, *The Black Panthers: A Story of Race, War and Courage—The 761st Tank Battalion and WWII* (Yardley, PA: Westholme Publishing, 2014). Though Taylor is not directly mentioned, Phil Bertelsen's recent History Channel documentary, *The 761st Tank Battalion: The Original Black Panthers* (2023), executive produced by and featuring Morgan Freeman, is excellent.

2. This phrase "one foot on campus, one foot in the community" was first used by Larry Clark in our phone interview, June 28, 2016.

3. "Herschensohn's *Eulogy to 5:02:* Today's featured digital object," *Pepper-dine Library News*, October 24, 2011. The film, *Eulogy to 5:02*, is part of Pep-perdine's Bruce Herschensohn Collection, which also includes correspondence between Elyseo Taylor and Herschensohn regarding the production of *5:02*. Bur-ton at this time was on his fourth Oscar nomination, aptly for a film called *The Spy Who Came in from the Cold* (dir. Martin Ritt, 1965).

4. Elyseo Taylor's remarks are from a talk he gave at the Bellagio Study and Conference Center in Lake Como, Italy, September 20, 1976. The Rockefeller Center archives do not possess a full draft of the speech but the conference sum-mary, "Report on the 311th Conference, September 16–21, 1976" for the confer-ence titled "The Role of the Mass Media in Enlisting Public Support for Marginal Groups," sponsored by the European Centre for Social Welfare and Training, Vienna, contains lengthy quotes/transcriptions from a number of the conference guest speakers. Thanks to Mary Ann Quinn, archivist at the Rockefeller Archive Center, for uncovering this report.

5. I don't have exact causal evidence for his relocation to the United States; perhaps it was watching Watts in flames from abroad (similar to Baldwin's

return from Europe during key campaigns of the civil rights movement), perhaps it was driven by professional hopes to work again with Herschensohn and his Hollywood connections . . . maybe both.

6. Elyseo Taylor's short film *Black Art, Black Artists* is presented/produced by the University Extension of UCLA and features an important September 1966 exhibit on UCLA's campus, *The Negro in American Art*, which suggests that Taylor had some relations with UCLA prior to his formal post in the film department. The film's date is 1971, and this makes me wonder if there's also a chance that he did not actually shoot the exhibit photography, but received director credit for assembling it, writing/conducting the interview with Van Slater, and perhaps shooting the footage of Slater at work.

7. Allyson Nadia Field, Jan-Christopher Horak, and Jacqueline Najuma Stewart, eds., *L.A. Rebellion: Creating a New Black Cinema* (Oakland: University of California Press, 2015), 7. The editors of this collection state that Young recruited Taylor to the faculty at UCLA and to be a part of the Media Urban Crisis planning committee after becoming aware of his "education efforts with young people in Watts."

8. Colin Young, email, August 3, 2016.

9. Peña made a reel-to-reel audio recording of an early Doors show in 1966 at the London Fog that may be the band's earliest live recording; it was released by Rhino Records in 2016. Her student films, *Cum Joyn Us* and *The Wonderful World of Wigs*, were well received especially the comedy, *Cum Joyn Us*, about her Mexican American family and their Jewish gardener in Echo Park. In an email on July 16, 2024, Peña explains that where she lived most of her neighbors were Jewish and had Mexican gardeners, so the film playfully reversed this and includes Harry Belafonte's rendition of "Hava Nagila." Grant's talent as a cinematographer motivated the film department to hire him to teach camera courses after he graduated. He was also on the camera crew for Stan Lathan's *Save the Children* (1973) and Denis Sanders's *Soul to Soul* (1971). In an email he expressed to me some regret about his student work not focusing more on Black life.

10. Colin Young explained to me that he went after federal funding for the program and "federal funds meant no exclusions, so officially we excluded nobody." But he said by locating the work "in the 'hood' I hoped to discourage white students applying . . . and it happened not to my surprise that we didn't get any [applications] from the white students." Not one person I interviewed mentioned any white students as formally part of Ethno, but there were white classmates who worked on their film projects and vice versa.

11. "UCLA Students Will Film Aspects of Ghetto Life as Means to Dialog," *Los Angeles Times*, January 4, 1970. In an archival document titled "Resume of Elyseo Jose Taylor" shared by his daughter, Karen Taylor, the education section states: "1947 until 1953, undergraduate and early graduated studies at the

University of Chicago"; also "Studied at the Universities of Heidelberg, Grenoble and Perugia, the German, French and Italian languages and literatures, as well as economics, sociology and philosophy." My deepest thanks to Karen Taylor, who I connected with in the eleventh hour of this writing. There were many aspects of her father's professional career for which she did not have details; yet, the materials, photos, postcards she shared from his early life were tremendously valuable.

12. This could be a reference to a very short lived Ethno precursor called "The New Communicators" which started in the summer of 1968. See Chon Noriega, *Shot in America: Television, the State and the Rise of Chicano Cinema* (Minneapolis: University of Minnesota Press, 2000), 100–4, and a book by New Communicator alum Jesús Salvador Treviño, *Eyewitness: A Filmmaker's Memoir of the Movement* (Houston: Arte Publico Press, 2001), 59–64.

13. George Stoney and his National Film Board of Canada "Challenge for Change" program are also mentioned in Colin Young's "Film and Social Change," *Journal of Aesthetic Education* 3, no. 3 (July 1969). This must have been a significant model for both men in their thinking about the MUC program.

14. "UCLA Students Will Film Aspects." Through the UC Extension media center, Schnitzler produced a series of educational documentaries, co-sponsored by the National Institute for Mental Health (NIMH), called *The Social Seminar*. He hired early MUC/Ethno students (Brian Maeda, Wendell Handy, Clifford Stewart, Richard Wells) to crew and in one case even direct these shorts, so there is an overlap between what Schnitzler was doing and what Taylor at this point was proposing in the *LA Times* piece. I discuss Richard Wells's short *Teddy* (1971), part of the Social Seminar series, later in this chapter.

15. Richard Hawkins, oral history interview by Allyson Field, October 14, 2010, L.A. Rebellion Oral History Project, UCLA Film and Television Archive.

16. The Regents of the University of California, Berkeley (06900231), 1969 March 03–1970 March 02. Ford Foundation records, Grants Them-Tw (FA732H) Reel 1937; 2097.

17. There is mention in Elyseo Taylor's December 2, 1969, "Media Urban Crisis Staff Report" that six students, including Esparza, Rufus Howard, and Yasu Osawa (they are the first three names listed; the next three do not appear to have stayed with the program) had been hired as a student planning staff, paid monthly from October to December of 1969. Administrative files of Franklin D. Murphy, 1935–1971, University of California, Los Angeles. Office of the Chancellor, Record Series 401, box 18 (hereafter Murphy files).

18. Elyseo Taylor, "Project Report on Communicating and Learning Through Film Production Project," July 2, 1970. The Regents of the University of California, Berkeley (06900231), 1969 March 03–1970 March 02. Ford Foundation records, Grants Them-Tw (FA732H) Reel 1937; 2097.

19. See Thomas Waugh, et al., *Challenge for Change: Activist Documentary at the National Film Board of Canada* (McGill-Queen's University Press, 2010), which includes Alan Rosenthal, *"You're on Indian Land:* Interview with George Stoney."

20. See Colin Young, "Film and Social Change"; and Elyseo J. Taylor, "Film and Social Change in Africa South of the Sahara," *American Behavioral Scientist* 17, no. 3 (January/February 1974). On May 4, 1970, the two men were scheduled to give a lecture titled "Cinema and Social Change," which one can only assume was canceled due to the protest over the Kent State shootings that day. See "UC Faculty Lectures Will Probe Theater," *Los Angeles Times,* April 12, 1970. The calendar for a series of Monday night lectures, with the theme "The Theater: Reality and Illusions," is listed here, with May 4 featuring "Prof. Colin Young, chairman of the theater arts department and Elyseo Jose Taylor, assistant professor of theater arts." See also "Students, Faculty to join war protests," *Daily Bruin,* May 5, 1970, and "State of Emergency: Massive Student Action Suppressed by Police," *Daily Bruin,* May 6, 1970.

21. Colin Young, personal interview, February 27, 2017. For recent writing on Grierson, see Angela J. Aguayo, *Documentary Resistance: Social Change and Participatory Media* (New York: Oxford University Press, 2019), 34–35, where she confirms that for social change documentary, "by most accounts, British filmmaker John Grierson led the charge" (34).

22. Again, double 'c' MUCC refers to the Media/Urban Crisis Committee, made up of the administrators and faculty included in the planning stages of the pilot program; the single 'c' MUC refers to the program itself.

23. Henry W. McGee Jr., et al, to Vice Chancellor Paul O. Proehl, March 16, 1970, Murphy files, box 18.

24. Paul O. Proehl, letter to Henry W. McGee, et al., March 18, 1970, Murphy files, box 18.

25. Charles Z. Wilson, letter to Dr. David Saxon, March 18, 1970, Murphy files, box 18.

26. "Minutes of the Standing Committee on Ethno-Communications," May 26, 1970, Murphy files, box, 18.

27. In the 1973–74 course catalog, the name of the second course is changed to "History of African, Asian and Latin American Film." After 1974 the catalog continues to list the courses for several years without a professor named, but eventually Teshome Gabriel assumed both courses.

28. In contrast, Ronald Takaki's denial of tenure at UCLA was widely covered in the *Daily Bruin,* for example in Rick Keir, "Takaki: pioneered black studies courses," *Daily Bruin,* Tuesday, November 17, 1970, which describes reported reasons for the "popular" history teacher's tenure denial.

29. This title card was omitted from the version of Caldwell's *I & I: An African Allegory* that is included in the *L.A. Rebellion Creating a New Black Cinema*

DVD anthology produced by the UCLA Film and Television Archive. However, you can still visit the campus and request to see an original copy of the film that includes the controversial title card.

30. A memo by Elyseo Taylor, "Media Urban Crisis Staff Report" dated December 2, 1969, includes the following first-year admit names (including typos/sic): AFRO-AMERICAN; James Johnson, Rufus Howard, Wendel Handy, Stewart and Wells. AMERICAN INDIAN; Tom Nelford, Sandy Johnson, Ted Hollappa, Lorene Bennett, Arch Henry White. ASIAN AMERICAN; Yasu Osawa, Danny Quan, Ernest Harada, Daniel Norbori, Peter Takeuchi. MEXICAN AMERICAN; Moctezuma Esparza, Xavier Reyes, Francisco Martinez, Gloria Gutierrez, David Lazarin. Howard may have come the second year, as there are photos taken by Robert Nakamura of a class trip with second-year Ethno students such as Larry Clark, Eddie Wong, and Steve Tatsukawa, and Rufus Howard appears in those photos. Marie Kodani appears in the archival record as having attended a meeting of the Ethno-Communications Committee in May of 1970, and other classmates remember her, but she does not appear the original list of first-year admittees. Clark remembers shooting one of her short student films, but I have not been able to find any films where she has a directing credit. Lilian Wu presented me with a snapshot of herself with Kodani and Native American MA student Rita Keshena from the "Ethno days" for my article "Searching for Betty Chen: Rediscovering the Asian American Filmmakers of UCLA in the Seventies," *Film Quarterly* 73, no. 3 (2020). Kodani did camera work on Lilian Wu's film *In Transit: The Chinese in California* (1977).

31. Much more could be said about the connections between these movement magazines and the key Ethno filmmakers who worked for each of them. For example, Garza and Esparza worked for *La Raza*. Laura Ho is one of the founding editors of *Gidra* and at least Mary Uyematsu Kao, Eddie Wong, and Duane Kubo contributed writing and photography. Sandra Osawa was the editor for *Talking Leaf* in the years between UCLA and *The Native American Series*, and she regularly covered issues such as police brutality against Native Americans in Southern California.

32. Luis Garza, personal interview, May 27, 2016.

33. Note: in this chapter I use the term "Muccers" or "Mother Muccers" to indicate the first class of students in the program, which in its first year was commonly referred to as the Media Urban Crisis program and had not yet been given the "Ethno-Communications" name. In this chapter I will tend to refer to the second class as the Ethno filmmakers, as they were the first group of students to enter in the fall of 1970 under the new Ethno-Communications name. This distinction is more important in this chapter than the others, where I may casually use the terms interchangeably.

34. Luis Garza, personal interview.

35. Moctesuma Esparza, personal interview, June 7, 2016.

36. Moctesuma Esparza, personal interview.

37. Moctesuma Esparza, personal interview.

38. This Esparza quote is from the KCET documentary "L.A. Rebellion: A Cinematic Movement," *Artbound*, Season 14, Episode 3, 2023. Some of the original twelve mention being recruited in different ways, as shared in this chapter.

39. Moctesuma Esparza, personal interview.

40. Moctesuma Esparza, personal interview.

41. Charles Burnett, email, June 3, 2016.

42. Ben Caldwell, personal interview, June 9, 2016. When Caldwell says he was a student of Haile, he is referring at least in part to Gerima's technical role as a graduate student Teaching Assistant (TA).

43. For more on Caldwell and Kaos see the magnificent new book/work of art collaboration between Robeson Taj Frazier and Ben Caldwell, *Kaos Theory: The Afrokosmic Ark of Ben Caldwell* (Angel City Press, 2023).

44. Richard Wells, personal interview, June 11, 2016.

45. Mario da Silva remembers this project too, but as being part of "Upward Bound" where they worked with youth on a film in Sacramento (email, August 25, 2016).

46. Noriega details how a number of Ethno students, including Betty Chen, became involved in this and other Chicano public affairs programs, in some cases dropping out of UCLA to do so (*Shot in America*, 114–17). See also Mary Beltran, *Latino TV: A History* (New York: New York University Press, 2022).

47. Brian Maeda, personal interview, June 2, 2016.

48. Danny Kwan and Luis Garza, personal interview, June 7, 2016.

49. I was fortunate to trade emails with Colombian filmmaker Luis Ospina before he died, and he shared a similar sense about the Chicana/o vs the Latin American film students at UCLA at the time: "At the time we were sort of on the same wavelength: politics. Us Latin Americans were considered as "Latinos" along with the Chicanos. And of course we shared a common language" (email, May 31, 2016). Ospina also provided a roll call of the Latin American film students, including Jorge Prelorán (Argentina), Rodolfo Restifo (Venezuela), Jorge Cosío (Mexico), and Jean-Louis Jorge (Dominican Republic).

50. Brian Maeda, personal interview.

51. Nobuko Miyamoto and Chris Iijima were part of an early Asian American movement musical group with Charlie Chin sometimes called "Yellow Pearl." This is yet another example of musician activists in the community scoring or providing soundtracks for Ethno films. Nobuko is often referred to by just her first name, like Beyoncé or Cher.

52. Mary Uyematsu Kao, personal interview, June 27, 2017.

53. Sandra Osawa, email, June 28, 2016.

54. Daniel Cobb, ed., *Say We Are Nations: Documents of Politics and Protest in Indigenous America since 1887* (Chapel Hill: University of North Carolina Press, 2015), 259.

55. Victor Payan, "'Listen to your Own Voice!' An Interview with Native American Independent Filmmaker, Sandra Osawa," *In Motion Magazine*, 1997, http://www.inmotionmagazine.com/osawa.html.

56. Sandra Osawa, personal interview, March 16, 2019.

57. Sandra Osawa, email, October 1, 2014. Going forward, when speaking about Sandra Johnson Osawa and Yasu Osawa I will for the sake of clarity refer to them as Sandra and Yasu. Some writings and archival material will refer to her as Sandy Johnson. Sandra's memory of Yasu as T.A. goes along with Brian Maeda's memory that Yasu organized a trip for the Muccers to Manzanar, and seemed to be in a leadership position.

58. I invited Sandy and Yasu Osawa to a talk I gave at SCMS in 2019 in Seattle and visited privately with them the following day. We spoke a second time in August of 2023 in Seattle.

59. Saza Osawa, "An Upstream Journey: An Interview with Sandra Osawa," *Native Americans on Film: Conversations, Teaching, and Theory*, ed. M. Elise Marubbio and Eric L. Buffalohead (Lexington: University Press of Kentucky, 2013).

60. Yasu Osawa, personal interview, March 16, 2019.

61. See Nicolas Rosenthal, *Reimagining Indian Country: Native American Migration and Identity in Twentieth-Century Los Angeles* (Chapel Hill: University of North Carolina Press, 2012), 133–34.

62. Osawa offered these memories after learning that Bunny Lindquist died in 2022. Bunny's name also appears in UCLA-trained anthropologist Joan Weibel-Orlando's research on Native Americans and alcohol, where her tribal affiliation is listed as Seneca; see Joan Weibel-Orlando, "Indians, Ethnicity and Alcohol," in *The American Experience with Alcohol: Contrasting Cultural Perspectives*, edited by Linda A. Bennett and Genevieve M. Ames (New York: Plenum Press, 1985).

63. See Rita Keshena, "The Role of American Indians in Motion Pictures," *American Indian Culture and Research Journal* 1, no 2 (1974). Keshena's obituary was printed in the Wisconsin paper *The Shawano Leader*, http://www.shawano leader.com/content/keshena-remembered-dedication-menominee-tribe.

64. Thanks to Allyson Nadia Field for sharing Orie Medicinebull's 1980 film *Colliding Worlds* with me. It is streaming on the California State Library site "California Revealed" at https://californiarevealed.org/do/b266799f-aadc-4e49-9620-567c6ef5c56f. Medicinebull received her MFA in film at UCLA a decade after Sandra Osawa had entered and left the program. Diné filmmaker Arlene Bowman also received an MFA in filmmaking in 1986.

65. Robert Nakamura, personal interview, June 1, 2016.

66. Reported by Tatsukawa (1949–1984) in Renee Tajima, "Ethno-Communications: The Film Program that Changed the Color of Independent Filmmak-

ing," in *The Anthology of Asian Pacific American Film and Video* (New York: Third World Newsreel, 1985).

67. Larry Clark, oral history interview by Jacqueline Stewart and Jan-Christopher Horak, June 2, 2010, L.A. Rebellion Oral History Project, the UCLA Film and Television Archive,.

68. Clark, oral history.

69. As an actor, Whitfield also appears in Haile Gerima's *Ashes and Embers* (1982). As himself, he appears in Camille Billops and James Hatch's documentary *Finding Christa* (1991).

70. Margaret B. Wilkerson, "The Black Theatre Experience: PASLA (Performing Arts Society of Los Angeles)," in *Theatre West: Image and Impact*, ed. Dunbar H. Ogden with Douglas McDermott and Robert K. Sarlós (Amsterdam: Rodopi, 1990), 69–83.

71. Wilkerson's essay unlocks the mystery of the name "Jita Hadi." PASLA had a tradition of giving its members African or Black names "as a type of tribal identification. Motojicho, which means 'eyes that see all,' was the name given to Whitfield by the group" (79). And she says that Jitahadi (sic), the name given to Taylor, Whitfield's assistant, meant "determination."

72. Field, Horak, and Stewart, *L.A. Rebellion*, 27.

73. Larry Clark, phone interview, June 28, 2016.

74. See David E. James, "Anticipations of the Rebellion: Black Music and the Politics in Some Earlier Cinemas," and Morgan Woolsey, "Re/soundings: Music and the Political Goals of the L.A. Rebellion," both in Field, Horak, and Stewart, *L.A. Rebellion*. See also Daniel Widener, *Black Arts West: Culture and Struggle in Postwar Los Angeles* (Durham: Duke University Press, 2010), and Alessandra Raengo's work, "Encountering the Rebellion: liquid blackness Reflects on the Expansive Possibilities of the L.A. Rebellion Films" in Field, Horak, and Stewart, *L.A. Rebellion*, in conjunction with her Georgia State University–based research group, liquid blackness (liquidblackness.com). They have done tremendous symposia and exhibits centering Clark's work, especially *Passing Through*.

75. This happens again, most notably with June and Dan Kuramoto first scoring early Visual Communications projects and later appearing in Duane Kubo's UCLA thesis *Cruisin' J-Town* (1975). Also, Clora Bryant created music for Zeinabu irene Davis's *Cycles* (1989) and is the subject of her feature-length documentary *Trumpetistically Clora Bryant* (2005). Though she is more of a singer/songwriter, called "The Chicana First Lady of Song," Carmen Moreno wrote jazz-tinged original music for Sylvia Morales's *Chicana* (1979) and Moreno also appears and performs in Moctesuma Esparza's McGraw Hill series, *La Raza*, in an episode co-directed by Esperanza Vasquez (1973).

76. He was working on a second feature documentary, *To Promote the General Welfare* (1972), that features incredible footage of welfare rights champion

Johnnie Tillmon. I have only seen raw footage of this film, but the *L.A. Rebellion* editors list it as complete. Images of Tillmon and Alicia Escalante, both iconic welfare rights activists, also appear in Sylvia Morales's *A Crushing Love*, discussed in chapter 3.

77. Robert Hardgrave, "Editor's Introduction," *American Behavioral Scientist* 17, no. 3 (January/February 1974).

78. Ben Caldwell, personal interview.

79. In my interview with Larry Clark he relayed this nickname to me.

80. Sylvia Morales, personal interview, January 29, 2016.

81. Pamela Jones, oral history interview by Jacqueline Stewart, May 29, 2011, L.A. Rebellion Oral History Interviews, UCLA Film and Television Archive. Jones was a film student and discusses her student films in this interview; unfortunately there are no available screening copies. Therefore when she is described as part of the L.A. Rebellion it is usually in reference to her acting. She also appeared in Hollywood films, such as *Buck and the Preacher* (1972). Her reference to the Black Brazilian activist and founder of Teatro Experimental do Negro Abdias do Nascimento is also interesting and speaks of the Third World connections Rebellion and Ethno film students were making, in part due to the very cinema Elyseo Taylor was bringing to campus.

82. Gail Yasunaga, email, March 23, 2018.

83. Bobby Roth, phone interview, July 12, 2018. Roth has a had a prolific career as both a feature film director and episodic television director. His thesis film for UCLA, *Independence Day* (1976), starred a young Henry Sanders, in a role that he claims impressed Charles Burnett enough to cast him as the lead in *Killer of Sheep* (1977).

84. Bernard Nicolas, personal interview, August 12, 2016.

85. Mario di Silva, email, August 25, 2016.

86. Ntongela Masilela, email, August 3, 2016.

87. Ntongela Masilela, email, July 16, 2016.

88. Molefi Asante, personal interview, August 9, 2016.

3. RELATIONAL FILMOGRAPHIES OF REBELLION

1. Sekou Sundiata, "Droppin' Revolution," *Longstoryshort*, 2000, Righteous Babe Records.

2. Roseann Liu and Savannah Shange, "Toward Thick Solidarity: Theorizing Empathy in Social Justice Movements," in *Radical History Review* 131 (May 2018).

3. M. Jacqui Alexander, *Pedagogies of Crossing: Meditations on Feminism, Sexual Politics, Memory, and the Sacred* (Durham: Duke University Press, 2005), 268–69.

4. Toni Cade Bambara, "Foreword," in *This Bridge Called My Back: Writings by Radical Women of Color*, ed. Cherríe Moraga and Gloria Anzaldúa, 2nd ed. (New York: Kitchen Table: Women of Color Press, 1983), vi–vii. The "Sisters of the yam, rice . . . " etc, is a reference to the women of color collective Bambara created in her own novel, *The Salt Eaters* (1980).

5. Cherríe Moraga, "Preface," in Moraga and Anzaldúa, *This Bridge Called My Back*, xiii–xiv. For an analysis of the train passage in Moraga's preface see also Grace Kyungwon Hong and Roderick Ferguson's introduction to their co-edited *Strange Affinities: The Gender and Sexual Politics of Comparative Racialization* (Durham: Duke University Press, 2011), 9–10.

6. Moraga, "Preface," xxiv.

7. Thanks here go to Roderick Ferguson for his chapter "On the Specificities of Racial formation: Gender and Sexuality in Historiographies of Race," in *Racial Formation in the 21st Century*, ed. Daniel Martinez HoSang, Oneka LaBennett, and Laura Pulido (Berkeley: University of California Press, 2012). Ferguson suggests that "the genre of the anthology seemed particularly adept at capturing the heterogeneity of interests, aesthetic forms and racial subjectivities within women-of-color and queer-of-color formations" (51). Ferguson notes here C. G. Franklin's excellent work, *Writing Women's Communities: The Politics and Poetics of Contemporary Multi-Genre Anthologies* (Madison: University of Wisconsin Press, 1997), where she argues that the "crossings of generic boundaries enabled the unfixing of other boundaries as well," such as boundaries between the theoretical and the creative, between academic and non-academic readership (4–5).

8. Toni Cade Bambara, "Reading the Signs, Empowering the Eye: *Daughters of the Dust* and the Black Independent Cinema Movement," in *Black American Cinema*, ed. Manthia Diawara (New York: Routledge, 1993), 120.

9. Bambara, "Reading the Signs," 122.

10. Bambara, "Reading the Signs," 132–33.

11. Haile Gerima interviewed by Elvis Mitchell, March 28, 2016, KCRW.com.

12. Volumes could be written on Mae Huettig Churchill and her activism, which included raising funds for the Community Alert Patrol in Los Angeles, the organization that significantly inspired the Black Panthers' police-patrolling practices, as well as her earlier academic life, which included earning a PhD in Economics from the University of Pennsylvania. Her 1942 dissertation was called "Economic Control of the Motion Picture Industry: A Study in Industrial Organization." She was also the wife of Robert Churchill of the educational film company Churchill Films, and mother to director/cinematographer Joan Churchill. See W. D. Phillips, "A Maze of Intricate Relationships: Mae D. Huettig and Early Forays into Film Industry Studies," *Film History* Volume 27, Number 1 (2015).

13. See Jesús Salvador Treviño, *Eyewitness: A Filmmaker's Memoir of the Chicano Movement* (Houston: Arte Público Press, 2001) for his descriptions of the

New Communicators. See also Chon Noriega, *Shot in America: Television, the State and the Rise of Chicano Cinema* (Minneapolis: University of Minnesota Press, 2000). He describes Esperanza Vasquez and Francisco Martinez as former New Communicators who joined the UCLA filmmakers and "whose work would . . . define Chicano Cinema"(104). Esparza explained to me in our interview that Vasquez was an art student when she was at UCLA. Francisco Martinez was officially part of the Ethno-Communications program. Vasquez's career warrants greater research as she was also part of Sidney Poitier's efforts to recruit minority trainees for his films *Brother John* and *Buck and the Preacher*.

14. Moctesuma Esparza, personal interview, June 7, 2016.

15. Martinez speaks in Spanish; she was expertly dubbed by the beloved actress/community activist Carmen Zapata, most well-known for starring in the first bilingual children's show on PBS, *Villa Allegre*. Zapata also offered both the English and Spanish voice-over narration for Sylvia Morales's *Chicana* (1979).

16. Moctesuma Esparza, email, February 17, 2018.

17. *Claiming a Voice: The Visual Communications Story* (dir. Arthur Dong, 1990). Because of the early challenges getting access to a number of the short films by the Asian American students in Ethno, I initially saw only footage from films like *Wong Sinsaang* and *Cruisin' J-Town* in excerpts included in Dong's documentary.

18. James Naremore, *Charles Burnett: A Cinema of Symbolic Knowledge* (Oakland: University of California Press, 2017), 23.

19. Jeff Furumura, email, February 8, 2018.

20. Eddie Wong interviewed in *Claiming a Voice*.

21. See also Josslyn Luckett, "Searching for Betty Chen: Rediscovering the Asian American Filmmakers of UCLA in the Seventies," *Film Quarterly* 73, no. 3 (2020).

22. See Luckett, "Searching for Betty Chen."

23. The UCLA Film and Television Archive's copy of this animation was not dated, so we have only the sense from the subject matter that the film was likely made in 1970. The film now streams on the archive's youtube channel with the kind permission of Chen's family. See also Josslyn Luckett, "The Effervescent Artist, Educator, Activist Betty Chen," August 24, 2023, https://cinema.ucla. edu/blogs/archive-blog/2023/08/24/ the-effervescent-artist-educator-activist-betty-chen.

24. Bryan Brown, "Tragedy at Kent State," *New York Times Upfront*, March 30, 2015, 16–19.

25. This short animated piece is narrated by Nobuko Miyamoto, who wrote and sang the original music. June Kuramoto also co-produced the music for this project. In 2021 the short was re-edited and currently streams on the Smithsonian Folkways page: https://www.youtube.com/watch?v = K0tL8-j_i9Q.

26. See Raul Ruiz's "testimonio" in Mario T. Garcia, *The Chicano Generation: Testimonios of the Movement* (Oakland: University of California Press, 2015), 73, which explains that the National Chicano Moratorium Committee convened in the fall of 1969 and they organized two earlier anti-war demonstrations in December of 1969 and February of 1970.

27. See Mario T. Garcia's introduction to *Ruben Salazar, Border Correspondent: Selected Writings, 1955–1970* (Berkeley: University of California Press, 1996), 1–3, and also Chon Noriega, "Requiem for Our Beginnings," *Aztlán: A Journal of Chicano Studies* 41, no. 2 (2016).

28. Moctesuma Esparza, personal interview.

29. Jason C. Johansen, "Chicano Film History in the Making," *Los Angeles Times*, March 27, 1978.

30. Laura Ho Fineman, email, November 3, 2019.

31. A million thanks to Suzi Wong who in 2021 shared with me (via Zoom) meaningful reflections of her own experience of re-watching *Sleepwalker* fifty years later, from her tender memories of the girl she played with, to the expansive reflections on the volatile politics of the time for community organizers such as herself, her brother Eddie, and Laura.

32. This "Asian American Ethnos" curation by VC's Abraham Ferrer included Brian Maeda's student film, *Yellow Brotherhood* (1970), which is discussed in detail along with the other Asian Ethnos' work in Ming-Yuen S. Ma's fantastic essay, "Claiming a Voice: Speech, Self-Expression, and Subjectivity in Early Asian American Independent Media," in *The Routledge Companion to Asian American Media*, ed. Lori Kido Lopez and Vincent N. Phan (London: Routledge, 2017).

33. Laura Ho Fineman, personal interview, August 12, 2016.

34. Eddie Wong describes both the formation of ARM and the sit-in that led to these arrests in an oral history project conducted by the Asian American Study Center at UCLA called "Collective Memories: Founders of Asian American Studies and the Asian American Movement in Southern California," July 21, 2018, www.aasc.ucla.edu/aasc50/cm_eddiewong.aspx.

35. Tanya Hamilton's narrative feature film *Night Catches Us* (2010) was the first to come to mind, but on the documentary side there are many—from Grace Lee's *American Revolutionary: The Evolution of Grace Lee Boggs* (2013) and Damani Baker's *House on Coco Road* (2016), about his activist mother, Fannie Haughton, to Christina D. King and Elizabeth Castle's documentary on Lakota activist Madonna Thunder Hawk and her family, *Warrior Women* (2018).

36. *Chicana* was named by the Library of Congress to its National Film Registry list in 2021.

37. Sylvia Morales, "Filming a Chicana Documentary," in *Chicanos and Film: Representation and Resistance*, ed. Chon Noriega (Minneapolis: University of

Minnesota Press, 1992), 309. Musician/composer/"Chicana first lady of song" Carmen Morena provided an exquisite original score and is quoted in this article describing the "sense of self-respect" she hoped to infuse in her music for the inspiring project, "a story about us, Chicanas!" (310).

38. Rosa Linda Fregoso, "Chicana Film Practices: Confronting the 'Many-Headed Demon of Oppression,'" in Noriega, *Chicanos and Film*, 172.

39. See "Elizabeth (Betita) Sutherland Martinez: A Chronology," *Social Justice* 39 Issue 2/3 (2012): 3–11. As far back as the late 1940s, she was working at the UN as a researcher on decolonial struggles in West Africa. She was one of two Chicanas active in the Student Non-Violent Coordinating Committee (SNCC), working as the director of the NYC SNCC office and as editor/writer of key SNCC publications such as *The Movement: Documentary of a Struggle for Equality* (New York: Simon and Schuster, 1964) and *Letters from Mississippi* (New York: McGraw Hill, 1965). Martinez passed away at the age of 95, on June 29, 2021.

40. Sylvia Morales, personal interview, January 29, 2016.

41. For more on these solidarity struggles see historian Rosie Bermudez's work on Alicia Escalante, including "Chicana Militant Dignity Work: Building Coalition and Solidarity in the Los Angeles Welfare Rights Movement," *Southern California Quarterly* 102, no. 4 (2020).

42. I'm aware that I do not engage in cross-racial/intertextual echo work with Moraga's storyline in *Crushing* because there frankly is not a parallel story within the films I discuss as part of the wider Ethno filmography that deals as directly as she does with queer desire, with coming out, with co-parenting between women. There are certainly works by and about queer women of color who did NOT attend UCLA in the '70s or '80s, that fully dwell in the realm of desire that Moraga describes in her monologue in *Crushing*. I am thinking especially of Bay Area filmmaker Aarin Burch's *Spin Cycle* from 1989 and of course the work of Cheryl Dunye. Michelle Parkerson mentions both of these filmmakers' works along with her own in her 1991 essay "Birth of a Notion: Toward Black, Gay, and Lesbian Imagery in Film and Video," reprinted in *Sisters in the Life: A History of Out African American Lesbian Media Making*, ed. Yvonne Welbon and Alexandra Juhasz (Durham: Duke University Press, 2018).

43. See Bermudez, "Chicana Militant Dignity Work," and Robin D. G. Kelley, "Getting to Freedom City," *Boston Review*, October 7, 2020.

4. USES OF ETHNO

Epigraph: Audre Lorde, "Uses of the Erotic, the Erotic as Power," in *Sister Outsider* (Trumansburg, NY: Crossing Press, 1984), 49.

1. Lorde, "Uses of the Erotic," 51–52.

2. Josslyn Luckett, "Rebellion Musics: The Reel Multiracial Jazz Archive Way out West," in *Rebel Musics, Volume 2: Human Rights, Resistant Sounds, and the Politics of Music Making*, ed. Daniel Fischlin and Ajay Heble (Montreal: Black Rose Books, 2021).

3. The Anthony Macías quotes in this paragraph are from "California Composer Laureate: Gerald Wilson, Jazz Music, and Black-Mexican Cultural Connections," *Boom: A Journal of California* 3, no. 2 (2013): 34–51. See also Luckett, "Rebellion Musics."

4. Keith Jarrett, "'Jazz'; 40 Years Missing," *New York Times*, January 21, 2001, italics mine.

5. Scott DeVeaux, "Constructing the Jazz Tradition: Jazz Historiography," *Black American Literature Forum* 25, no. 3 (1991): 525. To dig deeper into the debates in jazz historiography see the amazing Guthrie Ramsey, *The Amazing Bud Powell: Black Genius, Jazz History, and the Challenge of Bebop* (Berkeley: University of California Press, 2013).

6. Amiri Baraka, "'Jazz and the White Critic': Thirty Years Later," in *Digging: The Afro-American Soul of American Classical Music* (Berkeley: University of California Press, 2009), 150–51.

7. Sherrie Tucker, "Big Ears: Listening for Gender in Jazz Studies," *Current Musicology*, no. 71-73 (2001-2002), 375.

8. Tucker, "Big Ears," 377.

9. Tucker, "Big Ears," 377–78.

10. "Viewers like you" is an established tag line for PBS programming. In 2022 documentary filmmaker Grace Lee launched a podcast critiquing the stated 'inclusivity' of the network called "Viewers like Us: Restoring the Public in Public Television"; see https://viewerslikeus.com.

11. David Hajdu, "Not Quite All that Jazz," *The New York Review of Books*, February 8, 2001.

12. Peter J. Paris, *The Spirituality of African Peoples: The Search for a Common Moral Discourse* (Minneapolis: Fortress Press, 1995), 147.

13. Paris, *The Spirituality of African Peoples*, 148.

14. Daniel Fischlin, Ajay Heble, and George Lipsitz, *The Fierce Urgency of Now: Improvisation, Rights, and the Ethics of Cocreation* (Durham: Duke University Press, 2013), 231.

15. Jan-Christopher Horak, "Tough Enough: Blaxploitation and the L.A. Rebellion," in *L.A. Rebellion: Creating a New Black Cinema*, ed. Allyson Nadia Field, Jan-Christopher Horak, and Jacqueline Najuma Stewart (Oakland: University of California Press, 2015), 142. Horak quotes French critic Raphaël Bassan.

16. "*I am Horace Tapscott, and I am not for sale*" is a refrain from a poem by one of Tapscott's long time Pan Afrikan People's Arkestra poets Kamau Daáood,

called "PAPA, the Lean Griot: for Horace Tapscott, pianist, arranger, composer, mentor, community arts activist, beloved patriarch," in *Language of Saxophones: Selected Poems* (San Francisco: City Lights, 2005), 95–99.

17. Both the title of Tapscott's biography and of his 1978 solo piano LP.

18. Arkestra member Roberto Miranda played bass in the "People's Quintet," the ensemble credited for providing the score for Gerima's student film *Child of Resistance* (1972).

19. See Steven L. Isoardi, *The Dark Tree: Jazz and the Community Arts in Los Angeles* (Berkeley: University of California Press, 2006), 93.

20. See also Horace Tapscott, *Songs of the Unsung: The Musical and Social Journey of Horace Tapscott*, ed. Steven Isoardi (Durham: Duke University Press, 2001), 17–18.

21. Daáood, *Language of Saxophones*, 98.

22. For more on Clora Bryant see her entry in the book she co-edited, *Central Avenue Sounds: Jazz in Los Angeles* (Berkeley: University of California Press, 1998), 342–68.

23. A five-minute version of *Trumpetistically Clora Bryant* was produced in 1989, and the feature-length version was completed in 2005.

24. For more on Kuramoto's life and activism, see Susan Asai, "Sansei Voices in the Community: Japanese American Musicians in California," in *The Music of Multicultural America: Performance, Identity, and Community in the United States*, ed. Kip Lornell and Anne Rasmussen (Jackson: University Press of Mississippi, 2016).

25. *Cruisin' J-Town* received the honor of being inducted into the Library of Congress's National Film Registry in 2023, the same year as Ethno classmate Larry Clark's *Passing Through*.

26. It is important to point out that Johnny Mori's interview in *Cruisin'* segues to performance footage of his drumming with the Kinnara Taiko ensemble. As Kubo points out whenever he screens the film, this footage features the vanguard of Asian American Taiko players, including Kinnara founder Rev Masao "Mas" Kodani, Qris Yamashita, Wendy Mori, and the globally renowned Taiko musician/teacher Kenny Endo, in one of his earliest Taiko performances. For more on Asian American Taiko see Deborah Wong, *Louder and Faster: Pain, Joy, and the Body Politic in Asian American Taiko* (Oakland: University of California Press, 2019).

27. Thanks to S. Pearl Sharp's documentary *Fertile Ground: Stories from the Watts Towers Arts Center* (2004), I learned of this concert from the inclusion of a shot of a pink flyer that reads: "Simon Rodia/Watts Towers Jazz Festival, July 1st and 2nd, 1978 . . . featuring Henry Franklin, Hiroshima, Frank Morgan, Horace Tapscott Arkestra."

28. Saza Osawa, "An Upstream Journey: An Interview with Sandra Osawa," in *Native Americans on Film: Conversations, Teaching, and Theory*, ed. M. Elise

Marubbio and Eric L. Buffalohead (Lexinton: University Press of Kentucky, 2013), 320. Here Sandra is interviewed by her daughter, and the other films of hers she refers to are *Maria Tallchief* (2007) and *On and Off the Res' with Charlie Hill* (2000).

29. See Ron Welburn, "Native Americans in Jazz, Blues, and Popular Music," in *Indivisible: African-Native American Lives in the Americas,* ed. Gabrielle Tayac (Washington, DC: National Museum of the American Indian, 2009). See also Jeff Berglund, Jan Johnson, and Kimberli Lee, eds., *Indigenous Pop: Native American Music From Jazz to Hip Hop* (Tucson: University of Arizona Press, 2016). For Bailey see also the thrilling music documentary *Rumble: The Indians Who Rocked the World* (dir. Catherine Bainbridge and Alfonso Maiorana, 2017).

30. Moore (Pima/Akimel O'odham, 1912–1983) played in several iterations of Armstrong's band, including the 1964 Armstrong All Stars who recorded "Hello, Dolly." For the purposes of this chapter's effort to call for a reconsideration of the other people of color in this music it should be noted that Armstrong and Moore shared the bandstand with drummer Danny Barcelona, who was a Filipino musician from Hawai'i. Watch his epic solo in Armstrong's performance in *Jazz on a Summer's Day* (Bert Stern, 1959). For all the screen time and talk of Armstrong in Ken Burns's *Jazz,* including lengthy discussions of "Hello, Dolly," there is no mention of the thoroughly multiracial All Star band.

31. Chad Hamill, "American Indian Jazz: Mildred Bailey and the Origins of America's Most Musical Art Form," in Berglund, Johnson, and Lee, *Indigenous Pop,* 33.

32. Jonathan Kirshner, *Hollywood's Last Golden Age: Politics, Society, and the Seventies Film in America* (Ithaca: Cornell University Press, 2012), 2.

33. Nathan Abrams and Gregory Frame, "Introduction," in *New Wave, New Hollywood: Reassessment, Recovery, and Legacy,* ed. Nathan Abrams and Gregory Frame (New York: Bloomsbury, 2021), 6–7.

34. Kirshner, *Hollywood's Last Golden Age,* 2.

35. Much has been written about the shortcomings of this New Hollywood filmography as it relates to gender and white women both in front of and behind the camera; see the important work of Maya Montañez Smukler, *Liberating Hollywood: Women Directors and the Feminist Reform of 1970s American Cinema* (New Brunswick: Rutgers University Press, 2019).

36. Christopher Sieving, *Soul Searching: Black-Themed Cinema from the March on Washington to the Rise of Blaxploitation* (Middletown, CT: Wesleyan University Press: 2011), 163 and 184. He makes the point of the collaboration between a white director and Black screenwriter, but also emphasizes that of the "white filmmakers who sustained an auteurist-based movement . . . known variously as the New Hollywood cinema or Hollywood Renaissance" only Robert Altman's *Nashville* (1975) "makes use of black actors (Timothy Brown and Robert DoQui) in what might charitably be classified as featured parts." He points

out that of the "secondary entries" in the canon Ashby's *The Last Detail* and Schrader's *Blue Collar* use Black actors (Otis Young, Richard Pryor, and Yaphet Kotto) in leading roles (184).

37. Marsha Goodman also directed an earlier student project, *Spirit Song* (1976), about Alison Mills Newman. Newman's long-out-of-print novel *Francisco* has recently resurfaced and been championed by Saidiya Hartman, who wrote a foreword to the 2023 edition. Hopefully more readers can connect the "rediscovered" author to Goodman's warm-hearted student film about Mills Newman's young life as a singer and actress in Los Angeles.

38. Ashby's 1978 Vietnam War drama, *Coming Home,* shot south of Los Angeles, must also be reflected on as piece that gestures nobly toward addressing Black and Latino quadriplegics wounded in that war, but after the first spectacular, largely improvised pool table scene, there is hardly a line of dialogue spoken by any vet who is not white. For a "more perfect" consideration of Vietnam on film, I often screen *Coming Home* alongside *Ashes and Embers* (Gerima, 1982) and *Requiem 29* (Garcia, 1970), both addressed in chapter 3.

39. See R. B. Pippin, *Filmed Thought: Cinema as Reflective Form* (Chicago: University of Chicago Press, 2019). Pippin points out that if Jake "had heard anything other than the mispronunciation, he would already have had the film's most important clue" (104). See also Ralph Armbruster-Sandoval's analysis of *Chinatown* in "A People's History of Los Angeles: Teaching the Brown/Black Metropolis—Is Another Los Angeles Possible?," *Latino Studies* 8 (2010): 271–83.

40. *In Transit* was digitally restored by UCLA Film and Television Archive in 2023 and received a public screening at the Hammer Museum followed by a q&a with Lilian Wu, as part of a new student film restoration initiative called "Present Preserving the Past," https://www.cinema.ucla.edu/events/2023/12/1 /ucla-student-film-restorations-present-preserving-past.

41. Hong and Quo are two of the lead narrators, but there are others. Laura Ho, the director of *Sleepwalker,* also spoke with me about the support and encouragement she received from Beulah Quo.

42. There are a number of wonderful anecdotes about supportive Hollywood talent—from TV regulars Carmen Zapata and Pat Li, to film actress Lonette McKee—rolling up to the set in fancy Mercedes vehicles, willing to work for pennies. See for example the introduction to *Illusions* in Phyllis Klotman, ed., *Screenplays of the African American Experience* (Bloomington: Indiana University Press, 1991), 193.

43. In "L.A. Rebellion Oral Histories," a chapter in *L.A. Rebellion: Creating a New Black Cinema,* Dash explains, "we [she and Moroccan cinematographer Ahmed El Maanouni] shot *Illusions* on black-and-white reversal and I was going for that 1940s film noir, very rich, rich velvety Black (sic) look, so we used

reversal stock. And when I brought it to the labs here, they said, 'Oh, this is . . . underexposed'. . . 'No it's not . . . it's film noir'" (335–36).

44. Jans Wager does a great reading of the incest secret of Faye Dunaway's Mulwray in comparison to the racial lineage secret of Jennifer Beals's Daphne Monet in Carl Franklin's *Devil in a Blue Dress*. See *Dangerous Dames: Women and Representation in the Weimar Street Film and Film Noir* (Athens: Ohio University Press, 1999), 125.

45. Consider Mulwray/Dunaway's veil in the restaurant meeting with Gittes/ Nicholson forty-five minutes into the film.

46. Julie Dash, email, July 12, 2024.

47. Stephen Farber, "Couples," *The Hudson Review* 23, no. 1 (1970): 103.

48. Kirshner, *Hollywood's Last Golden Age*, 77.

49. "Real world" is the phrase that Farber uses to describe the "day to day living" Bob and Carol return to after their retreat.

50. Though *A Different Image* was finished before the 1983 chart-topping single "Walking in L.A.," by Missing Persons, was released, Larkin's film—with its multiple scenes of Black women and men walking in L.A.—stands as such a respectful counter to the repetitive erasure of the pop tune's lyric "nobody walks in L.A."

51. *Cinco Vidas/Five Lives,* Esparza's UCLA thesis film (directed by José Luis Ruiz), was aired on NBC and won a local Emmy. See Lorenza Munoz, "The Warrior Within: Producer Moctesuma Esparza, a veteran Chicano activist, still fights for Latino rights. But as the years have passed, he has learned to soften his approach," *Los Angeles Times,* September, 5, 1999. The quote in the text is a line from the show's narration.

52. Farber, "Couples," 106.

53. Kirshner, *Hollywood's Last Golden Age*, 78.

54. Sam Wasson, *Paul on Mazursky* (Middletown, CT: Wesleyan University Press), 6.

55. Monaco is quoted in Wasson, *Paul on Mazursky, 3.*

56. See Josslyn Luckett, "Digging and Bluing with Billy Woodberry," *Film Quarterly* 70, no. 4 (2017), where Woodberry describes the creation of the scene as collaborative and improvisational, with only an outline provided by scriptwriter Charles Burnett (69).

57. Samantha Sheppard, "The Art of Feeling: The Presence and Performance of Kaycee Moore," the lead essay in the Milestone booklet for their DVD release of the restored print of *Bless Their Little Hearts,* 2019. See also Samantha Sheppard, "Bruising Moments: Affect and the L.A. Rebellion," in Field, Horak, and Stewart, *L.A. Rebellion.* Shepperd's designation of Moore as a co-creator of the project parallels the frequent assessment of Rowlands's co-creator status with Cassavetes on multiple projects.

58. Paris, *The Spirituality of African Peoples*, 147.

CONCLUSION

1. Renee Tajima-Peña, personal interview, February 1, 2016.

2. Sankofa Video, Books and Café, located a stone's throw from Howard University in DC, was founded by Haile and Shirikiana Gerima in 1998, named after the film they produced, *Sankofa,* in 1993. Their website defines the space as "liberated territory . . . where thoughtful consideration of the past and future can take place via books, films, and programming particularly generated by and about people of African Descent" (https://www.sankofa.com). Haile Gerima recently retired after over four decades of teaching film at Howard.

3. See Jacqueline Stewart, "Defending Black Imagination," in *Now Dig This!: Art and Black Los Angeles, 1960–1980,* ed. Kellie Jones (Los Angeles: Hammer Museum, 2011).

4. Kellie Jones, "Now Dig This! An Introduction," in Jones, *Now Dig This!,* 24.

5. Nakamura playfully explains his "early midlife crisis" in an interview for Arthur Dong's documentary, *Claiming a Voice: The Visual Communications Story* (1990).

6. Karen Higa, "Black Art in L.A.: Photographs by Robert A. Nakamura," in Jones, *Now Dig This!,* 51–55. Visit this essay, which is also available on the Hammer Museum webpage (https://hammer.ucla.edu/now-dig-this) to see six of Nakamura's photographic portraits. Higa's essay cites Robert Fogelson's work *The Fragmented Metropolis: Los Angeles, 1850–1930* (Berkeley: University of California Press, 1983), yet it also calls to mind Mike Davis, *City of Quartz* (New York: Verso, 1990).

7. To clarify, the Asian American Studies department at UCLA houses the Center for EthnoCommunications that was founded by Ethno alum Robert Nakamura in 1996 and is surely inspired by the original multiracial Ethno-Communications Program in the film school. Its website does not mention the Ethno program started by Elyseo Taylor; see https://www.aasc.ucla.edu/ethno/about.aspx.

8. Fischlin et al., *The Fierce Urgency of Now: Improvisation, Rights, and the Ethics of Cocreation,* 234.

9. Lawson Inada, letter to author, May 23, 2016. Inada also relayed to me that he felt a kind of kinship to Eddie Wong as the only Chinese American member of the four central co-founders of Visual Communications (with Robert Nakamura, Duane Kubo, and Alan Ohashi), as Inada was the one Japanese American in the foursome that included Shawn Wong, Frank Chin, and Jeffery Paul Chan who collectively edited *Aiiieeeee! An Anthology of Asian-American Writers,* which—speaking of multiracial crossings—was first published by Howard University Press in 1974.

10. See the symposium website at https://voices.uchicago.edu/sojourner. Also see Hayley O'Malley, "The 1976 Sojourner Truth Festival of the Arts: A Specula-

tive History of the First Black Women's Film Festival," *Feminist Media Histories* 8, no. 3 (2022).

11. O.Funmilayo Makarah, "Fired Up!," in *Black Women Film and Video Artists,* ed. Jacqueline Bobo (New York: Routledge, 1998), 136.

12. Robin D. G. Kelley, *Freedom Dreams: The Black Radical Imagination* (Boston: Beacon Press, 2002), ix. John Marquez, *Black-Brown Solidarity: Racial Politics in the New Gulf South* (Austin: University of Texas Press, 2013), guided me back to Kelley, within Marquez's larger critique of the tension between scholars of social movements and "the activists who create, participate in, and maintain them" (35).

Selected Filmography

This filmography represents an ongoing labor of love. It primarily includes work by filmmakers of color who were students in or closely associated with either the MUC program and/or the Ethno-Communications Program. It also contains films from the L.A. Rebellion filmography that I address or mention in this book. I have also included one film by a UCLA film school student, Marsha Goodman, who was not directly linked with either program, but whose thesis film was associate-produced by an Ethno student, Francisco Martinez. I am exceptionally grateful for the model of the filmography assembled by Allyson Nadia Field, Jan Christopher Horak, and Jacqueline Najuma Stewart at the conclusion of their book *L.A. Rebellion: Creating a New Black Cinema*. I also hope to steer readers to the DVD collection they produced in conjunction with the UCLA Film and Television Archive and which has been in circulation since 2015 (https://www.cinema.ucla.edu/la-rebellion-dvd). My aim is to provide a working list for future researchers and to give as much information as I can about where and how to see and in a few instances stream these films. Many thanks to Maya Montañez Smukler and Mark Quigley at the UCLA Film and Television Archive for lending their empowered eyes to this list. Thank you also to the filmmakers who generously provided me with materials and temporary links of their films from their personal archives.

Shirikiana Aina

> *Brick by Brick*, 1982 (33 min), UCLA Film & Television Archive, L.A. Rebellion DVD anthology

Melvonna Ballenger

Rain (Nyesha), 1978 (16 min), UCLA Film & Television Archive, L.A. Rebellion DVD anthology

Carroll Parrott Blue

Varnette's World: A Study of a Young Artist, 1979 (25 min), Third World Newsreel, streaming Internet Archive

Charles Burnett

Several Friends, 1969 (22 min), Milestone Films (DVD), UCLA Film & Television Archive, L.A. Rebellion DVD anthology

The Horse, 1973 (14 min), Milestone Films (DVD)

Killer of Sheep*, 1977 (81 min) Milestone Films (DVD), streaming Kanopy

Ben Caldwell

I & I: An African Allegory, 1979 (32min), UCLA Film & Television Archive, L.A. Rebellion DVD anthology

Betty Chen

Portraits of a Young Girl, 1970? (2 min), streaming UCLA Film & Television YouTube channel

Rainbow Car Wash, 1977? (19 min) UCLA Film & Television Archive

Larry Clark

Tamu, 1970 (12 min), UCLA Film & Television Archive

As Above, So Below, 1973 (52 min), UCLA Film & Television Archive, L.A. Rebellion DVD anthology

Passing Through*, 1977 (111 min) UCLA Film & Television Archive

Julie Dash

Four Women, 1975 (7 min), Women Make Movies, streaming Kanopy

Diary of an African Nun, 1977 (15 min), Women Make Movies, streaming Kanopy, also UCLA Film and Television Archive, L.A. Rebellion DVD anthology

Illusions*, 1982 (36 min), Women Make Movies, streaming Kanopy

Daughters of the Dust*, 1991 (112 min), Cohen Film Collection, streaming Kanopy

Zeinabu irene Davis

Cycles, 1989 (17 min), Women Make Movies, UCLA Film & Television Archive, L.A. Rebellion DVD anthology

Trumpetistically Clora Bryant, 2005 (57 min)

Spirits of Rebellion: Black Independent Cinema from Los Angeles, 2017 (101 min), The Cinema Guild (DVD/Blu-ray).

Jeff Furumura

I Don't Think I Said Much, 1971 (16 min), from the collection *Beyond the Japanese Garden: Short Stories and Documentaries* (Japanese American National Museum DVD, 2007).

David Garcia (d) Moctesuma Esparza (p)

Requiem 29*, 1970 (32 min), UCLA Film & Television Archive

Haile Gerima

Hour Glass, 1971 (13 min), Mypheduh Films, available as bonus feature on DVD of *Bush Mama*, also UCLA Film & Television Archive, L.A. Rebellion DVD anthology

Child of Resistance, 1972 (36 min), Mypheduh Films, available as bonus feature on DVD of *Bush Mama*.

Bush Mama*, 1975 (97min), Mypheduh Films (DVD)

Wilmington 10—USA 10,000, 1979 (120 min)

Ashes and Embers, 1982 (129 min), Mypheduh Films (DVD)

Marsha Goodman

Not Gone, Not Forgotten, 1982 (30 min), streaming YouTube

Laura Ho

Sleepwalker, 1971 (13 min), UCLA Film & Television Archive

Duane Kubo

Cruisin' J-Town*, 1975 (24 min), New Day Films, Visual Communications Archives

Something's Rotten in Little Tokyo, 1977 (co-directed with Eddie Wong, color, 38 min), Visual Communications Archives

Hito Hata: Raise the Banner, 1980 (co-directed with Robert Nakamura, color, 90min), Third World Newsreel, Visual Communications Archives

Danny Kwan

Homecoming Game, 1970 (21 min), UCLA Film & Television Archive

Alile Sharon Larkin

The Kitchen, 1975 (7 min), UCLA Film & Television Archive YouTube channel

A Different Image, 1982 (51 min), Women Make Movies, UCLA Film & Television Archive

Brian Maeda

Yellow Brotherhood, 1970 (20 min), UCLA Film and Television Archive

O.Funmilayo Makarah

Define, 1988 (5 min), UCLA Film & Television Archive

Creating a Different Image: Portrait of Alile Sharon Larkin, 1989 (5min), UCLA Film & Television Archive

Diversity, 1989 (12 min), UCLA Film & Television Archive

L.A. in My Mind, 2006 (4 min), UCLA Film & Television Archive, L.A. Rebellion DVD anthology

Barbara McCullough

Water Ritual #1: An Urban Rite of Purification, 1979 (6 min), Third World Newsreel, UCLA Film & Television Archive, L.A. Rebellion DVD anthology

The World Saxophone Quartet, 1980 (5 min), Third World Newsreel, UCLA Film & Television Archive

Shopping Bag Spirits and Freeway Fetishes: Reflections on Ritual Space, 1981 (60 min), Third World Newsreel, UCLA Film & Television Archive

Horace Tapscott: Musical Griot, 2017 (color, 72 min)

Sylvia Morales

Chicana*, 1979 (23 min), Women Make Movies, streaming Kanopy

A Crushing Love: Chicanas, Motherhood and Activism, 2009 (58 min), Women Make Movies, streaming Kanopy

Robert Nakamura

Manzanar*, 1971 (16 min), Visual Communications Archive

Wataridori: Birds of Passage, 1977 (37 min), New Day Films, Visual Communications Archive

Hito Hata, 1980 (see Kubo)

Bernard Nicolas

Daydream Therapy, 1977 (8 min), UCLA Film & Television Archive YouTube channel

Sandra Osawa

Curios, 1970 (2 min), Upstream Productions

In the Heart of Big Mountain, 1988 (28 min), Upstream Productions (DVD)

Pepper's Pow Wow, 1997 (59 min), Upstream Productions (DVD)

Maria Tallchief, 2007 (57 min), Upstream Productions (DVD)

Jose Luis Ruiz (d) and Moctesuma Esparza (p, w)

Cinco Vidas, 1973 (51 min), UCLA Film & Television Archive

Elyseo Taylor

Black Art, Black Artists, 1971 (16 min), UCLA Film & Television Archive, L.A. Rebellion DVD anthology

Esperanza Vasquez (d) Moctesuma Esparza (p)

Agueda Martinez, 1977 (17 min), Moctesuma Esparza Productions, UCLA Film & Television Archive

Richard Wells

Teddy, 1971 (16 min), University of California Los Angeles, Extension Media Center, streaming Internet Archive

Eddie Wong

> *Wong Sinsaang*, 1971 (12 min), New Day Films, Visual Communications
> Archive
>
> *Something's Rotten in Little Tokyo*, 1977 (see Kubo)

Billy Woodberry

> *Bless Their Little Hearts**, 1984 (84 min), Milestone Films, streaming
> Kanopy

Lilian Wu

> *In Transit: The Chinese in California*, 1977 (25 min), UCLA Film &
> Television Archive YouTube channel

*indicates the film has been named to the Library of Congress National
Film Registry List

Bibliography

Abrams, Nathan, and Gregory Frame, eds. *New Wave, New Hollywood: Reassessment, Recovery, and Legacy.* New York: Bloomsbury, 2021.

Aguayo, Angela J. *Documentary Resistance: Social Change and Participatory Media.* New York: Oxford University Press, 2019.

Alexander, M. Jacqui. *Pedagogies of Crossing: Meditations on Feminism, Sexual Politics, Memory, and the Sacred.* Durham: Duke University Press, 2005.

Alvarez, Luis. "From Zoot Suits to Hip Hop: Towards a Relational Chicana/o Studies." Latino Studies 5 (2007): 53–75.

Anderson, Trezzvant W. *Come Out Fighting: The Epic Tale of the 761st Tank Battalion, 1942–1945.* Salzburg: Salzburger Druckerei und Verlag, 1945.

Armbruster-Sandoval, Ralph. "A People's History of Los Angeles: Teaching the Brown/Black Metropolis—Is Another Los Angeles Possible?" *Latino Studies* 8 (2010): 271–83.

Asai, Susan M. "Sansei Voices in the Community: Japanese American Musicians in California." In *The Music of Multicultural America: Performance, Identity, and Community in the United States,* edited by Kip Lornell and Anne K. Rasmussen, 368–94. Jackson: University of Mississippi Press, 2016.

Bambara, Toni Cade. "Foreword" to *This Bridge Called My Back: Writings by Radical Women of Color,* edited by Cherríe Moraga and Gloria Anzaldúa, vi–viii. New York: Kitchen Table: Women of Color Press, 1983.

———. "Preface" to Daughters of the Dust: *The Making of an African American Woman's Film*, by Julie Dash, xi–xvi. New York: New Press, 1992.

———. "Reading the Signs, Empowering the Eye: *Daughters of the Dust* and the Black Independent Cinema Movement." In Diawara, *Black American Cinema*, 118-144.

Baraka, Amiri. "'Jazz and the White Critic': Thirty Years Later." In *Digging: The Afro-American Soul of American Classical Music*, 145–54. Berkeley: University of California Press, 2009.

Beltran, Mary. *Latino TV: A History*. New York: New York University Press, 2021.

Berglund, Jeff, Jan Johnson, and Kimberli Lee, eds. *Indigenous Pop: Native American Music From Jazz to Hip Hop*. Tucson: University of Arizona Press, 2016.

Bermudez, Rosie. "Chicana Militant Dignity Work: Building Coalition and Solidarity in the Los Angeles Welfare Rights Movement." *Southern California Quarterly* 102, no. 4 (2020): 420–55.

Biondi, Martha. *The Black Revolution on Campus*. Berkeley: University of California Press, 2012.

Biskind, Peter. *Easy Riders, Raging Bulls: How the Sex-Drugs-And-Rock 'n' Roll Generation Saved Hollywood*. New York: Simon and Schuster, 1998.

Bobo, Jacqueline. *Black Women as Cultural Readers*. New York: Columbia University Press, 1995.

Bobo, Jacqueline, ed. *Black Women Film and Video Artists*. New York: Routledge, 1998.

Bogle, Donald. *Toms, Coons, Mulattoes, Mammies and Bucks: An Interpretive History of Blacks in American Films*. 4th ed. New York: Bloomsbury, 2001.

Brown, Elaine. *A Taste of Power: A Black Woman's Story*. New York: Anchor Books, 1992.

Brown, Scot. *Fighting for US: Maulana Karenga, the US Organization, and Black Cultural Nationalism*. New York: New York University Press, 2003.

Bryant, Clora, Buddy Collette, William Green, Steven Isoardi, Jack Kelson, Horace Tapscott, Gerald Wilson, and Marl Young, eds. *Central Avenue Sounds: Jazz in Los Angeles*. Berkeley: University of California Press, 1998.

Cobb, Daniel, ed. *Say We Are Nations: Documents of Politics and Protest in Indigenous America Since 1887*. Chapel Hill: University of North Carolina Press, 2015.

Collison, Craig. "The Fight to Legitimize Blackness: How Black Students Changed the University." PhD dissertation, University of Washington, 2008.

Critical Ethnic Studies Editorial Collective. "Introduction: A Sightline." In *Critical Ethnic Studies Reader*, edited by Nada Ellis, David Hernandez, Jodi Kim, Shana L. Redmond, Dylan Rodriguez, and Sarita Echavez See, 1–15. Durham: Duke University Press, 2016.

Daáood, Kamau. *The Language of Saxophones: Selected Poems of Kamau Daáood*. City Lights, 2005.

Davis, Mike. *City of Quartz: Excavating the Future in Los Angeles*. New York: Verso, 2006.

DeVeaux, Scott. "Constructing the Jazz Tradition: Jazz Historiography," *Black American Literature Forum*, Literature of Jazz, 25, no. 3 (Autumn, 1991): 525–60.

Diawara, Manthia, ed. *Black American Cinema*. New York: Routledge, 1993.

DiNicolo, Gina M. *The Black Panthers: A Story of Race, War and Courage—the 761st Tank Battalion and WWII*. Yardley, PA: Westholme Publishing, 2014.

Drinnon, Richard. *Keeper of Concentration Camps: Dillon S. Myer and American Racism*. Berkeley: University of California Press, 1987.

"Elizabeth (Betita) Sutherland Martinez: A Chronology." *Social Justice* 39, Issue 2/3 (2012): 3–11.

Ellison, Ralph. *Shadow and Act*. New York: Random House, 1964.

Elsaesser, Thomas. "The Pathos of Failure: American Films of the 1970s, Notes on the Unmotivated Hero." In *The Last Great American Picture Show: New Hollywood Cinema in the 1970s*, edited by Thomas Elsaesser, Alexander Horwath, and Noel King. Amsterdam: Amsterdam University Press. 2004.

Escobedo, Elizabeth R. *From Coveralls to Zoot Suits: The Lives of Mexican American Women on the World War II Home Front*. Chapel Hill: University of North Carolina Press, 2013.

Farber, Stephen. "Couples." *The Hudson Review* 23, no. 1 (1970).

Ferguson, Roderick A. "On the Specificities of Racial Formation: Gender and Sexuality in Historiographies of Race." In *Racial Formation in the 21st Century*, edited by Daniel Martinez HoSang, Oneka LaBennett, and Laura Pulido, 44–56. Berkeley: University of California Press, 2012.

Field, Allyson Nadia. "Rebellious Unlearning: UCLA Project One Films (1967–1978)." In Field, Horak, and Stewart, *L.A. Rebellion: Creating a New Black Cinema*, 83-118.

Field, Allyson Nadia, Jan-Christopher Horak, and Jacqueline Najuma Stewart, eds. *L.A. Rebellion: Creating a New Black Cinema*. Oakland: University of California Press, 2015.

———. "L.A. Rebellion Oral Histories." In Field, Horak, and Stewart, *L.A. Rebellion: Creating a New Black Cinema*, 321-53.

Fischlin, Daniel, and Ajay Heble. *Rebel Musics, Vol 2: Human Rights, Resistant Sounds, and the Politics of Music Making*. Montreal: Black Rose Books, 2021.

Fischlin, Daniel, Ajay Heble, and George Lipsitz. *The Fierce Urgency of Now: Improvisation, Rights, and the Ethics of Cocreation*. Durham: Duke University Press, 2013.

Floyd, Jacob. "History Lives in the Present." *Film Comment*, October 30, 2023.

Fogelson, Robert. *The Fragmented Metropolis: Los Angeles, 1850–1930.*
Berkeley: University of California Press, 1983.

Ford, Tanisha. *Our Secret Society: Mollie Moon and the Glamour, Money, and Power Behind the Civil Rights Movement.* New York: Amistad, 2023.

Franklin, Cynthia G. *Writing Women's Communities: The Politics and Poetics of Contemporary Multi-Genre Anthologies.* Madison: University of Wisconsin Press, 1997.

Frazier, Robeson Taj, and Ben Caldwell. *Kaos Theory: The Afrokosmic Ark of Ben Caldwell.* Angel City Press, 2023.

Fregoso, Rosa Linda. "Chicana Film Practices: Confronting the 'Many-Headed Demon of Oppression." In Noriega, *Chicanos and Film*, 168–82.

Garcia, Mario. *The Chicano Generation: Testimonios of the Movement.* Oakland: University of California Press, 2015.

———. "Introduction." In *Ruben Salazar, Border Correspondent: Selected Writings, 1955–1970,* edited by Mario Garcia, 1–28. Berkeley: University of California Press, 1996.

Gelmis, Joseph. "Francis Ford Coppola: Free Agent within the System." In *Francis Ford Coppola: Interviews,* edited by Gene D. Phillips and Rodney Hill, 3–16. Jackson: University of Mississippi Press, 1998.

Glick, Joshua. *Los Angeles Documentary and the Production of Public History, 1958–1977.* Oakland: University of California Press, 2018.

Hamill, Chad. "American Indian Jazz: Mildred Bailey and the Origins of America's Most Musical Art Form." In *Indigenous Pop: Native American Music from Jazz to Hip Hop,* edited by Jeff Berglund, Jan Johnson, and Kimberli Lee, 33–46. Tucson: University of Arizona Press, 2016.

Hardgrave, Robert. "Editor's Introduction." *American Behavioral Scientist* 17, no. 3 (January/February 1974): 325–27.

Harjo, Joy. "The Path to the Milky Way Leads Through Los Angeles." In *A Map to the Next World: Poems and Tales.* New York: W.W. Norton & Company, 2000.

Higa, Karin. "Black Art in L.A. Photographs by Robert Nakamura." In *Now Dig This!: Art and Black Los Angeles, 1960–1980,* edited by Kellie Jones, 51–56. Los Angeles: Hammer Museum, 2011.

Hitch, Charles, J. "President Hitch's Inaugural Address at UCLA." *University Bulletin: A Weekly Bulletin for the Staff of the University of California* 16, no. 34 (May 27, 1968).

Hong, Grace Kyungwon, and Roderick A. Ferguson, eds. *Strange Affinities: The Gender and Sexual Politics of Comparative Racialization.* Durham: Duke University Press, 2011.

Horak, Jan-Christopher. "Tough Enough: Blaxploitation and the L.A. Rebellion." In Field, Horak, and Stewart, *L.A. Rebellion: Creating a New Black Cinema,* 119–55.

Horne, Gerald. *Fire This Time: The Watts Uprising and the 1960s*. New York: Da Capo Press, 1997.

Inada, Lawson Fusao. *Legends from Camp: Poems*. Minneapolis: Coffee House Press, 1993.

Isoardi, Steven L. *The Dark Tree: Jazz and the Community Arts in Los Angeles*. Berkeley: University of California Press, 2006.

James, David E. "Anticipations of the Rebellion: Black Music and the Politics in Some Earlier Cinemas." In Field, Horak, and Stewart, *L.A. Rebellion: Creating a New Black Cinema*, 156–70.

———. *The Most Typical Avant-Garde: History and Geography of Minor Cinemas in Los Angeles*. Berkeley: University of California Press, 2005.

Johnson, Gaye Theresa. *Spaces of Conflict, Sounds of Solidarity: Music, Race, and Spatial Entitlement in Los Angeles*. Berkeley: University of California Press, 2013.

Jones, Kellie. "Now Dig This! An Introduction." In *Now Dig This!: Art and Black Los Angeles, 1960–1980*, edited by Kellie Jones, 15–28. Los Angeles: Hammer Museum, 2011.

Kao, Mary Uyematsu. *Rockin' the Boat: Flashbacks of the 1970s Asian Movement*. Los Angeles: UCLA Asian American Studies Center, 2020.

Kelley, Robin D. G. *Freedom Dreams: The Black Radical Imagination*. New York: Beacon Press, 2003.

———. "Getting to Freedom City." *Boston Review*, October 7, 2020.

Keshena, Rita. "The Role of American Indians in Motion Pictures." *American Indian Culture and Research* 1, no. 2 (1974).

Khor, Denise. *Transpacific Convergences: Race, Migration, and Japanese American Film Culture before World War II*. Chapel Hill: UNC Press, 2022.

Kirshner, Jonathan. *Hollywood's Last Golden Age: Politics, Society, and the Seventies Film in America*. Ithaca: Cornell University Press, 2012.

Klotman, Phyllis Rauch, ed. *Screenplays of the African American Experience*. Bloomington: Indiana University Press, 1991.

Krämer, Peter. "Afterword: New Wave, New Hollywood, New Research." In *New Wave, New Hollywood: Reassessment, Recovery and Legacy*, edited by Nathan Abrams and Gregory Frame. New York: Bloomsbury Academic, 2021.

Kun, Josh, and Laura Pulido, eds. *Black and Brown in Los Angeles: Beyond Conflict and Coalition*. Berkeley: University of California Press, 2014.

Kurashige, Scott. *The Shifting Grounds of Race: Black and Japanese Americans in the Making of Multiethnic Los Angeles*. Princeton: Princeton University Press, 2008.

Lemus, Nery Gabriel. "On Fallen Nature and the Two Cities." In Kun and Pulido, *Black and Brown in Los Angeles*, 341–45.

Liu, Roseann, and Savannah Shange. "Toward Thick Solidarity: Theorizing Empathy in Social Justice Movements." *Radical History Review* 131 (May 2018): 189–98.

Lorde, Audre. "Uses of the Erotic: The Erotic as Power." In *Sister Outsider: Essays and Speeches*, 53–59. Berkeley: Crossing Press, 1984.

Luckett, Josslyn. "Digging and Bluing with Billy Woodberry." *Film Quarterly* 70, no. 4 (2017): 67–76.

———. "Rebellion Music: The Reel Multiracial Jazz Archive Way Out West." In Fischlin and Heble, *Rebel Musics, Volume 2*, 75–94.

———. "Searching for Betty Chen: Rediscovering the Asian American Filmmakers of UCLA in the Seventies." *Film Quarterly* 73, no. 3 (2020): 34–40.

MacDougall, David. "Colin Young, Ethnographic Film, and the Film Culture of the 1960s." *Visual Anthropology Review* 17, no. 2 (2001–2002): 81–88.

Macías, Anthony. "California's Composer Laureate: Gerald Wilson, Jazz Music, and Black-Mexican Connections." *Boom: A Journal of California* 3, no. 2 (Summer 2013): 34–51.

———. *Chicano Chicana Americana: Pop Culture Pluralism*. Tucson: University of Arizona Press, 2023.

———. *Mexican American Mojo: Popular Music, Dance, and Urban Culture in Los Angeles, 1935–1968*. Durham: Duke University Press, 2008.

Makarah, O.Funmilayo. "Fired Up!." In *Black Women Film and Video Artists*, edited by Jacqueline Bobo, 125–38. New York: Routledge, 1998.

Manzarek, Ray. *Light My Fire: My Life with the Doors*. New York: Putnam, 1998.

Márquez, John D. *Black-Brown Solidarity: Racial Politics in the New Gulf South*. Austin: University of Texas Press, 2013.

Masilela, Ntongela. "The Los Angeles School of Black Filmmakers." In Diawara, *Black American Cinema*, 107–17.

Massood, Paula J. *Black City Cinema: African American Urban Experiences in Film*. Philadelphia: Temple University Press, 2003.

Mimura, Glen M. *Ghostlife of Third Cinema: Asian American Film and Video*. Minneapolis: University of Minnesota Press, 2009.

Mitchell-Kernan, Claudia, ed. *40 Years of Ethnic Studies at UCLA*. Los Angeles: UCLA Graduate Division, 2010.

Miyagawa, Irene. "UCLA Sells Out." *Gidra* 1, no. 6 (September 1969).

Miyamoto, Nobuko. *Not Yo' Butterfly: My Long Song of Relocation, Race, Love, and Revolution*. Edited by Deborah Wong. Oakland: University of California Press, 2021.

Moraga, Cherríe, and Gloria Anzaldúa, eds. *This Bridge Called My Back: Writings by Radical Women of Color*. New York: Kitchen Table: Women of Color Press, 1981.

Morales, Sylvia. "Filming a Chicana Documentary (1979)." In Noriega, *Chicanos and Film: Representation and Resistance*, 308–11.

Murase, Mike. "Ethnic Studies and Higher Education for Asian Americans." In *Counterpoint: Perspectives on Asian America,* edited by Emma Gee, 205–23. Los Angeles: Asian American Studies Center, University of California, 1976.

Murashige, Mike. "Haile Gerima and the Political Economy of Cinematic Resistance." In *Representing Blackness: Issues in Film and Video,* edited by Valerie Smith, 183–204. New Brunswick: Rutgers University Press, 1997.

Naremore, James. *Charles Burnett: A Cinema of Symbolic Knowledge.* Oakland: University of California Press, 2017.

Noriega, Chon A. "City of Dreams." *Aztlán: A Journal of Chicano Studies* 37, no. 1 (2012): 1–3.

———. *Shot in America: Television, the State, and the Rise of Chicano Cinema.* Minneapolis: University of Minnesota Press, 2000.

———, ed. *Chicanos and Film: Representation and Resistance.* Minneapolis: University of Minnesota Press, 1992.

Okada, Jun. *Making Asian American Film and Video: History, Institutions, Movements.* New Brunswick: Rutgers University Press, 2015.

O'Malley, Hayley. "The 1976 Sojourner Truth Festival of the Arts: A Speculative History of the First Black Women's Film Festival." *Feminist Media Histories* 8, no. 3 (2022): 127–54.

Osawa, Saza. "An Upstream Journey: An Interview with Sandra Osawa." In *Native Americans on Film: Conversations, Teaching, and Theory,* edited by M. Elise Marubbio and Eric L. Buffalohead, 303–21. Lexington: University Press of Kentucky, 2013.

Paris, Peter J. *The Spirituality of African Peoples: The Search for a Common Moral Discourse.* Minneapolis: Fortress Press, 1995.

Parkerson, Michelle. "Birth of a Notion: Toward Black, Gay, and Lesbian Imagery in Film and Video." In *Sisters in the Life: A History of Out African American Lesbian Media Making,* edited by Yvonne Welbon and Alexandra Juhasz, 21–25. Durham: Duke University Press, 2018.

Payan, Victor. "'Listen to your Own Voice!' An Interview with Native American Independent Filmmaker, Sandra Osawa." *In Motion Magazine,* 1997.

Petrie, Duncan. "Colin Young: Interview." *Journal of British Cinema and Television* 7, no. 2 (2010): 311–323.

Phillips, W. D. "A Maze of Intricate Relationships: Mae D. Huettig and Early Forays into Film Industry Studies." *Film History* 27, no. 1 (2015): 135–63.

Pippin, R. B. *Filmed Thought: Cinema as Reflective Form.* Chicago: University of Chicago Press, 2019.

Prashad, Vijay. *The Darker Nations: A People's History of the Third World.* New York: The New Press, 2007.

Pulido, Laura. *Black, Brown, Yellow, and Left: Radical Activism in Los Angeles.* Berkeley: University of California Press, 2006.

Raengo, Alessandra. "Encountering the Rebellion: *liquid blackness* Reflects on the Expansive Possibilities of the L.A. Rebellion Films." In Field, Horak, and Stewart, *L.A. Rebellion: Creating a New Black Cinema*, 291–318.

Ramsey, Guthrie P. *The Amazing Bud Powell: Black Genius, Jazz History, and the Challenge of Bebop.* Berkeley: University of California Press, 2013.

Reid, Mark A. *Redefining Black Film.* Berkeley: University of California Press, 1993.

Rojas, Fabio. *From Black Power to Black Studies: How a Radical Social Movement Became an Academic Discipline.* Baltimore: Johns Hopkins University Press, 2007.

Rooks, Noliwe M. *White Money/Black Power: The Surprising History of African American Studies and the Crisis of Race in Higher Education.* Boston: Beacon Press, 2006.

Rosenthal, Nicolas G. *Reimagining Indian Country: Native American Migration and Identity in Twentieth-Century Los Angeles.* Chapel Hill: University of North Carolina Press, 2012.

Sanchez, George J. *Becoming Mexican American: Ethnicity, Culture, and Identity in Chicano Los Angeles (1900–1945).* New York: Oxford University Press, 1993.

———. "Why Are Multiracial Communities So Dangerous? A Comparative Look at Hawai'i; Cape Town, South Africa; and Boyle Heights, California." *Pacific Historical Review* 86, no. 1 (2017): 153–70.

Sandoval, Denise M. "The Politics of Low and Slow/Bajito y Suavecito: Black and Chicano Lowriders in Los Angeles from the 1960s through the 1970s." In Kun and Pulido, *Black and Brown in Los Angeles*, 176–200.

Schulberg, Budd. *From the Ashes: Voices of Watts.* New York: Meridian Books, 1969.

Sheppard, Samantha N. "The Art of Feeling: The Presence and Performance of Kaycee Moore." In *Bless Their Little Hearts,* Milestone DVD booklet, 2021.

———. "Bruising Moments: Affect and the L.A. Rebellion." In Field, Horak, and Stewart, *L.A. Rebellion: Creating a New Black Cinema*, 225–50.

———. "A Profound Edge: Collectivism and The New Negress Film Society." *Film Quarterly* 77, no. 1 (2023): 25–37.

Sieving, Christopher. *Soul Searching: Black Themed Cinema from the March on Washington to the Rise of Blaxploitation.* Middletown, CT: Wesleyan University Press, 2011.

Slide, Anthony. *Nitrate Won't Wait: Film Preservation in the United States.* Jefferson, NC: McFarland, 1992.

Smith, Valerie, ed. *Representing Blackness: Issues in Film and Video.* New Brunswick: Rutgers University Press, 1997.

Smukler, Maya Montañez. *Liberating Hollywood: Women Directors and the Feminist Reform of 1970s American Cinema.* New Brunswick: Rutgers University Press, 2019.

Sragow, Michael. "Godfatherhood." In *Francis Ford Coppola: Interviews,* edited by Gene D. Phillips and Rodney Hill, 167–84. Jackson: University of Mississippi Press, 1998.

Stewart, Jacqueline. "Defending Black Imagination: The 'L.A. Rebellion' School of Black Filmmakers." In *Now Dig This!: Art and Black Los Angeles 1960–1980,* edited by Kellie Jones, 41–50. Los Angeles: Hammer Museum, 2011.

Sundiata, Sekou. "Droppin' Revolution." *Longstoryshort.* Righteous Babe Records, 2000.

Tajima, Renee. "Ethno-Communications: The Film Program that Changed the Color of Independent Filmmaking," in *The Anthology of Asian Pacific American Film and Video.* New York: Third World Newsreel, 1985.

———. "Lights, Camera . . . Affirmative Action." *The Independent,* March 1984, 16–18.

Tapscott, Horace. *Songs of the Unsung: The Musical and Social Journey of Horace Tapscott.* Edited by Steven Isoardi. Durham: Duke University Press, 2001.

Tasch, Jacqueline. "The Long Road Home: Forty Years of Ethnic Studies at UCLA." In *Forty Years of Ethnic Studies at UCLA,* edited by Claudia Mitchell-Kernan. Los Angeles: UCLA Graduate Division, 2009.

Taylor, Clyde. "The L.A. Rebellion: A Turning Point in Black Cinema." *The New American Filmmakers Series* 26. New York: Whitney Museum of American Art, 1986.

———. "New U.S. Black Cinema." *Jump Cut* 28 (April 1983).

———. "The Next Wave: Women Film Artists at UCLA." *Black Collegian,* April/May 1980.

———. "Once Upon a Time in the West . . . L.A. Rebellion." In Field, Horak, and Stewart, *L.A. Rebellion: Creating a New Black Cinema,* ix–xxiv.

———. "Passing Through. An Underground Film about Black Music Underground." *Black Collegian,* February/March 1980.

Taylor, Elyseo J. "Film and Social Change in Africa South of the Sahara." *American Behavioral Scientist* 17, no. 3 (January/February 1974).

Treviño, Jesús Salvador. *Eyewitness: A Filmmaker's Memoir of the Chicano Movement.* Houston: Arte Público Press, 2001.

Tucker, Sherrie. "Big Ears: Listening for Gender in Jazz Studies." *Current Musicology* 71–73 (2001–2002): 375–408.

Wager, Jans. *Dangerous Dames: Women and Representation in the Weimar Street Film and Film Noir.* Athens: Ohio University Press, 1999.

Wald, Gayle. *It's Been Beautiful:* Soul! *and Black Power Television.* Durham: Duke University Press, 2015.

Wasson, Sam. *Paul on Mazursky.* Middletown, CT: Wesleyan University Press, 2011.

Waugh, Thomas, et al. *Challenge for Change: Activist Documentary at the National Film Board of Canada*. Toronto: McGill-Queen's University Press, 2010.

Welburn, Ron. "Native Americans in Jazz, Blues, and Popular Music." In *Indivisible: African-Native American Lives in the Americas*, edited by Gabrielle Tayac, 201–10. Washington, DC: National Museum of the American Indian, 2009.

Weibel-Orlando, Joan. *Indian Country, L.A.: Maintaining Ethnic Community in Complex Society*. Urbana: University of Illinois Press, 1999.

———. "Indians, Ethnicity, and Alcohol." In *The American Experience with Alcohol: Contrasting Cultural Perspectives*, edited by Linda A. Bennett and Genevieve M. Ames, 201–26. New York: Plenum Press, 1985.

Widener, Daniel. *Black Arts West: Culture and Struggle in Postwar Los Angeles*. Durham: Duke University Press, 2010.

Wilderson, Frank B., III. *Red, White, and Black: Cinema and the Structure of U.S. Antagonisms*. Durham: Duke University Press, 2010.

Wilkerson, Margaret B. "The Black Theatre Experience: PASLA (Performing Arts Society of Los Angeles)." In *Theatre West: Image and Impact*, edited by Dunbar H. Ogden, Douglas McDermott, and Robert K. Sarlos, 69–83. Amsterdam: Rodopi, 1990.

Wilson, Charles Z. *Crossing Learning Boundaries by Choice, Black People Must Save Themselves: A Memoir*. Bloomington, Indiana: Authorhouse, 2008.

Wong, Deborah. *Louder and Faster: Pain, Joy, and the Body Politic in Asian American Taiko*. Oakland: University of California Press, 2019.

Wong, Eddie. "Opinion: Shuck 'n Jive." *Gidra* 1, no. 6 (September 1969).

Woolsey, Morgan. "Re/soundings: Music and the Political Goals of the L.A. Rebellion." In Field, Horak, and Stewart, *L.A. Rebellion: Creating a New Black Cinema*, 171–95.

Young, Colin. "Film and Social Change." *Journal of Aesthetic Education* 3, no. 3 (Special Issue: Film, New Media, and Aesthetic Education) (July 1969): 21–27.

———. "Observational Cinema." In *Principles of Visual Anthropology*, edited by Paul Hockings, 99–113. New York: Mouton de Gruyter, 2003.

———. "Teaching Film at UCLA." *Journal of the University Film Producers Association* 16, no. 4 (1964).

Young, Cynthia A. *Soul Power: Culture, Radicalism, and the Making of a U.S. Third World Left*. Durham: Duke University Press, 2006.

Zinnemann, Fred, John Houseman, Irvin Kershner, Kent Mackenzie, Pauline Kael, and Colin Young. "Personal Creation in Hollywood: Can it be Done?" *Film Quarterly* 15, no. 3, Special Issue on Hollywood (Spring 1962): 16–34.

Index

Founded in 1893,
UNIVERSITY OF CALIFORNIA PRESS
publishes bold, progressive books and journals
on topics in the arts, humanities, social sciences,
and natural sciences—with a focus on social
justice issues—that inspire thought and action
among readers worldwide.

The UC PRESS FOUNDATION
raises funds to uphold the press's vital role
as an independent, nonprofit publisher, and
receives philanthropic support from a wide
range of individuals and institutions—and from
committed readers like you. To learn more, visit
ucpress.edu/supportus.